PRECARIOUS PRIVILEGE

PRECARIOUS PRIVILEGE

Race and the Middle-Class Immigrant Experience

Irene Browne

Russell Sage Foundation
New York

The Russell Sage Foundation

The Russell Sage Foundation, one of the oldest of America's general purpose foundations, was established in 1907 by Mrs. Margaret Olivia Sage for "the improvement of social and living conditions in the United States." The foundation seeks to fulfill this mandate by fostering the development and dissemination of knowledge about the country's political, social, and economic problems. While the foundation endeavors to assure the accuracy and objectivity of each book it publishes, the conclusions and interpretations in Russell Sage Foundation publications are those of the authors and not of the foundation, its trustees, or its staff. Publication by Russell Sage, therefore, does not imply foundation endorsement.

ROR: https://ror.org/02yh9se80
DOI: https://doi.org/10.7758/hvda9363

Library of Congress Cataloging-in-Publication Data

Names: Browne, Irene, author.
Title: Precarious privilege : race and the middle-class immigrant experience / Irene Browne.
Other titles: Race and the middle-class immigrant experience
Description: New York : Russell Sage Foundation, [2024] | Includes bibliographical references and index. | Summary: "Precarious Privilege demonstrates how social class permeates all aspects of the racialization of illegality in Atlanta today, from the stigmatized image of the "typical Latine" as a working-class undocumented Mexican to the political and media elites that construct this image to the heritage belief systems, identities, and markers of prestige that middle-class Latine immigrants deploy to resist such stigmatization. As the intensifying state-sponsored racialization of illegality throughout the United States threatens the status of Latine professionals, many marshal transnational middle-class status to combat it. To understand how social class privilege shapes both the experience of racialization of illegality and middle-class Latine immigrants' reactions and responses, Irene Browne addresses two guiding questions: First, how do first-generation middle-class Mexican and Dominican immigrants experience the racialization of illegality in Atlanta? Second, how does social class factor into this experience of racialization, and into the strategies that Mexican and Dominican immigrants deploy to negotiate and resist it? The book will aid policymakers and scholars in efforts to address anti-immigrant racism and benefit professionals such as teachers, healthcare workers, and counselors by highlighting the diversity within the Latine immigrant population and identifying the difficulties that this population faces. It will also help activists by explaining how middle-class Latine immigrants situate themselves within the U.S. landscape of race and inequality and the gen-

eral public by offering a more complex picture of Latine immigrants"-- Provided by publisher.
Identifiers: LCCN 2023041115 (print) | LCCN 2023041116 (ebook) | ISBN 9780871545206 (paperback) | ISBN 9781610449250 (ebook)
Subjects: LCSH: Hispanic Americans--Social conditions. | Hispanic Americans--Race identity. | Hispanic Americans--Legal status, laws, etc. | Immigrants--United States--Social conditions. | Racism--United States. | United States--Race relations.
Classification: LCC E184.S75 B76 2024 (print) | LCC E184.S75 (ebook) | DDC 305.868/073--dc23/eng/20231023
LC record available at https://lccn.loc.gov/2023041115
LC ebook record available at https://lccn.loc.gov/2023041116

The paper used in this publication meets the minimum requirements of American National Standard for Information Sciences--Permanence of Paper for Printed Library Materials. ANSI Z39.48-1992.

Text design by Suzanne Nichols.

RUSSELL SAGE FOUNDATION
112 East 64th Street, New York, New York 10065
10 9 8 7 6 5 4 3 2 1

To Dad and Miriam

Contents

DOI: https://doi.org/10.7758/hvda9363.4527

Illustrations

FIGURES

TABLES

About the Author

Irene Browne is associate professor of sociology at Emory University.

Acknowledgments

FIRST AND FOREMOST, I owe a large debt of gratitude to the individuals who took the time to participate in the study and recount their stories. I am especially grateful to the two Dominican key informants who passed away during the research period.

I was fortunate to receive financial support from the National Science Foundation, the Russell Sage Foundation, and the Emory University Research Committee. My fellowship at the Emory Fox Center for Humanistic Inquiry provided me with the necessary circumstances to write a first draft of the manuscript. Karen Stolley provided much-needed input on my application to the Fox Center. She helped me connect my work to the humanities and wrote a letter of recommendation. Helen Marrow also took the time to write a recommendation on my Fox Center application. I thank the Fox Center director, Walter Melion, and the other fellows for their feedback on the preliminary chapters. I was also fortunate to attend a lovely Emory writing retreat to work on a later version of the manuscript; there I received helpful advice from Allison Adams, the director of the Emory Center for Faculty Development and Excellence (CFDE). The CFDE and the Emory Sociology Department provided funds for hiring professional copyeditors Michelle Hiskey and Rachel Fudge from *Ideas on Fire*. Thank you, Michelle and Rachel.

Emory also sponsored a month-long stay in Salamanca, Spain, where I was able to strengthen my Spanish-language skills. I appreciate Karen Stolley's instruction during the trip, especially the afternoon seminars on the history of Spain.

I thank my editor at the Russell Sage Foundation Press, Suzanne Nichols, for her unwavering support for the project from the initial rough drafts through to the final manuscript. From her comment that the first draft contained "too much jargon" to her observation that the next draft was "too descriptive," she helped guide the manuscript to a version with both more theoretical heft and greater accessibility to a broad audience.

Three anonymous external reviewers also offered critical evaluations that helped me deepen the theoretical engagement and flow of the book. I appreciate the care with which they evaluated the manuscript.

My sociology colleagues also provided constructive feedback. I appreciate my walks with Cathy Johnson when we talked about social psychology and its applicability to my interviews. Tim Dowd, Karen Hegtvedt, and Frank Lechner also generously provided suggestions, questions, and comments on book chapters. As department chair, Tim Dowd offered steadfast encouragement on the project.

I am grateful for the participation of Selina Gallo-Cruz, who conducted the majority of the interviews, then translated and transcribed many of them (with support from the National Science Foundation). Selina also provided invaluable feedback on the proposal draft for the second NSF award. Other graduate students who conducted, translated, or transcribed interviews include: Jimena de Gregoria, Sergio Gutiérrez Negrón, Neal Gupta, Emily Lemón, Marisela Martinez-Cola, and Ricardo Menu-Cerrutti. I was fortunate to have the contributions of gifted undergraduates to the project: Amelia Ándujar, Teresa Appel, Monse Juárez, Eleanor Ma, Julybeth Murillo, Ivy Pomerantz, Branca Sanchez, Javiér Trujillo, and Rubén Diaz Vasquez.

I thank my co-PI on the project, Belisa González. Her collaboration and insights were vital for the success of the study. I also thank my coauthors on the publications that form the backbone of this book: Natalie Delia-Deckard, Belisa González, Mary Odem, and Katharine Tatum. I appreciate the thoughtful comments of the journal editors and reviewers, both those who accepted the manuscript and those who deemed it not ready for publication. Maggie Hagerman and Katharine Tatum did herculean work in coding the interviews, and Katharine took the lead in some of the analyses for the papers. Other students who assisted with data analysis, information searches for the book, or feedback on chapters include: Clark Brinson, Kate Hawks, Michaela Jenkins, Allison Sullivan, and Adria Welcher.

I also am thankful for the rounds of detailed comments from my writing group. I am honored to be a member of this dream team of scholars: Maggie Hagerman, Helen Marrow, Joya Misra, Yami Rodriguez, Cinzia Solari, and Natasha Warikoo. My Faculty Support Program team—Sara McKay, Julia Moore, and Evelyn Rodriguez—also provided an abundance of encouragement and a place for weekly accountability.

My parents and extended family lent their emotional support in weekly Zoom calls during the pandemic. Thanks to my sister, Nancy Baum, for insisting on (I mean, setting up) the Zoom calls and for cheering me on as I wrote. Thanks to my father, Joseph Browne, for his faith in me. Thanks to my nephew, Michael Baum, who read multiple chapters and offered constructive feedback. Other family members provided much-needed moral support: Danny Baum, Patty Jackson, David Baum, Kirsten Baum, Pamela Hammer, Bob Conroy, and Linda Richardson. I hold a special appreciation for my stepbrother, Kevin Richardson. My lifelong friends Janet Franklin, Beth Blosser, Rosie Roemer, and Lisa Wade also read chapter drafts and supported me throughout the project (and the pandemic).

Lastly, I thank my daughter, Miriam. She provided the initial inspiration for the book and kept me grounded. Central to my life, Miriam reminds me of the importance of family each day.

1 | Middle-Class Latine Immigrants, the Racialization of Illegality, and Precarious Privilege

Corporate manager Santiago migrated to Atlanta from Mexico in the 1990s. During his 2010 interview, Santiago told us about the time his daughters called him from the community pool. They were being denied entry even though they were members and had a pass to swim. They did not have their key. This was Santiago's response:

> So I went to the [neighbor who was guarding the pool entrance,] and I said, "Look, my friend . . . you are harassing us . . . because we are Latinos, and . . . if you don't like Latinos, we've got a problem. And don't think that . . . we are not educated. If you want to go to my office to see my diplomas—by the way I have one from Mexico and one from here—come to my office."
>
> . . . And this is part of the problem. Ten years ago it was very open-minded, the society here in Georgia. Actually, it was hot being Latino ten years ago. When I came here, actually, it was very nice being Latino because everybody opened the doors for you and said, "Ah, you're Latino, my friend! Where [do] you come from by the way?"
>
> . . . The problem now is not about the color of the skin. It's the attire, because they are not used to seeing Mexicans with ties and suits and well dressed. Well, that is the misconception about Mexican people. It's like the misconception about all Latinos that we are from Mexico.

Santiago voiced three provocative claims: that his family was being harassed because they were Latine, that the atmosphere for Latines in Atlanta had shifted from welcoming to a problem, and that this problem was tied to the invisibility of middle-class Latines "with ties and suits." Further, Santiago implied that all Latines are not simply assumed to be Mexican;

DOI: https://doi.org/10.7758/hvda9363.5964

they are assumed to all be *poor* Mexicans.[1] To counter this ethnoracial and class stereotype, Santiago marked his membership in the global middle class by highlighting his diplomas from multiple countries.[2]

In another interview, conducted in 2009, Juan, a Dominican engineer, recounted how speaking Spanish could trigger anti-Latine prejudice in Atlanta.[3] Juan and a group of his professional Dominican friends were at a restaurant enjoying a lively conversation in Spanish. A drunk patron approached their table:

> At some point that person talked to us and said, "You're in the United States. Why are you speaking Spanish? You need to be speaking English. Stop that talking." And we were like, *Whoa, wait a minute. Is this guy out of his mind?* "This is a free country," we told him. "We speak whatever we want to speak." And then one of us, I can't remember who, told him, "You know what? We speak English, we speak Spanish, and we speak French. What do you speak? Hello?"

Juan and his friends turned fluency in Spanish from a stigmatizing marker of "foreignness" into a sign of cosmopolitan sophistication, temporarily elevating their social status above that of the American detractor.[4]

Dominican professionals such as Juan often find that speaking Spanish in Atlanta not only is scorned but also prompts the automatic assumption that they are Mexican and undocumented.[5] According to Felipe, a Dominican physician who moved to Atlanta in 2008 after accepting a research job, "the experience that I have had with many North Americans [in Atlanta] is that . . . all Hispanics are Mexican until you can demonstrate to the contrary." He added: "They believe that all of the people that are physically Hispanic are Mexican and that they are undocumented or that they are illiterate and uneducated."

Echoing Santiago's narrative, Felipe believed that the presumption of a Mexican origin includes stereotypes associated with undocumented legal status and low social class—being "illiterate and uneducated." These assumptions can be countered only by "demonstrating to the contrary," that is, displaying middle-class assets or otherwise communicating one's "not Mexican" Latine identity.[6] Further, the link between being working-class and being undocumented is so tight in Atlanta that signaling middle-class status may preclude assumptions that one is undocumented.[7] For instance, Santiago used his two diplomas to assert a privileged social status even though he was living in the United States without authorization. (Juan and Felipe were both U.S. citizens.)

Santiago, Felipe, and other professional, middle-class immigrants from Mexico and the Dominican Republic faced a harsh new obstacle to their aspirations in the United States: stereotyping that was not solely based on where they came from or how they looked, but that wrongly assigned their social class and attached it to assumptions about their citizenship status. One aspect of this stereotyping already has a name: the "racialization of illegality." The term refers to the social forces that transform a Mexican identity (real or perceived) into a racial category that is equated with undocumented status.[8]

A central aim of this book is to show how social class permeates all aspects of the racialization of illegality in Atlanta today—from the stigmatized image of the "typical Latine" as a working-class undocumented Mexican to the political and media elites who construct this image, to the heritage belief systems, identities, and markers of prestige that middle-class Latine immigrants deploy to resist such stigmatization.[9] As the intensifying state-sponsored racialization of illegality throughout the United States threatens the status of Latine professionals, many marshal their transnational middle-class status to combat it.[10]

I first became interested in the racial and class dilemmas facing middle-class Latine immigrants such as Santiago, Juan, and Felipe in 2005, after I had adopted a child from Guatemala. I was looking for a new place to live with better schools, and I remarked to a friend that I did not want my daughter to be the only person of color in the neighborhood. (I'm white.)[11] "Oh, race doesn't matter anymore," the (white) friend replied. "She'll be fine wherever you settle." My fourteen years of research as a sociologist had told me, however, that race *did* matter. All around us, bias against Latines in Georgia was becoming so severe that journalists and scholars had begun referring to "Juan Crow" policies and an incipient "Latine backlash."[12]

The contrast between my friend's perceptions of race and my reading of the scholarship spurred me to investigate experiences among well-resourced Latine immigrants, such as Santiago, who had supposedly "made it" into the middle class.[13] Before 2005, a Latine immigrant was in fact more likely to be embraced or at least tolerated in Atlanta and other places where immigrants were a relatively new and rapidly growing segment of the population in what the literature calls the "new immigrant destinations" of the early twenty-first century.[14] That atmosphere chilled between 2005 and 2016 as southern states ramped up anti-immigrant policy and immigration enforcement. The public increasingly associated Mexican origin (and consequently the perception of "Mexicanness") with undocumented status.[15] An economic recession and Donald Trump's 2016 presidential campaign further cemented this misperception.[16]

Although well-educated immigrants such as Santiago, Juan, and Felipe by many measures had achieved the "American dream," the racialization of illegality potentially transformed their social position from privileged to precarious.[17] Latines in Atlanta today are at risk of being labeled a working-class undocumented Mexican, even if they are not from Mexico, even if they have authorized legal status, even if they hold multiple university diplomas, even if they speak three languages, and even if they are "well dressed."[18] This precarity motivates middle-class Latines in Atlanta to try to avoid or negotiate possible stigma and to reestablish an esteemed social status within the city's social landscape of race and immigration.[19] How do they do this? They signal that they are middle-class.

I define social class as a position in an economic and social hierarchy that comes with resources, mannerisms, worldviews, and ways of thinking.[20] I rely on the work of the sociologist Pierre Bourdieu to make sense of the effect of middle-class status on Latines who migrate to the United States with quite divergent experiences, resources, and national identities. Unlike Karl Marx and Max Weber, who situated class hierarchies within economic forces and labor market relations, Bourdieusian scholars identify an additional dimension of class where symbolic resources circulate. Symbolic resources are practices and possessions that carry social prestige, such as speaking French, attending an exclusive private school, or collecting fine wine. These symbolic resources generate status, or the hierarchical ordering of individuals and dimensions of social life according to their social value.[21]

Status processes are central to the ongoing construction of classes and the boundaries between them. The ability to create those boundaries and to distribute, withhold, and determine the value of resources increases the higher one sits in the class hierarchy. That is, the middle class is situated relationally, exercising greater power, resources, and social status than the working class and the poor, but having lower status and access to fewer resources compared to the elite.[22] In research, "middle-class" standing often includes the prestige and material benefits of a college degree and/or professional occupation along with the social connections, skills, tastes, and dispositions that accompany those credentials.[23] That is, "middle-class" positioning has social, economic, and power dimensions.

Beyond access to higher prestige and more resources, middle-class status may neutralize the attribution of undocumented legal status. In most situations, U.S.-born individuals assume an immigrant's legal status based on social cues. René Flores and Ariela Schachter report that in addition to a Mexican appearance, two of the most salient cues triggering assumptions about legal status are education and occupation—that is, social class.[24] In Flores and Schachter's experiments, low-educated Latine immigrants are assumed to be undocumented, and well-educated Latine immigrants are assumed to be documented.[25]

I argue that middle-class status is not simply one "positive identity" among many. Rather, middle-class status is a fundamental axis of social stratification that carries social worth and privilege. I build on Michael Bratton's definition of "class privilege" as "a self-reproducing and legally sanctioned financial, material, social and relational advantage that affect one's opportunities for income, well-being, social standing, and life chances."[26] To signal class privilege is to advocate for one's position on the social class hierarchy during social interactions, potentially reproducing that hierarchy.[27]

Paradoxically, my in-depth interviews reveal that in their efforts to rectify working-class assumptions and reassert class privilege, middle-class Latine immigrants often reinforce class and race inequality.[28] Although Federico and his wife immigrated from the Dominican Republic with advanced educational degrees "under our arms" but "no money," they did, he suggested, bring "*something to offer worth.* . . . If somebody doesn't have education, especially here in the U.S., it's very difficult. Not only to have something, but even to *be somebody.*"

By attaching assessments of social worth to a college education ("to be somebody"), respondents such as Federico reinscribed the boundaries that distinguish middle-class Latine immigrants not only from working-class and class-privileged Latine immigrants but also from working-class Americans.[29] This book explores how they do this.[30]

To understand how social class privilege shapes both the experience of the racialization of illegality and middle-class Latine immigrants' reactions and responses, this study addresses two guiding questions:

> How do first-generation, middle-class Mexican and Dominican immigrants experience the racialization of illegality in Atlanta?
>
> How does social class factor into this experience of racialization and into the strategies deployed by Mexican and Dominican immigrants to negotiate and resist it?[31]

WHY MIDDLE-CLASS MEXICANS AND DOMINICANS?

I expose the centrality of social class within the U.S. racial system by comparing middle-class Mexicans and Dominicans in Atlanta. Including Mexicans in my study is fundamental to capturing the lives of Atlanta's middle-class Latine immigrants, for at least three reasons. First, the metro area's 131,949 foreign-born Mexicans comprise over half of Atlanta's Latine population, providing a prototypical case of "Latine immigrants in

Atlanta."[32] Second, the constant replenishment of the large Mexican population by new immigration for several decades has reinforced the preeminence of a prototypical Mexican nationality within the Atlanta Latine landscape.[33] Third, given that the racialization of illegality is based on a constellation of stereotypes that include Mexican identity, a focus on Mexicans can reveal how middle-class status affects the negotiation strategies of first-generation Latine immigrants. Is Santiago's strategy of communicating a middle-class identity sufficient for Mexican immigrants' attempts to dispel negative stereotypes associated with working-class and undocumented status?

Adding Atlanta's 9,079 foreign-born Dominicans strengthens the study significantly by enabling me to interrogate the claim that, with the racialization of illegality, "all" Latine immigrants are assumed to be Mexican, irrespective of their national origin.[34] I ask: How do middle-class Dominicans distance themselves from assumptions about the illegality of Mexican nationality? How do Dominicans and Mexicans form social bridges and express solidarity with other Latine immigrants in Atlanta? How does social class figure into these efforts?

Dominicans' unique positioning with respect to the U.S. black-white binary also offers a critical perspective on middle-class Latine immigrants and the U.S. racial system. Many Dominicans fit within an Afro-Latine subpopulation, and the U.S.-born regularly associate Dominicans with African Americans.[35] Yet Dominicans come from a national tradition that explicitly rejects a "black" racial identity.[36] In the Dominican Republic, state-sponsored stigmatization of a "black" racial identity has associated that identity with Haitians. Consequently, Dominicans frequently reject a "black" racial self-categorization in favor of a "mixed" or "indio" self-categorization.[37] In cities such as New York, Philadelphia, and Boston, first-generation Dominicans often emphasize their immigrant status and express anti-blackness.[38]

In contrast to these locales, Atlanta's unique history and demographics offer attractive opportunities for Dominicans to align with African Americans and to embrace a black identity. Atlanta's Dominicans can join a large and vibrant black middle class. They can work for black-owned enterprises, move to elite black neighborhoods, and send their children to elite private schools that are racially diverse. They can reap the economic rewards of participating in black social networks.[39]

Conversely, the historic anti-black racism that runs through the metropolis's white community could motivate middle-class Dominicans in Atlanta to follow co-nationals in other cities in rejecting black affiliations. They could stress their immigrant or Latine status. However, with Atlanta's predominantly Mexican Latine population, the racialization of illegality has caused the designation of "Latino immigrant" to carry its own stigmatized connotations and led to possible distancing from other Latines as well.

Middle-class Dominicans therefore join Mexicans in facing incentives to engage in "classic assimilation strategies" by using their credentials and financial resources to center their lives in predominantly white settings.[40] Occupying these privileged spaces ("white spaces") carries a cost: as the number of whites in any given setting rises, so do the chances of being exposed to racial discrimination. Louwanda Evans and Wendy Moore push the question of discrimination further with their argument that predominantly white professional settings buttress white dominance by simultaneously generating racial discrimination and extinguishing challenges to racism through an insistence that "racial dynamics do not exist."[41] This contradiction opens the door for Mexican and Dominican immigrants to downplay or deny racism as an assimilation strategy in their encounters with U.S.-born whites.[42]

THE RACIALIZATION OF ILLEGALITY IN THE AMERICAN SOUTH

Before delving further into the strategies used by Mexicans and Dominicans to negotiate the racialization of illegality in Atlanta, we first need a basic understanding of the U.S. racial system. How are various features of daily American life organized and treated with respect to race?

A popular belief is that racism is a property of individuals, but sociologists reject this idea.[43] Instead, sociologists focus on racialization as an ongoing process in which individuals and larger entities (particularly government agencies, but also schools and the media), through their actions, create categories such as "white," "black," and, increasingly, "Latine" and imbue them with meaning.[44] Often these groupings are based on physical attributes (such as skin tone), but they can also encompass social attributes such as nationality, language, and even social class.[45] Racialization arranges racial categories in a hierarchy of social value that favors the dominant social group.[46] In the United States, whites remain at the top and blacks consistently occupy the bottom rung.

Since the mid-2000s, scholars have been using the "racialization of illegality" as a term to describe the racialization of undocumented legal status through its association with Latines or Mexicans. Some scholars focus on supposedly "race-neutral" immigration policies that are selectively enforced to target Latines and their communities. Douglas Massey has traced how the policies undergirding the racialization of illegality affect migration streams from Latin America by making return migration much more difficult.[47] Other scholars have explored the stigmatization of stereotypes equating "Mexican" with "illegal" through institutions such as the media.[48] Scholars have also documented how the racialization of illegality intrudes upon the daily lives of Latines, from an increased risk of traffic stops to the perception by non-Latine whites of supposed "illegals" as threats.[49]

In 2021 Cecilia Menjívar brought together the various writings to develop a comprehensive, multilayered articulation of the racialization of illegality: "This strong association between being Latina/o and undocumented, broadcast in the media and cemented through [policy] enforcement practices, has led scholars to examine experiences of 'illegality' through a lens of race, and to conceptualize illegality as racialized."[50] I add to Menjívar's framework by showing that the racialization of illegality is also "classed"—that is, it is associated with working-class undocumented Latines. The class dimension presents to middle-class Latine immigrants an array of status-enhancing negotiation strategies. My approach allows us to see that their responses to the racialization of illegality are embedded within a class hierarchy and may actually reproduce that hierarchy.

Although the "racialization of illegality" is a recently coined term, the processes behind it are not. For over 150 years, U.S. immigration policy has contributed to defining national groups as "races."[51] Through actions such as establishing strict quotas based on nationality, U.S. immigration policy in the late nineteenth and early twentieth centuries prescribed who was "welcome" (groups from northern Europe) and who was an "outsider" (migrants from Latin America, the Caribbean, Africa, and Asia).[52] Mexicans were exempted from the quota system. Allowed into the United States to work the fields, they experienced ongoing racial and class discrimination while they were in the country.[53] Federal immigration policy shifted with the 1965 Hart-Celler Act, which prioritized refugees, educationally and occupationally skilled immigrants, and immigrants with connections to family members living in the United States.[54] Caps on visas were now extended to Mexicans, which prompted more undocumented Mexican migration.[55]

The 1986 Immigration Reform and Control Act (IRCA), which provided a route for undocumented immigrants to obtain legally sanctioned status, combined with rising local border enforcement and an anti-immigrant backlash in California to produce a surplus of Latine immigrants in Los Angeles. That surplus contributed to the "push" factors for sending Latine immigrants to new immigrant destinations. At the same time, the economic restructuring of the South opened up job opportunities and created "pull" factors.[56] Atlanta became one of the premier new immigrant destinations, and many employers and residents welcomed the Latine newcomers.[57] In Atlanta throughout the 1990s, as Santiago observed, "it was hot being Latino." So what changed after that?

In Georgia and other new immigrant destinations in the American South, sharp increases in the Latine population combined with the elevation of immigration on the Republican political agenda and national media coverage after 2005 to foster a particularly hostile climate for newly arrived Latine immigrants.[58] Scholars describe this souring climate as part of a larger system of "crimmigration" that integrated immigration control into the criminal justice system, thus coordinating a "war on immigrants" with a "war on crime."[59] Although undocumented presence in the United States historically had been considered an administrative violation ("entry without inspection"), unauthorized presence in the United States was increasingly criminalized and policed within key social institutions, including the polity, the media, the schools, and the labor market.[60] The targeting of poor Latine immigrants has racialized this policing.[61] Enforcing immigration policy generates two seemingly contradictory patterns: it homogenizes all Latines into a single stigmatized group—undocumented working-class Mexicans[62]—and it reinforces the legal and social divides between Latine immigrants who are unauthorized ("undeserving") and those who are authorized ("deserving").[63] Those on the undeserving side of the moral boundary are branded as "illegals."[64]

Since 2005, the South's Latine immigrants have had to cope with new attention from local sheriff's departments and police now involved in immigration policy enforcement; intensified anti-Latine rhetoric at the local, state, and national levels; and fewer material resources during an economic recession.[65] These shifts in policy, rhetoric, and labor market conditions provide important context for understanding the experiences of Santiago, Juan, Felipe, and other middle-class authorized immigrants as they became caught up in the racialization of illegality.

Central to the racialization of illegality has been the nationally directed 287(g) program, which has earned the dubious moniker of "the gold standard of racial profiling."[66] Enacted in 1996 as section 287(g) of the federal Illegal Immigration Reform and Immigrant Responsibility Act but not implemented until the early to mid-2000s, the 287(g) program substantially increased the precarity of the day-to-day lives of undocumented immigrants.[67] Through this program, U.S. Immigration and Customs Enforcement (ICE) officials authorize and train local law enforcement to ascertain individuals' legal status and to hold anyone they cite or arrest; individuals without documentation are detained for ICE. Joining the 287(g) program was optional for state and local law enforcement. In 2002, southern states began signing on to 287(g), with Florida leading the way. In 2007, Cobb County, a populous suburb of Atlanta, joined the program. Interviews with police officers show that after 287(g) went into effect, traits such as country of origin and language became salient reasons for arrest.[68] This policy racialized illegality by allowing someone to be arrested based on where they were from, the language they spoke, and other markers of race. Reinforcing these activities was a 1976 Supreme Court ruling that deemed it legal for immigration officers to stop individuals at the border who appeared to be of Mexican origin.[69] Judicial conceptions of "Mexican appearance" included speaking Spanish or heavily accented English in addition to bearing class and race markers, such as looking poor, being "of small stature and [having] darker skin tone and hair colour."[70]

The racialization of illegality was further energized by the anti-immigrant rhetoric buttressing the 287(g) program and other Republican-led immigration policies. Pundits and politicians proclaimed that "illegal aliens" were producing an urgent and life-threatening crisis. In 2004, Georgia U.S. representative Tom Tancredo warned a crowded town hall meeting in Atlanta: "If Republicans don't do something about the border, Republicans can't say, 'We're doing all we can to protect you [from immigrants]. . . .' They are looking for jobs, yes, but there are people coming into this country to kill you and your children. Maintaining the borders is essential to our survival."[71] When Tancredo and other political officials refer to "the border," they almost always mean the border with *Mexico*, not the border with Canada.[72] For instance, included among the policies that Tancredo was advocating was a "demand [for] the extradition of Americans of Mexican descent who commit crimes in the United States and flee to Mexico."[73]

In 2005, the U.S. House of Representatives advanced a major policy initiative against undocumented Latine immigrants by passing HR 4437, the Border Protection, Antiterrorism, and Illegal Immigration Control Act. This bill imposed stiffer penalties on employers that hired undocumented immigrants, pumped funds into fencing the U.S.-Mexico border, and changed undocumented status from a misdemeanor to a felony.[74] The title of the bill defined the threat: the southern U.S. border needed protection from illegal immigrants, thus associating them with a sense of menace.[75] Although HR 4437 failed in the Senate, the bill intensified the criminalization of undocumented status and marked a strong shift in the public discourse by labeling Latin American immigrants (not just Mexican immigrants) as threats in need of "control."[76]

Undocumented immigrants and their supporters took to the streets in protest against HR 4437, and their increased visibility ignited a backlash from U.S. citizens.[77] Whites in Atlanta and many new immigrant destinations perceived the protesters as undeserving interlopers demanding government handouts. Whites' attitudes toward immigration changed from "diffuse and confused" to "racialized, resentful, and threatened."[78] African Americans remained split on whether they perceived Latine immigrants as direct competitors for jobs or partners in the struggle against racism.[79]

Media stories around HR 4437 and the ensuing protests drew the spotlight of national and local media. Immigration coverage in the national press spiked, and the public became aware of immigration as an important political issue in localities across the United States (what Daniel Hopkins calls "politicized places").[80]

The national and local publicity around HR 4437 and related political mobilization strengthened U.S.-born residents' perceptions of immigrant threat and paved the way for state legislatures, particularly those near the southern border, to step into the conflict.[81] These lawmakers, frustrated with the lack of federal immigration reform when HR 4437 failed, proposed and passed their own anti-immigrant policies.[82] In Georgia, the Republican-dominated state legislature passed two omnibus bills (SB 529 and HB 87) aimed at making daily life for unauthorized Latine immigrants so difficult that they would "self-deport."[83] In 2006, with the passage of SB 529, Georgia had taken the "most aggressive and sweeping action at the time to control illegal immigration of any state in the nation."[84] Later, other states, including South Carolina, Alabama, and Arizona, would look to Georgia as a model and follow in its racializing footsteps.

Consequently, all Latine immigrants and their children living in Georgia and other new immigration destinations in the South were made vulnerable to racial profiling. Undocumented immigrants faced arrest and deportation under these laws.[85] Their situation worsened with the 2008 global recession.[86] Between December 2007 and June 2009, unemployment rose rapidly and jobs in traditional immigrant employment sectors, such as construction, fell steeply.[87] Undocumented immigrants in particular suffered from the contraction of economic opportunities, the erosion of job quality and earnings, and the expansion of restrictive immigration policies.[88]

Presenting an additional obstacle to working, the implementation of the E-Verify program caused severe economic hardship for undocumented immigrants. Local jurisdictions that adopted the program required that employers check the immigration status of employees against a national database. With employers now also helping to enforce immigration law, E-Verify became another tool of racialized illegality.[89] In turning to work in the informal sector, like fruit vending, undocumented Latine workers became even more vulnerable. In Los Angeles, for instance, as Rocío Rosales points out, "[undocumented Mexican fruit vendors] were willing to take jobs with no pay and/or incur debt because of limited [local] opportunities . . . and the potential of greater exploitation in other Los Angeles industries."[90]

In the hostile atmosphere created by the federal passage of E-Verify, southern states' attempts to showcase their anti-immigrant and enforcement chops, and other shifts in the public narrative, daily life changed for Georgia's middle-class immigrants such as Santiago, Juan, and Felipe. No longer were they "hot," enjoying a positive image of "hardworking immigrants." Now they were facing the stigmatizing stereotype of "illegals."[91] As Santiago reflected:

> We have this bad situation. . . . If you were to review the polls of immigration, you would realize that, in national crisis, society tends to blame someone. In the beginning of the twentieth century, in the 1910s were Irish, the 1910s, '20s, and '30s were Irish, Italians, Polish. Now in the 2010s, we are Latinos, you know? . . . Last week the state Congress created a bill against illegal alien workers, so the climate is very hard.

Georgia's was not the only state legislature enacting harsh omnibus immigration legislation. In 2010, Arizona's SB 1070 contained provisions so draconian that they were deemed unconstitutional.[92] Georgia immediately proposed a similar bill, reworking aspects of the Arizona law to pass constitutional muster with the courts, as did Alabama, Indiana, South Carolina, and Utah.[93] All successfully passed their own omnibus immigration bills.[94]

In 2011, immigration enforcement at the state and local levels further increased when the U.S. Department of Homeland Security (DHS) launched the Secure Communities program.[95] This policy enabled local law enforcement agents to match any fingerprints in ICE records with other government documents. The technology became a powerful tool for building a deportation case against any undocumented person, and in Georgia the deportees were largely Mexican. Between 2010 and 2019 in Georgia, 66 percent of individuals deported under the Secure Communities act were Mexican nationals; over 92 percent of those deportees were from Mexico, Honduras, Guatemala, and El Salvador.[96] Mexicans were much more heavily targeted for deportation in Georgia compared to Dominicans, despite the increase over time in the number of Dominicans living in the state. This situation increased incentives for Dominicans to eschew being perceived as "Mexican."

Although Barack Obama campaigned on a platform that was sympathetic to undocumented immigrants and that endeavored to attract Latine voters, total deportations actually increased under his administration.[97] As the ICE data presented in figure 1.1 show, Georgia deportations reached their highest levels in 2010. Georgia deported relatively few individuals before 2006. (Trends for all deportations follow the trends for Mexicans. See table A.1 for raw numbers.)

In 2016, anti-immigrant sentiment and rhetoric and the racialization of

Figure 1.1 Deportations of Mexicans and Dominicans in Georgia, 2003–2019

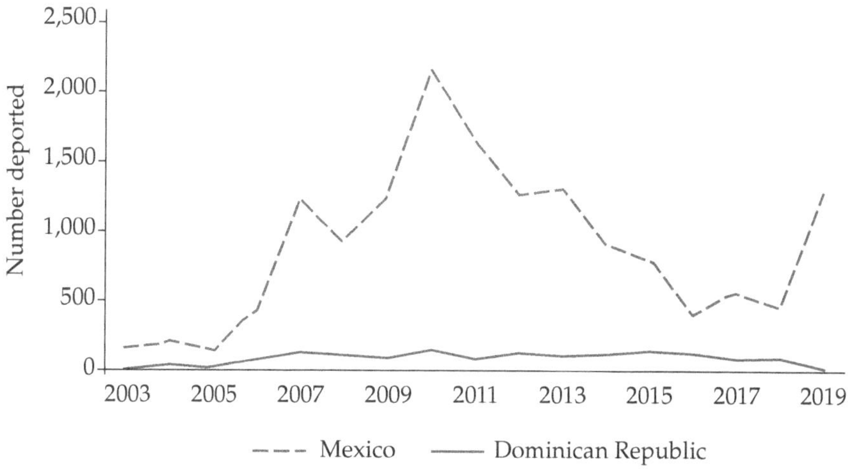

Source: TRACImmigration 2021. "Latest Data: Immigration and Customs Enforcement Removals."

illegality reached a new apex with the political rise of Donald Trump.[98] As *Time* reported:

> Donald Trump kicked off his presidential bid [in 2015] with harsh words for Mexico. "They are not our friend, believe me," he said, before disparaging Mexican immigrants: "They're bringing drugs. They're bringing crime. They're rapists. And some, I assume, are good people."[99]

Along with portraying Mexican immigrants as dangerous criminals and rapists, Trump promised to build a wall at the U.S.-Mexico border to quell the threat. The wall did more than pose a physical barrier for immigrants from Mexico and Latin America: as a symbol connecting Mexicans even more with Latine immigrants, the wall conveyed the same message to both: *You do not belong in the United States.*[100]

Latine immigrants in Georgia and other new immigrant destinations in the South were and continue to be especially hard hit by the growing public anti-immigrant hostility and the racialization of illegality.[101] Scholars show that low-income Latine immigrant families in these locales have experienced *downward* mobility. By losing the gains they made in attempting to succeed in the United States, their American dream has become a "hope turned sour."[102] As Blanca noted: "Unfortunately, if you don't have papers here, you are nobody, you are worth nothing." She identified becoming "worthless" as the social toll exacted from immigrants by undocumented legal status.

Authorized Latine immigrants are affected indirectly too, both because they are sometimes treated as if they are undocumented and because many have family members who experience the racialization directly.[103] These conditions can put enormous strains on households. Children fear arriving home to find that a parent is gone, and documented family members may suddenly become responsible for raising children when an undocumented parent is deported.[104]

Scholarship focused on undocumented Latine immigrants tends to home in on low-income families and does not answer questions raised by the experiences of the population I investigated: Santiago, Juan, Felipe, and other middle-class Latine immigrants who may have more resources to marshal in defending themselves in response.[105] The experiences of first-generation, middle-class Latine immigrants show us whether and how racial discrimination creates obstacles that prevent ethnoracial minorities from fully achieving the American dream for themselves and their children.[106] Representing the group that assimilation theory deems the most successful, middle-class Latine immigrants are arguably in the best position to be upwardly mobile and to prosper. With more economic resources, they can live in well-resourced and exclusive neighborhoods, send their children to "better" schools, join prestigious groups and organizations, and forge advantageous social connections.[107] Yet, as the stories of Santiago, Juan, and Felipe illustrate, they also may be treated like outsiders and have their privileged social class status undermined.

Why Atlanta?

Although observers couch the racialization of illegality within national trends, some studies illustrate the importance of nationality, place-based demographics, and local racial history to understanding the impact of race and class on the experiences of middle-class Latine immigrants.[108] Yet almost all of these studies are based in traditional immigrant destinations. New immigrant destinations such as Atlanta have unique conditions that have fundamentally shaped their racial systems. Atlanta's system includes a history of black-white political struggles, a prominent black civil rights legacy alongside entrenched white supremacist groups, a political culture steeped in the conservatism of the South, and a growing constituency of Democrats.[109]

Atlanta's "demographic explosion" has transformed it from a black-white city to a black-white-Latine city where no one racial group holds a majority.[110] Between 1980 and 2000, Atlanta's Latine population grew 995 percent, jumping from 1 percent of the population in 1980 to 7 percent in 2000.[111] These newcomers, from Mexicans to Dominicans to Puerto Ricans to Argentines, represent a rich diversity of national origins and social classes. African Americans have also been moving to the city in unprecedented numbers, expanding the metro's black middle class. White residents have been moving out.[112]

The 1996 Olympics in particular, by giving Atlanta international visibility, contributed to the city's demographic explosion, and construction of the Olympic venues attracted thousands of Latine immigrant workers.[113] With the Games "just a year away," the *Atlanta Journal-Constitution* reported, "construction of Olympic venues was behind schedule. Organizers were desperate for construction workers to finish the work." The city's hosting of the Olympics had already given local businesses a boost; now they were encouraged "to look the other way while immigrants—some of whom would be in the United States illegally—bailed the city out of a jam."[114]

The Olympics also drew middle-class Latine immigrants who decided to stay after watching the games as well as those who encountered opportune business prospects while they were in the city. In 1990, before the Olympics, 52,377 Latines lived in Atlanta. In 2000, after the Olympics, Latine representation had grown 800 percent to a population of 249,218. Approximately 12 percent of the Latines living in Atlanta in both decades held college degrees (see chapter 2 for more detail).[115]

Atlanta houses the corporate headquarters of some top Fortune 500 companies such as Coca-Cola Corporation, Home Depot, Delta Airlines, and United Parcel Service (UPS).[116] These companies have done more than provide opportunities for Latin American professionals to make Atlanta their home; they have also sponsored them for H-1B visas, which facilitate legal migration.[117] Educated workers from across Latin America work for these Atlanta companies, but the racialization of illegality often leads the public to perceive them as undocumented Mexicans.

Atlanta represents an ideal new immigrant destination in which to tackle my research questions because here we find insights into immigration patterns throughout the U.S. South. With rapid demographic changes occurring earlier than in other new destination states, Georgia has been identified as a "harbinger of where other new [immigrant] destinations may be headed demographically, politically, and legislatively."[118] For authorized Latine professionals, economic opportunities are flourishing in Atlanta, but undocumented immigrants encounter adverse conditions. How bad is it? The journalist Joel Rose describes Atlanta as one of the "toughest place[s] in the U.S. to be an undocumented immigrant."[119] Rose attributes this dubious distinction to a combination of exceptionally harsh immigration laws, high deportation rates, the eager cooperation of local law enforcement with ICE, and judges who rarely side with immigrants.

STIGMA, PRECARIOUS PRIVILEGE, AND OTHER KEY CONCEPTS

Identifying the ways in which the racialization of illegality undermines or challenges class-based advantages—and the resources that privileged Latine immigrants can deploy to avoid, resist, or remake racialization—provides crucial information about persistent social inequality in the United States.[120] As Khiara Bridges emphasizes in her study of middle-class African Americans, understanding the U.S. racial system requires interrogating "the fraught [social] space within which class-privileged racial minorities exist—the disadvantage within their privilege."[121] Bridges argues that understanding this disadvantage requires "theorizing the non-economic injuries" that wealthier people of color experience. When middle-class minority members are absent in our research, racial discrimination across class lines remains invisible. This invisibility can lead to the mistaken assumption that poverty and a lack of resources undergird racism and that upward mobility, by implication, is the route away from experiences of racism.

I draw on this concept of "disadvantage within privilege" by attending to the unique "precarious privilege" of middle-class Latine immigrants subject to the racialization of illegality. My respondents confronted being misperceived as occupying a low-status identity—an undocumented, working-class Mexican—that did not fit their own self-categorization as middle-class. This misperception raised an ever-present potential for stigmatization—stigma being defined here as an "attribute that is deeply discrediting" to one's social esteem and prestige.[122] My respondents' social privilege became precarious because they ran the risk of encountering this stigma at any moment and during any of their many face-to-face interactions.

My concept of "precarious privilege" most closely aligns with Stillerman's (2023) use of the term in his study of the middle class in Chile. "While others have used the concept of precarious privilege to understand lifestyle migration or labor activism," he writes, "I have used the concept of precarious privilege to examine the contradictory circumstances of middle-class families in Chile's free market context."[123] For Stillerman, occupational instability within the Chilean economy produces economic precarity among the middle class. He is interested in how middle-class Chileans respond to the "contradictory position" through consumption (market practices). Similar to Stillerman, I consider precarity in terms of "contradictory circumstances," but my focus is the U.S. system of racialization and contradictory social status positions. I home in on how precarity is experienced as the stigma attached to the image of the "typical Latine." Further, while Stillerman is interested in how middle-class individuals create social boundaries through consumption, I highlight stigma-reducing identity work strategies during social interaction.

As I discussed earlier, the stigmatized image of the "typical Latine" as an undocumented working-class Mexican immigrant is the result of political processes and the U.S. racial system.[124] Seen through this lens, stigma is not just an unpleasant individual experience of losing esteem during a given social encounter. It is also part of a larger "stigmatizing social system" that collectively upholds inequality.[125]

Indeed, as the public health scholars Bruce Link and Jo Phelan explain, stigma is connected to social institutions and social systems through five specific processes. First, "people distinguish and label human differences." Second, "dominant cultural beliefs link labeled persons to undesirable characteristics and to negative stereotypes." Third, labeled persons are cast as an out-group that separates "them" from "us." Fourth, labeled persons experience status loss and discrimination that lead to unequal outcomes. Finally, Link and Phelan emphasize that "stigma is entirely dependent on social, economic, and political power." Only those with power can systematically label and disapprove of, exclude, reject, and discriminate against out-group members.[126]

The racialization of illegality fits all these criteria. As one way of labeling human differences, "Latine" has become a racialized category in the United States that defines human difference. The pejorative term "illegals" encapsulates the negative stereotypes associated with Latine immigrants. Symbols of not belonging that separate "us" from "them," such as a wall built at the U.S.-Mexican border, remind Latine immigrants that they are seen as "outsiders" by native-born Americans.[127] Latine immigrants experience potential status loss in discriminatory experiences, from being denied entrance to a community pool to being told to "stop speaking Spanish." The racialization of illegality—and the consequent stigmatization of all Latines as undocumented working-class Mexicans—is produced in white-dominated institutions by the actions of powerful actors, such as policymakers, judges, police, employers, pundits, and media professionals.[128] These groups maintain the racial hierarchy with whites at the top.

My study builds upon Link and Phelan's framework by illustrating how class privilege complicates the stigmatization process. I show that middle-class Latine immigrants can both practice discrimination toward stigmatized members of immigrant groups, particularly undocumented working-class Latines, and experience discrimination themselves from the (white non-Latine) U.S. majority. While suffering from their perceived association with the "illegal" other, they simultaneously benefit from their social and economic distancing from this increasingly criminalized group.

I offer a fresh perspective to understand how Atlanta's middle-class Latine immigrants navigate potential stigmatization, on the one hand, and opportunities for pan-Latine solidarity, on the other hand, by combining three concepts: racialization despite assimilation, typicality, and identity work. My approach shows that the day-to-day interactions of middle-class Latine immigrants are tied to larger systems of class and race inequality.

Racialization despite Assimilation

Although middle-class Latine immigrants reap material and status benefits from their class position, they often are exposed to structural disadvantages such as anti-Latine prejudice and limited access to white neighborhoods, schools, and workplaces.[129] The sociologist Jessica Vasquez describes this predicament as "racialization despite assimilation," explaining that "[Latine] immigrant families [are] included in the mainstream on various levels (education, linguistics, occupation, culture) while also maintaining ethnic cultural values, beliefs, practices, and social circles." At the same time, they "face the constraint of racialization. [Middle-class Latine immigrants] are restricted by the way others perceive, treat, and racialize them."[130]

Within a racialization-despite-assimilation situation, social connections to other Latine immigrants become converted into "ethnic capital," an especially important resource for economic mobility.[131] For instance, in her groundbreaking study, Jody Agius Vallejo reports that middle-class Mexican Americans living in Southern California encounter barriers to full participation in white-dominated spaces. Blocked opportunities prompt middle-class Mexican Americans to adopt a "minority culture of mobility." As Agius Vallejo explains, they rely on coethnics to engage in "group-specific mobility strategies embedded in ethnic communities, such as creating and joining ethnic community organizations."[132]

The value and availability of ethnic affiliations as a resource depend on local conditions.[133] Most U.S.-based research on the assimilation strategies of middle-class Latine immigrants focuses on traditional destinations such as Los Angeles, Miami, and New York.[134] Compared to Latine immigrants in these studies, Atlanta's middle-class Latine immigrants face a different set of economic, demographic, and political conditions. In most traditional destinations, the Latine population is large compared to the black population. For example, while almost half (45 percent) of Los Angeles residents are Latine, only 6 percent are (non-Hispanic) black.[135] Atlanta presents the opposite demographics. Almost one-third of the Atlanta metro area population is (non-Hispanic) black and 11 percent is Latine.[136]

Middle-class Latine immigrants in traditional destinations can access long-standing institutional and community supports that Atlanta does not offer. For example, in Los Angeles, approximately 12 percent of firms are Latine-owned and only 2 percent are black-owned.[137] In Atlanta, the proportions are reversed: a mere 4 percent of Atlanta businesses are Latine-owned, while 7 percent of the city's businesses are black-owned.[138]

Respondents in California could take advantage of business associations for upward mobility, and they could insulate their families from discrimination by living in predominantly Mexican middle-class neighborhoods.[139] Atlanta respondents did not have the option of moving to middle-class Latine enclaves. Instead, their residential choices were working-class Latine neighborhoods, middle-class white neighborhoods, middle-class black neighborhoods, or working-class black neighborhoods.

The middle-class Mexican and Dominican immigrants we interviewed opted for predominantly white spaces. Many of my Atlanta respondents explained that they chose to live in neighborhoods that had good schools and were close to work. Nevertheless, leaning into racialization despite assimilation, they took great pride in their Mexican or Dominican heritage, identifying as Mexican or Dominican rather than as white. (Strong attachment to a heritage identity is a common feature among first-generation immigrants across the United States.)[140] I predicted from existing research that their predominantly white environments would heighten their chances of being stereotyped or discriminated against by coworkers and neighbors.[141] However, frequent contact with whites might also have generated familiarity and a warm reception.[142] The interviews revealed an even more complicated picture.

My Mexican and Dominican respondents exhibited a curious tendency. Many of them described instances of non-Latines' negative treatment or automatic assumption that they were undocumented working-class Mexican immigrants. Some respondents even *anticipated* this stigmatizing assumption in their interactions with U.S.-born non-Latines.[143] Yet many respondents emphasized that they did not experience systemic discrimination, insisted that race was unimportant to their lives in Atlanta, and expressed optimism about their mobility prospects.[144] Further, exposure to other racialized groups sometimes led to feelings of warm welcome and facilitated social bridges with other Latine immigrants, blacks, and whites.[145] The other two concepts—typicality and identity work—allow us to make sense of these patterns.

Typicality and Identity Work

The racialization of illegality has fused the categories of Mexican, working-class, and undocumented to construct the "typical Latine" stereotype as experienced in Atlanta today. Research suggests that social class and race are tightly linked in white perceptions of middle-class minorities. In experiments, whites perceive subjects with Hispanic names as immigrants occupying a low SES position.[146] In studies of white perceptions of African Americans, cues that a person is middle-class lead whites to assume that the individual is white rather than black. When whites encounter cues that a person is working-class, they assume that the individual is black rather than white.[147] These perceptions are fueled by racial stereotypes and "status generalization" processes in which knowledge of overall black economic disadvantage translates into assumptions of low socioeconomic status and, concomitantly, inferior competence.[148] White perceptions can shift with social contact between whites and African Americans who are status equals.[149]

Social psychological theories of typicality suggest that non-Latines (out-group members) perceive the *combination* of race, nationality, and class characteristics rather than each attribute separately, the implication being that observers perceive degrees of membership, or "typicality."[150] That is, some people who appear to fit a category more than others can move away from the "typical Latine" image to differing extents.

For my respondents, the misperception that they were a "typical Latine" clashed with their self-concepts as middle-class. Self-concepts form the basis of social identities, or our sense of belonging to social groups.[151] We construct identities in dialogue with how we perceive ourselves (our self-concept) and how we are perceived by others (external classification).[152]

Identity work describes that dialogue and the efforts that we undertake to negotiate our social identities.[153] We tend to see our in-group in positive terms and to regard out-groups less favorably.[154] Through the identity work dialogue, we seek consistency and "the feeling that [we are] valued and accepted by others."[155] A mismatch between our self-concept and the stigmatizing perceptions of others undermines this feeling, leading us to experience a drop in self-worth. In response to—or anticipation of—the non-validation, stigmatized individuals engage in identity work strategies to move others' perceptions closer in line with their self-concept.[156] For instance, individuals often respond to stigmatization by emphasizing a higher-status aspect of their identity, drawing upon the class and cultural resources at their disposal.[157] This is the negotiation strategy that Santiago and Juan employed. They retained their "Latine" identity as they distanced themselves from the stigmatized "typical Latine" by signaling that they were middle-class.[158]

Latine immigrants also engage in identity work to distinguish themselves from stigmatized groups of Latines. While this often takes the form of distancing themselves from working-class Mexicans, the specific nationality treated as the "typical Latine" also depends on local demographics.[159] For example, Julie Dowling shows that middle-class Afro-Cubans living in New Mexico distance themselves from local Mexicans, who comprise almost half of the state's population. Her respondents looked to Cubans in Miami as their reference group and as the bearers of a positive identity.[160] Meanwhile, in Miami, individuals from "continental Latin America" distinguish themselves from Cubans, the largest Latine group, claiming that Cubans abuse the U.S. welfare system.[161]

Comparing Mexicans and Dominicans in Atlanta offers an excellent opportunity to understand processes of racialization despite assimilation, typicality, and identity work. Each of the three countries represented in my study—Mexico, the Dominican Republic, and the United States—has its own system of racial hierarchies, racial categories, and popular beliefs about race and class. Mexico and the Dominican Republic differ in the historically disadvantaged group that is most vigorously stigmatized: indigenous individuals in Mexico and Haitians in the Dominican Republic.[162] Their heritage and U.S. racial belief systems not only have been constructed to create social distance from these stigmatized groups but have also become symbolic resources that Latine immigrants can deploy to promote a positive identity. When my respondents insisted that race was "not an issue" in their lives, they drew upon both Mexican and Dominican beliefs about racial mixture (*mestizaje*) and U.S. colorblindness. (I discuss these racial belief systems in detail in chapter 3.)

Dominicans also may differ from Mexicans in physical appearance while still conveying distinct "embodied interactional cues" of the category "Latine."[163] Dominicans are more likely than Mexicans to have Afrocentric features, and members of the same Dominican family can vary greatly in phenotype, with some appearing "white" and others appearing "black."[164]

When I began comparing Dominicans and Mexicans for this book, I expected that, in line with studies conducted in other U.S. urban centers, Dominicans would most often engage a "black" racial identity. That is, assuming they would frequently be perceived as "black" by white and black U.S.-born individuals, I expected them to perform identity work through which they would explicitly embrace, reluctantly accept, or outwardly reject a black identity.[165] However, the Dominicans I interviewed were most likely to describe the salience of their external categorization as

Mexican during social interactions in Atlanta, and they seldom mentioned being externally identified as black. Indeed, one of the more surprising findings in my study was the high degree of similarity between the Mexicans and Dominicans in their experiences of and strategic responses to being racialized first and foremost as "illegal" working-class Mexicans.

Writings about immigrant traditional destinations also led me to expect that the respondents who experienced discrimination would be likely to recognize racism and take a critical stance toward the U.S. racial hierarchy.[166] A number of respondents, however, recounted negative or discriminatory experiences but continued to insist that race and U.S. racial dynamics did not affect their daily lives.

I also anticipated that respondents would react to the strong pejorative meanings attached to the term "illegal" by emphasizing their authorized status and drawing clear distinctions between themselves and unauthorized Latine immigrants. Although some respondents did so, many others did not even mention their legal status. Overall, signaling social class—particularly with references to education—was a much more common response to the racialization of illegality than signaling authorized legal status.[167]

Finally, existing scholarship suggests that both Mexicans and Dominicans are likely to attempt to enhance their social status by engaging in strategies that could bring them closer to whites and whiteness.[168] I find that this is indeed the case. But going even further, several of my respondents also pursued a distinctive status-enhancing trajectory in an attempt to position themselves *above*—not just alongside—U.S.-born whites.

Conducting the Interviews

To capture the dynamic and varied responses of middle-class Latine immigrants to constant racialization, a team of research assistants joined my colleague Belisa Gonzalez and me to carry out interviews that collected information from various respondents on what brought them to Atlanta; how they chose where to live, work, and send their kids to school; what their experiences had been like both initially and over time; and how they thought race had shaped those experiences.[169]

Between 2009 and 2016, Professor Gonzalez, a cadre of bilingual graduate research assistants, and I heard the stories of thirty-three college-educated Mexicans and thirty-five college-educated Dominicans.[170] This time frame allowed me to capture respondents' lives during watershed moments in the racialization of illegality. To include a few more voices in the contemporary moment as well, we followed up those interviews with seven more between 2021 and 2023.

Respondents' children ranged in age. While some respondents had grown up poor and obtained their college degree or professional job after arriving in the United States, many others had lived in middle-class comfort in Mexico or the Dominican Republic. A number of my respondents had parents who were college deans, judges, accountants, attorneys, pharmacologists, engineers, or physicians. We did not ask questions about legal status, but twenty Mexicans and twenty-five Dominicans informed us that they were authorized. Ten Mexicans and ten Dominicans did not volunteer any information on their legal status, so we assumed (albeit imperfectly) that they might not have been authorized. Three Mexican respondents stated that they were undocumented. In all of the analyses, I checked for differences between these three groups. There is surprising uniformity across all three groups in the distribution of their responses to our interview questions.

A bilingual first- or second-generation Latine conducted the majority of the interviews—forty-four out of sixty-eight—in Spanish. A female bilingual Latine graduate student conducted almost half (eighteen out of thirty-three) of the Mexican interviews. A male Dominican graduate student conducted close to one-third (thirteen out of thirty-five) of the interviews with Dominicans. Interestingly, he encountered some suspicion and reluctance to participate from potential female respondents. The female interviewers had more success recruiting and interviewing respondents. The more recent interviews were conducted by a Mexican student and a Dominican student. Interviews were translated and transcribed by the bilingual students who conducted the interviews as well as by a professional transcription service. These interviews, as will be seen throughout this book, revealed the importance of social class in both experiencing and negotiating the racialization of illegality.

THE ORGANIZATION OF THE BOOK

In the chapter that follows, I set the Atlanta stage to place the interviews in context. I show how race relations in Atlanta were originally built around the black-white color line but are now moving beyond that divide in the midst of a "diversity explosion."[171] I also show how Atlanta's unique racial politics combines with its flourishing economy to heighten a sense of "group threat" among U.S.-born whites.[172]

In chapters 3 through 5, I turn to my interviews to analyze my respondents' efforts to signal their class privilege in response to experiencing or anticipating the racialization of illegality.[173] In chapter 3, we see that respondents, when asked to racially identify, often constructed positive identities by drawing upon a heritage cultural system that elevates class distinctions over race-based categories. That is, while U.S. belief systems about racial inequality typically ignore systemic class hierarchies, both Mexican and Dominican racial ideologies emphasize class hierarchy as the foundation of national social inequality. My migrant respondents brought this ideological "baggage" with them to Atlanta.[174]

Following chapter 3's focus on how respondents saw themselves and negotiated their heritage and host identity categories, chapter 4 looks at the perception of them by the U.S.-born in everyday social encounters as "prototypical" undocumented, working-class, and Mexican "Latines" and at the ways in which they anticipated or attempted to change this misperception. As Juan, Santiago, and Felipe illustrate, respondents engaged in significant identity work to try to negotiate this stigmatizing image by signaling their nationality and/or social class categories. During interactions with U.S.-born Atlantans, Dominican respondents communicated that they were not Mexican and thus usually succeeded in also defusing the perception of them as undocumented and working-class. In contrast, some of Atlanta's Mexicans either tried to communicate that they were not working-class or explained to the U.S.-born that the "typical Latine" could also be middle-class. The latter strategy aimed to diffuse assumptions of undocumented status by endowing prototypical Latine identity in Atlanta with middle-class respectability.[175]

Finally, chapter 5 demonstrates that respondents did not simply symbolically position themselves on par with the dominant group representing the contemporary American dream—the U.S.-born white middle class.[176] Rather, respondents sometimes leveraged their cosmopolitan cultural resources to promote their social status *above* that of middle-class whites—as in Juan's reaction to being rebuked for not speaking in English: "How many languages do you speak?" My colleague Katherine Tatum and I refer to such efforts to turn the U.S. racial status hierarchy on its head as "one-up assimilation," and later in the chapter I tackle the question of whether such strategies are successful or not.[177]

Rather than perceiving their situation as bringing potential stigma, many respondents, as shown in chapter 6, felt secure in their esteemed middle-class status. In this chapter, I explore the multiple interpretations of these patterns within the context of current debates on assimilation. I reflect on the import of my study from an immigrant-centered perspective, paying particular attention to the consequences for the next generation.

My findings parallel the work of Crystal Fleming and her colleagues, who identify three strategies that African Americans deploy to respond to stigma: they confront the perpetrator; they ignore the slight or walk away; or they "educate" the perpetrator.[178] My middle-class Latine respondents used similar stigma-reducing strategies, which played out in a class-infused context, unique to Latines, that included the racialization of illegality and its assumptions about the working class as well as a Latin American racial ideology that prioritizes class hierarchies.

THE STUDY'S SIGNIFICANCE

My in-depth interviews with middle-class Latine immigrants exposed stigmatizing experiences and, by extension, the insidious dynamics that perpetuate U.S. racial hierarchies.[179] In this book, I explore the links between misperceptions about social class and the stereotyping and slights ("microaggressions") perpetrated in immigrants' day-to-day social interactions with U.S.-born non-Latines. Focusing on Atlanta, I add to the studies that have documented how these forms of "everyday racism" mark middle-class Latine immigrants as outsiders; simultaneously, I identify class-based strategies that rely on what Evans and Moore term "micro-resistance."[180] Adding complexity to the race-class-immigration nexus, I discern situations in which Atlanta's middle-class Latine immigrants distinguish themselves from other Latines and from African Americans rather than express solidarity with either group.

I hope that my study influences immigration scholars by spurring a more protracted and nuanced consideration of class privilege in relation to the racialization of illegality and by providing an approach to such an analysis. Understanding the workings of this system should aid policymakers and scholars in efforts to address anti-immigrant racism. My research also may benefit professionals such as teachers, health care workers, and counselors by highlighting the diversity within the Latine immigrant population and identifying the difficulties and dilemmas faced by this population. Activists hoping to forge coalitions with Latine immigrants may also profit from an understanding of how middle-class Latine immigrants situate themselves within the U.S. landscape of race and inequality. Finally, by countering the stereotypes embedded in the racialization of illegality and offering a more complete and complex picture of the Latine immigrant population, my study may influence policymakers, voters, and the general public.

Turning to the concerns about my daughter that originally motivated the project, I ask: What do my interviews suggest about what I may face as a white parent of someone who probably will have to navigate the racialization of illegality? A number of respondents explicitly told me that my daughter will be "fine" and that she will not experience negative encounters. Yet their stories also suggest that she is likely to be stereotyped as an undocumented working-class Mexican. Indeed, she is often asked where she is from and occasionally admonished to "go back to Mexico." I find that advising her on how to negotiate the racialization of illegality can be tricky. If she counters by saying that she is an educated (middle-class) U.S. citizen from Guatemala, not Mexico, she reinforces the distinction between the "typical Latine" and higher-status Latines. If she endeavors to confront native-born interlocutors and explain that they are ignorant about the class and ethnic diversity of the Latine population, she may exacerbate a tense situation.[181] If she mitigates conflict by "walking away" without comment, she leaves the assumptions about the "typical Latine" intact. Further, while my respondents could rely on their heritage view that "race doesn't matter," I was not raised in a Latin American racial belief system that my daughter can use to counter U.S. racialization.

Like my respondents and their children, my daughter is learning how to navigate her identity within a U.S. racial system that generates precarious privilege. My research showing that these experiences are part of a larger system of both racial and class inequality has helped me not only see the challenges that await her but also identify strategies that could be useful as she navigates them. My hope is that this book will help other families and inspire policymakers as they seek solutions to the racialization of illegality.

2 | Race, Class, and Latine Immigration in Atlanta: A Portrait

> Metro Atlanta has gained more than 650,000 jobs since 2010, up 29 percent, led by corporate jobs, health care and logistics. . . . Financial technology, always in the background in Georgia, is a top performer. In one recent year, Hollywood shot more motion pictures in Georgia than it did in California.
>
> —Scott Truby, *Atlanta Journal-Constitution*, January 2, 2020

> "The black Mecca" [Atlanta] leads the nation in numbers of African American millionaires; at the same time, it leads the nation in the percentage of its children in poverty.[1]
>
> —Robert Bullard, *The Black Metropolis in the Twenty-First Century* (2007), 151

> By almost any measure, [metro Atlanta] is one of the toughest places in America to be undocumented.
>
> —Joel Rose, *Morning Edition*, NPR, February 13, 2018

ANYONE ARRIVING at Hartsfield-Jackson Atlanta International Airport will encounter the metropolitan area's black-white divide immediately: the airport is named after a white mayor (Hartsfield) and the city's first black mayor (Jackson). As newcomers walk to baggage claim, they will see copies of the *Atlanta Journal-Constitution*—a mainstream publication with a majority-white readership—sitting alongside Atlanta's oldest black newspaper, the *Atlanta Daily World*. Driving into the city, visitors are guided by a sculpture of Dr. Martin Luther King Jr. onto John Lewis Freedom Park-

DOI: https://doi.org/10.7758/hvda9363.7855

way, dedicated to the civil rights activist and Georgia's much-beloved black congressional representative. New arrivals who continue on to suburban Stone Mountain, however, will encounter the largest Confederate memorial in the United States: the images of Confederate president Jefferson Davis and Confederate generals Thomas "Stonewall" Jackson and Robert E. Lee are carved into the side of the granite mountain at a scale surpassing Mount Rushmore.[2]

Newcomers will also immediately see evidence of Atlanta's changing demographics. In the airport, they will pass working-class Latine immigrants serving in the food venues and cleaning the airport facilities. They may spot Atlanta's Spanish-language newspaper, *El Mundo Hispánico*, on newsstands, and they are likely to hear Spanish spoken in public settings as they visit Atlanta tourist attractions, ride on public transportation, or shop at grocery stores.

ATLANTA IN THE TWENTIETH CENTURY

Over the past century, middle-class Latine immigrants have made a living in Atlanta amid shifting black-white race relations, stark racial residential segregation, racial politics, and a prospering economy. As in other cities in the U.S. Southeast, the profound legacy of black-white segregation in Atlanta has influenced which neighborhoods immigrants can choose to live in, the families they encounter in those neighborhoods, the composition and quality of their children's schools, and the reactions to immigrants from U.S.-born Atlantans.[3]

Between 1980 and 1990, 30,350 Latines moved to Atlanta, more than doubling the metro area's Latine population.[4] From 1990 through 2021, Atlanta's Mexican population grew even faster, increasing overall by 1,285 percent. This pushed Mexicans into the majority of metro Atlanta's Latine population by 2000. These numbers also cast the numerically dominant Mexicans as the group most often stereotyped as the "typical Latine."[5]

The Dominican population in Atlanta grew by a startling 27,001 percent from 1990 to 2021. This enormous percentage increase was partly due to how few Dominicans lived in Atlanta in 1990—only 711. The Dominican presence in Atlanta grew to 2,378 individuals in 2000 and 19,909 in 2021. Our interviews with respondents who arrived in the 1980s and 1990s gave us insight into these changes.

Overall Latine representation jumped from 1 percent to 7 percent of metro Atlanta's residents over the thirty-year period, with the majority coming from Mexico.[6] Atlanta's Latine population is currently 12 percent of the metro area's residents and growing. These "new faces in new places," as they attempt to gain a footing in institutions that developed around hardened black-white divisions, are transforming the famously black-white Atlanta metro into a multiracial metropolis.[7] As these changes advance, anti-immigrant groups are sounding the alarm that Georgia is in danger of becoming another "Mexifornia."[8]

In this chapter, I place immigration in the context of the history of race relations in Atlanta. I explain how the metro area's rapidly changing demographics are creating the conditions for the white perceptions of group threat that fuel the racialization of illegality. I describe the links between Atlanta's black-white racial history and its current demographic, economic, and political context of immigrant reception. The chapter presents important information for understanding the conditions that generate precarious privilege by simultaneously providing economic opportunities to middle-class Latine immigrants and potentially stigmatizing them.

Black-White Relations, 1865–2000

From the end of the Civil War through the civil rights era (1865–1968), Atlanta was marked by two major social and political forces: (1) efforts by white city leaders to systematically subordinate blacks and restrict black access to housing, schools, jobs, and economic opportunities; and (2) active black resistance to their suppression. Relations between this racial regime and the small group of Latine residents living in Georgia during this era were complex.[9]

After the Civil War, Atlanta's white citizenry used violence and intimidation to enforce black subordination. In 1906, for instance, Atlanta erupted in one of the worst race riots of the century, with whites attacking black business owners and residents.[10] The threat of lynching also was ever-present: there were 432 known lynchings in Georgia between 1875 and 1930.[11] Black citizens could find no redress in the legal system, as rulings on any dispute were made in favor of the white plaintiff by all-white juries and white judges.[12]

Under Jim Crow (1865 to the 1960s), racial residential segregation and black exclusion were codified into laws and local ordinances.[13] In what the historian Ronald Bayor identifies as "the most important of the segregation acts" in Atlanta, a 1922 racial zoning law divided most of the city's neighborhoods into black and white sections.[14] Other laws prevented blacks from purchasing or renting housing near white schools. Between the 1890s and 1970s, "black neighborhoods received fewer municipal services with many roads unpaved, water and sewer inadequate, social programs almost nonexistent, and schools overcrowded and underfunded."[15]

Black elites in Atlanta built their own institutions in response to repressive measures, violence, and Jim Crow segregation. Black businesses lined the streets of Auburn Avenue, black professionals served a black clientele, and black entrepreneurs supported black economic mobility by establishing companies such as the Atlanta Savings Bank, the Citizens Trust Bank, and the Atlanta Life Insurance Company.[16]

Atlanta also became a center of black intellectual life. During Reconstruction (1865–1871), the city's black elite had collaborated with northern philanthropists to found "the largest complex of Historically Black Colleges and Universities (HBCUs) in the nation."[17] This complex included Atlanta University, Morehouse College, Clark College, Spelman College, and Morris Brown College. At Atlanta University, W.E.B. Du Bois conducted the first sociological studies in the country and debated the national black leader Booker T. Washington.[18] Du Bois believed that well-educated blacks (the "talented tenth") would be a vanguard in the struggle for racial justice; Washington advocated black accommodation to segregation and promoted vocational training over a college education.[19] All of Atlanta's historically black colleges and universities stressed activism and a responsibility to serve the black community, as reflected in mottos such as "lifting as we climb," "culture for service," and "I'll find a way or make one."[20] African American institutions of higher learning also became sites of connection between members of the African diaspora: black elites from Africa, the Caribbean, and other parts of Latin America sent their children to HBCUs in Atlanta and elsewhere.[21] According to Hobson, "no force in the city had more political, social, cultural, and historical significance for blacks than the founding of these institutions of higher education."[22]

Throughout the Jim Crow era, seasonal migrant workers who primarily lived in rural areas outside of Atlanta made up Georgia's tiny Mexican population.[23] These Mexicans occupied an ambiguous place within Georgia's segregated anti-black institutions. The 1848 Treaty of Guadalupe Hidalgo guaranteed Mexicans residing in the United States "all the rights of citizens of the United States." In practice, however, this stipulation was applied unevenly.[24] In her study of the history of Mexicans in the U.S. Southeast, Julie Weise describes the complexity of the Mexican presence in the Jim Crow South:

> There was no easy, predictable continuity of whites' racial exclusion or inclusion of Mexicans, nor of African Americans' competition or solidarity with them. Rather, local actors engaged selectively with the regional and national politics of race, class, and citizenship to create a variety of outcomes throughout the twentieth century. In every case, white and African American southerners in different economic positions offered Mexicans complex combinations of acceptance and rejection, oppression and opportunity. Their attitudes

> and actions changed, in turn, as Mexicanos pursued their goals in ways that complemented, accepted, or resisted the local status quo.[25]

In the 1950s, Atlanta's small Latine population added a number of Cuban professionals and entrepreneurs who were fleeing Castro's rule.[26] These newcomers were settling in a city where segregation and racism were the order of the day and the Ku Klux Klan remained active.[27] At the same time, black activists, community leaders, and local residents were fighting the injustices of Jim Crow in the courts and in the streets.[28]

Home to Dr. Martin Luther King's Ebenezer Baptist Church and the headquarters for organizations such as King's Southern Christian Leadership Conference (SCLC) and the Student Nonviolent Coordinating Committee (SNCC), Atlanta became a hub for the civil rights movement in the 1960s.[29] Students from HBCUs often participated in direct actions in the city, including acts of civil disobedience such as sit-ins at "whites only" diners.[30] While SNCC and the SCLC were run by middle-class blacks, the emergence of the National Welfare Rights Organization (NWRO) gave voice to poor black women. Ethel Mae Mathews, president of the Atlanta NWRO chapter, advocated desegregation so that their children could have access to a quality education.[31] John Lewis, a key player in the civil rights movement, carried his activism into the halls of Congress by becoming a Georgia congressional representative.[32]

Although by the 1960s courts had ruled that "separate but equal" regimes were unconstitutional, Atlanta's white leaders resisted court-ordered mandates to integrate neighborhoods and schools, and according to Bayor, segregation in Atlanta actually widened during the civil rights era.[33] City planners built highways and public buildings that cordoned off black residents from whites and destroyed established black communities. Running east-west, Highway 20 divided the predominantly black southern neighborhoods from the predominantly white northern suburbs—a division that persists today. North-south Interstate 75/85 bisected the central city across Auburn Avenue, one of the flourishing black business centers.[34] Figure 2.1 depicts Atlanta's county boundaries and Latine population.

From the late 1960s through the 1970s and 1980s, Atlanta's black political and economic power expanded. Black economic advancement in Atlanta was strengthened by the enforcement of the antidiscrimination provisions of the Civil Rights Act of 1964. This policy created legal recourse to unfair treatment on the basis of race.[35] Meanwhile, opportunities for starting a business, building a professional career, or pursuing an advanced degree opened up for the metro area's middle-class blacks.[36] Indeed, Atlanta's prosperous economy and thriving local black institutions led *Ebony*

Figure 2.1 Atlanta Latine Population Density by Census Tract, 2021

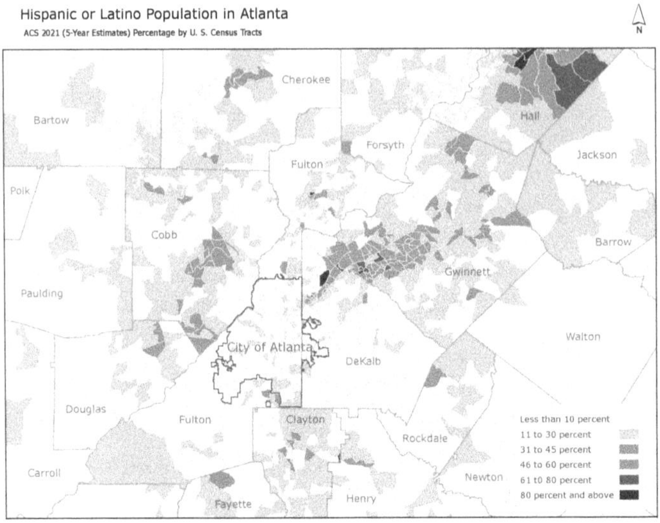

Source: American Community Survey, 2017–2021 (U.S. Census Bureau 2022a).

magazine to dub the city the "black Mecca" in 1971.[37] This reputation persisted through multiple decades. In 1974, blacks gained traction in Atlanta's politics when Maynard Jackson was elected the city's first black mayor. Jackson enacted landmark legislation to open up opportunities for black businesses to obtain city contracts.[38]

In 2003, *Atlanta* magazine announced that Atlanta had the "highest percentage of middle-class African Americans of any city in the nation—ushering in a new era of economic and political clout."[39] However, alongside the advances in political power and economic opportunities, the decades of black exclusion had produced a racially segregated city, disproportionately high black poverty rates, and persistent anti-black discrimination.[40]

The Impact of Immigration Policy on Latine Immigrant Settlement in Georgia, 1960s–2000

Beginning in the 1960s, as middle-class blacks were finding a place in Atlanta's growing economy and shifting political environment, prospects for working-class and middle-class Latine immigrants were also improving. In Georgia and throughout the United States, the inflow of immigrants from Latin America began accelerating following the passage of amendments to the 1965 Immigration and Nationality Act (Hart-Celler Act). As I discuss in chapter 1, this federal legislation changed the criteria for entering the United States from nationality-based quotas to family unification and job skills.

The majority of the Latine immigrants moving into Georgia in the 1960s and 1970s came from Mexico and settled in rural areas, not in Atlanta.[41] They filled jobs that black workers had left in pursuit of more lucrative manufacturing employment in Georgia and in the Rust Belt.[42] Black and white farmers in Georgia's rural areas increasingly depended on migrant labor and opposed restrictive immigration policy.[43] By 1975, half of the southwestern Georgia agricultural workforce was Mexican and Mexican American. Weise contends that "middle- and lower-middle class blacks trumpeted Mexicans' arrival into the agricultural fields as proof that black people had moved up in the world."[44]

With most Latine immigrants living in rural Georgia in 1970, Atlanta's foreign-born population remained small, comprising less than 2 percent of the metro's total inhabitants. Europeans represented the largest group of immigrants.[45] Sonia was one of several respondents who remarked on the scarcity of Latines living in Atlanta in the 1970s and 1980s: "When I came here [in the 1980s] . . . I guess I was the first Mexican between Midtown and Buckhead [the affluent area just north of Midtown]. . . . I mean there was nobody. I mean nobody. There was not one Hispanic soul in Piedmont Park [in downtown Atlanta] for like fifteen years."

Middle-class Latine immigrants such as Sonia were drawn to the growing economic opportunities that Atlanta offered to entrepreneurs and professionals. To assist the few Mexicans in Atlanta and address their relative isolation, fledgling organizations supporting Atlanta's Latine community began springing up in the 1970s.[46] For instance, in 1972 the Latin American Association was founded by sheriff deputy Angel Ortiz and Stratton Frank. This organization initially helped Latine immigrants find jobs and affordable housing.[47] A Mexican consulate established in Atlanta in the early 1970s primarily focused on business enterprises and trade.[48] In 1979, Atlanta's weekly Spanish-language newspaper, *El Mundo Hispánico*, was founded.

Mexicans increased their presence in Georgia and in other new immigrant destinations by unprecedented numbers after the passage of the federal 1986 Immigration Reform and Control Act (IRCA).[49] IRCA contained provisions to meet two goals: to stem the inflow of Mexican immigrants (by punishing employers who hired workers without documentation) and to grant legal status to a "modest number" of Mexican immigrants who had been living in the United States for a long time.[50] The first goal was not accomplished, but the second goal was quite successful. Through IRCA, approximately 2.3 million undocumented Mexicans were legalized.[51] IRCA had especially profound consequences for southern states such as Georgia, since the newly legalized Mexican immigrants could now travel across state lines in pursuit of work—a possibility that was not legally available to them when they were unauthorized.[52]

The 1994 North American Free Trade Agreement (NAFTA) put more pressures on Mexican workers to migrate to the United States, as many Mexican farmers were unable to subsist under NAFTA.[53] Other economic trends in the global economy also displaced workers in Mexico and low-income countries.[54]

A push away from traditional U.S. destinations toward new destinations such as Atlanta was spurred by crackdowns on immigrant labor and a shrinking number of jobs in traditional immigration gateways such as California, Arizona, and Texas.[55] At the same time, pull factors in Georgia included job opportunities in industrial niches such as poultry processing and carpet manufacturing, which attracted a growing number of Mexican immigrants from other parts of the United States and from Mexico.[56]

Worried by the rise in Latine immigrants throughout the United States, both federal officials and local white native-born constituencies lobbied for more restrictive policies. "The passing of the federal 1996 Illegal Immigration Reform and Immigrant Responsibility Act (IIRIRA) fundamentally transformed life for immigrants—undocumented, documented, and quasi-documented alike."[57] Weise explains that in conjunction with the 1996 Antiterrorism and Effective Death Penalty Act, the IIRIRA restricted immigrant movement and sent a message that undocumented immigrants were unwanted. Importantly, these policies redefined "aggravated felonies" as any violation that carried a penalty of at least one year in prison. Immigrants—including lawful permanent residents—convicted of an aggravated felony were automatically deported without a hearing.[58]

Section 287(g) of the IIRIRA also contributed to the racialization of illegality. Identified in chapter 1 as a cornerstone of the racialization of illegality, the 287(g) program vastly increased possible state and local law enforcement involvement in deportation.[59] After the September 11, 2001, World Trade Tower attacks, the U.S. government established the Department of Homeland Security and moved immigration enforcement under DHS auspices. With heightened rhetoric around U.S. vulnerability to "terrorists," state and local lawmakers enacted policies to funnel additional funds to policing (as discussed in chapter 1).[60]

Local and state immigration policies in Georgia following the passage of IIRCA included a mix of restrictive and integrative measures.[61] In the northern Atlanta suburbs, communities were passing local ordinances that prohibited day laborers from gathering (Cherokee County), revoked the licenses of landlords who rented to undocumented immigrants (Cherokee County), and "required contractors to ensure that undocumented workers were not hired on public works jobs" (Gwinnett County).[62] Some Georgia communities also enacted policies that provided resources to undocumented immigrants and generated a more inclusive context of reception.

Dalton offers a particularly clear example of an initially welcoming atmosphere in a Georgia city that became increasingly guarded. Located ninety miles north of Atlanta, Dalton prides itself on being the largest manufacturer of wall-to-wall carpet in the world.[63] In the 1990s, when the owners of Dalton's carpet manufacturers saw a rapidly increasing Mexican immigrant workforce in their factories, community leaders hired two social scientists to advise them on how to successfully integrate the Latine newcomers into the local neighborhoods, schools, and churches.[64] City officials poured resources into Dalton schools in particular, establishing programs that promoted the academic success of Latine students.[65] The new policies and resources not only facilitated the economic integration of new immigrants but also communicated a sense of inclusion and belonging.

However, alongside the integrative efforts of Dalton's leaders, some Dalton residents organized to resist the Latine newcomers. The local group Citizens Against Illegals and the Ku Klux Klan sponsored demonstrations in downtown Dalton, and citizens joined a campaign to send anti-immigrant and anti-Latine letters to the editor of the local paper.[66]

Dominican Migration to Atlanta, 1990–2000

Given the migration trends, the history of Georgia's Latine immigrants through the 1970s is primarily a history of Mexican migration. While a growing number of Mexican migrants moved to Dalton and other towns in rural Georgia to work in manufacturing or till the fields in the 1980s and 1990s, opportunities for working-class and middle-class Latine immigrants began to flourish in the Atlanta metro area.[67] Responding to these growing opportunities, Dominicans joined the more recent waves of Latine immigration.

The story of Dominican migration to Atlanta differs from the migration patterns of both Mexicans in the Atlanta metro area and Dominicans in traditional Dominican destinations such as New York, Miami, Providence, Washington, D.C., Boston, and Philadelphia.[68] Dominicans started migrating to New York before World War II in search of economic opportunities.[69] As Peggy Levitt explains in her study *The Transnational Villagers*, early Dominican migration to the United States was limited, and most migrants were wealthy families or refugees escaping dictator Rafael Trujillo's rule.

But "once begun, migration broadened to include a wide cross section of Dominican society."[70] Economic and political instability in the Dominican Republic from the 1960s through the 1980s also motivated Dominicans to leave the country and settle in traditionally favored U.S. destinations such New York and Miami.[71] During these decades, very few Dominicans were moving to Atlanta.

My interviews provide a window into the motivations behind the migration of the few middle-class Dominicans who made their way to Atlanta in the 1980s and 1990s. Three respondents reported that Atlanta was an appealing destination at that time precisely because of the lack of a large Dominican or Latine population. Lio, for instance, knowing that he wanted to move to the United States, chose Atlanta because there were so few Dominicans there. "My choices were not New York and not Miami," he said, "because it was already too many Dominicans there." When asked why he did not want to live in a city with a large number of Dominicans, he responded by noting differences in social class, which he perceived as creating differences in "culture":

> Most of the people that migrated from the Dominican Republic to New York, they did it in the sixties, when there was no visa or quota or anything like that. You just showed up. And the vast majority were from rural areas as opposed to professionals. So they would go there and then their jobs that they would do were, you know, fixing machines or that kind of blue-collar jobs. So the culture up there didn't quite relate to . . . to me, both in the sense of, excuse me, in sense of education and also culture.

Thus, his status as a middle-class professional and his attitudes toward the (undesirable) cultural differences of working-class Dominicans shaped Lio's decisions about moving to Atlanta. His perspective was not common among our Dominican respondents, the majority of whom were enthusiastic about their friendships with other educated Dominicans.

Francisco also invoked middle-class status when he explained why he moved to Atlanta in the 1980s. He saw the small number of Latines there as a bonus that would open up opportunities for himself and his children. The move to Atlanta, Francisco said, would bring "more security . . . better living, less Hispanic people. What would guarantee a future for my kids would be for them to develop in a growing society, where Hispanics were developing. They could . . . form part of the Hispanic leadership, like the labor force, like . . . like professionals."

Francisco envisioned his children not simply joining the middle class as professionals but as taking positions of leadership from which they would contribute to the growing Latine community and elevate their social and political status even further. Unlike Lio, who expressed a desire to live away from Dominicans, Francisco foresaw his family engaging with Atlanta's growing Latine population and perceived the benefits of being a "pioneer" ahead of the wave of Dominican migration to Atlanta.

The different years in which respondents migrated provide information on differences in their motivation to self-select and move to Atlanta over time. "Pioneers" such as Francisco moved to Atlanta in the 1980s, when there were very few Latines in the city. Some welcomed living in a place where their co-nationals were so sparse. Others were hoping to establish businesses that catered to a growing Latine population. As the Atlanta Latine immigrant population grew, a "chain migration" pattern emerged—respondents moving to Atlanta because they had a friend or relative living in the metro area. This pattern affected the racial composition of workplaces, schools, neighborhoods, and the social networks upon which respondents could rely.

ATLANTA IN THE TWENTY-FIRST CENTURY

Atlanta's "Diversity Explosion"

Given the economic growth of the metro area and its national reputation as a place of opportunity for black and Latine migrants of all social classes, Atlanta has moved to the forefront of the "diversity explosion" that is transforming the country from a majority-white nation to a country with a racially diverse population.[72] Between 2000 and 2021, Atlanta shifted from a black-white metropolis where 62 percent of the population was white and 28 percent was black to a white-black-Latine metro in which no group held a majority position. As figure 2.2 illustrates, the number and proportion of whites dropped over the past twenty years, while the black population rose to 34 percent of the metro area's population. Atlanta's Latine population doubled, from 5 percent to 12 percent, and continues to grow. The metro area's relatively small Asian population also doubled, from 3.3 percent in 2000 to 6 percent in 2021.

In some ways, the population trends in Atlanta mirror those in the United States as a whole. The white population is falling but remains in the plurality. The Latine and Asian populations are growing, though Latine representation in Atlanta, at 12 percent, is lower than the national average (20 percent). Atlanta diverges from national population trends, however, in one striking respect: blacks comprise 12 percent of the U.S. population, but represent one-third of Atlanta's population.

Figure 2.2 Atlanta's Demographic Composition, 2000 and 2021

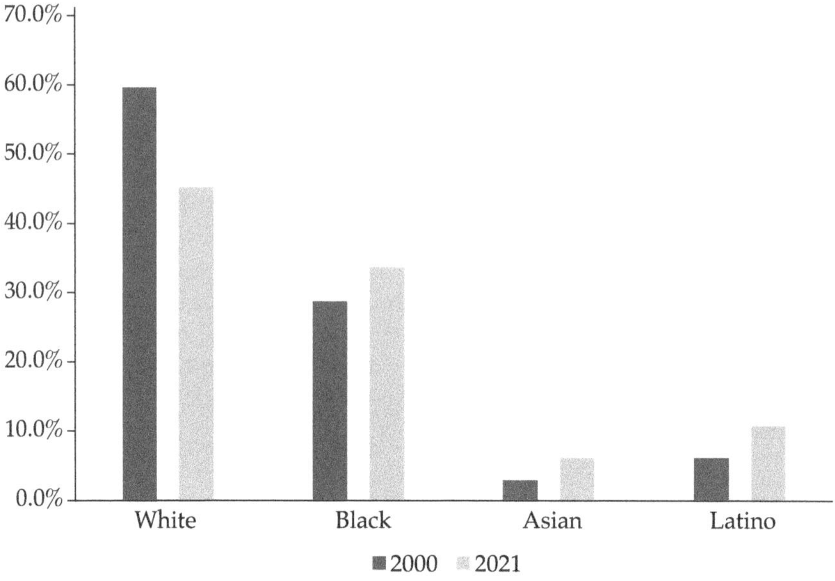

Source: U.S. Census Bureau 2001 and American Community Survey, 2017–2021 (U.S. Census Bureau 2022b).
Note: Groups are mutually exclusive in this table. "Whites" are non-Hispanic whites and "blacks" are non-Hispanic blacks.

Dramatic Shifts in the Demographic Profile of Local Communities

Table 2.1 illustrates the demographic shifts in the ten counties of the Atlanta metro area. Some of these counties showed especially dramatic changes in the racial mix of their population. For instance, in Gwinnett County, both the Latine population and the black population doubled between 2000 and 2021, while the white population fell by almost half. Rockdale County flipped from a predominantly white county to a predominantly black county with a small but growing population of Latines.

A Thriving Economy

An important draw for middle-class migrants is the national reputation Atlanta maintains as a city with some of the most favorable economic conditions for professionals in the United States—particularly for black profes-

Table 2.1 Atlanta's Demographic Composition by County, 2000 and 2021

County	2000			2021		
	Percentage Latine	Percentage White	Percentage Black	Percentage Latine	Percentage White	Percentage Black
North						
Cherokee	0.05	0.90	0.02	0.11	0.77	0.07
Cobb	0.08	0.69	0.19	0.13	0.50	0.27
DeKalb	0.08	0.32	0.54	0.09	0.29	0.52
Gwinnett	0.11	0.67	0.13	0.22	0.35	0.28
South						
Clayton	0.07	0.35	0.51	0.13	0.09	0.69
Douglas	0.03	0.76	0.18	0.10	0.37	0.47
Fayette	0.03	0.82	0.11	0.08	0.59	0.24
Fulton	0.06	0.45	0.44	0.07	0.39	0.43
Spanning North and South						
Henry	0.02	0.80	0.15	0.07	0.39	0.46
Rockdale	0.06	0.73	0.18	0.10	0.29	0.56
N	249,218	1,898,150	1,090,925	565,250	1,817,705	1,797,664

Source: 2000 Decennial Census and 2017–2021 American Community Survey (U.S. Census Bureau 2022a).
Note: Includes all ten counties comprising the Atlanta Metropolitan Region, as defined by the Atlanta Regional Commission.

sionals. For instance, the *Atlanta Journal-Constitution* has described Atlanta as a "center of black political power, wealth, and culture," and in 2020 *Forbes* put Atlanta on par with Washington, D.C., as the number-one metropolis in the nation where blacks were doing the best economically. *Forbes* also identified Atlanta as an "incubator for black entrepreneurs."[73] Atlanta finds appeal among big tech companies because of its relatively high number of black college graduates with degrees in computer science and engineering, as well as the "low taxes, few regulations, no unions, cheap housing, the airport and weather."[74]

The metro area's expanding population of black professionals, business owners, and entrepreneurs is part of "a Great Migration in reverse": returning south, some of the descendants of those who moved north in the twentieth century's Great Migration are finding a wealth of well-established black institutional structures and resources alongside growing opportunities.[75] Well-educated black parents can enroll their children in the elite black Jack and Jill clubs, they can reside in exclusive, predominantly black gated subdivisions, and they receive strong local political support for black-run ventures. Atlanta's rapidly growing black entertainment ventures have earned it a national reputation as the "new black Hollywood."[76]

Atlanta is also home to a growing number of black immigrants. As table 2.2 shows, the majority of the metro area's black immigrants are not Afro-Latine but hail instead from outside the Spanish-speaking Caribbean—Africa, Jamaica, and Haiti. The immigrant share is similar among Atlanta's college-educated black population.[77] Many black immigrants with low levels of education have settled in Clarkston, a city in the Atlanta metro area that houses more refugees per capita than any other city in the United States.[78] The city's large refugee population is the result of the combined efforts of local nongovernmental organizations (NGOs) targeting the city for affordable refugee resettlement and local officials advertising Clarkston as a "welcoming city."[79]

Latine professionals also are finding abundant economic opportunity in Atlanta.[80] As seen with our respondents, Atlanta-based corporations such as Coca-Cola, Home Depot, and UPS value cosmopolitan Latine professional employees who are fluent in multiple languages and comfortable interacting with clients from around the globe.[81] For instance, Jessica, from Mexico, headed a consulting company that assisted corporations in diversifying their workforce. She described middle-class immigrant skills, aptitudes, and backgrounds as the "secret sauce" possessed by educated Latine ("our community"). Her consulting company, she said,

> also developed our community advisory council, which is growing. That we launched . . . March of last year, um, which represents its different institu-

Table 2.2 Country of Birth for the Foreign-Born Population and the Black Foreign-Born Population, Atlanta Metropolitan Area, 2017–2021

	Percentage of Foreign-Born	Percentage of Black Population	Percentage of Black Foreign-Born	Percentage of Black Foreign-Born with a College Degree
Country of birth				
Mexico	15.55	0.07	0.71	0.42
Dominican Republic	1.19	0.12	1.24	0.39
Cuba	0.89	0.02	0.22	0.22
West Indies	8.81	3.60	36.55	40.25
Continent of birth				
Africa	12.38	4.85	49.29	45.62
North America (excluding the United States)	36.22	4.03	40.88	44.41
South America	8.30	0.31	3.11	3.68
Europe	10.50	0.54	5.51	5.62
Asia	32.20	0.11	1.12	0.68
Australia, Oceania	0.28	0.01	0.08	0.00
United States	—	90.15	—	—
N	33,213	61,300	5711	798

Source: 2017–2021 American Community Survey (U.S. Census Bureau 2022a) and Ruggles et al. 2022a.
Note: Percentages are weighted.

> tions, larger institutions in Atlanta, who understand diversity to be a value and kind of a secret sauce of our [Latine] community, and they recognize that that's very important to their business, so, um, it's Turner, UPS, Coca-Cola refreshments, Georgia Power, Chattahoochee Technical College, Georgia State University, Doraville police department, um, all of the Gwinnett County schools.

Several respondents mentioned the Coca-Cola Corporation as a source of professional employment. Horacio remarked, "There's a lot of Cuban, Colombian, Dominicans that . . . are very well established. They have businesses—I mean Coca-Cola has a great number of middle-class individuals that came here, actually some of them hired by Coca-Cola from within Latin America, and they just came here."

For Esteban, a Dominican, both his future wife's employment at Coca-

Cola and their perceptions of Atlanta's ample opportunities for professionals factored into their decision to relocate from Miami to Atlanta:

> So when I finished my PhD in Miami . . . at the time [my future wife] was working for Coca-Cola, and she felt that she liked the company, she had a lot of potential for a career there. And since I had an advanced degree and much more experience than she did, we felt that it would be easier for me to find a job here [in Atlanta], a good job, than it would be for her to find a job in Miami. So we decided to look . . . to stay. . . . I decided to relocate here, and we got married.

Residential Segregation and Settlement

Despite the class diversity of Atlanta's black population and the city's strong economic growth, years of segregationist policy—such as the concentration of public housing in the city of Atlanta, discriminatory lending practices toward blacks, and limited public transportation in the northern suburbs—have kept many of its neighborhoods racially segregated.[82]

Atlanta's southern suburbs and central city are home not only to the majority of Atlanta's poor and working-class blacks but also to many of the metro's wealthy black families. For instance, the Cascade Corridor neighborhood, located in Atlanta's southern suburbs, earned this appealing description in *Atlanta* magazine:

> Want to rub elbows with the likes of Atlanta mayors, civil rights hero C. T. Vivian, singer Janelle Monáe, and top execs such as Coca-Cola's Carl Ware? Then head to southwest Fulton County and the tony neighborhoods of the Cascade Road corridor. . . . Like similar suburban communities, the Cascade area has strong homeowner associations, verdant cul-de-sacs, active megachurches, golf courses, and tennis leagues.[83]

The advertisement signals class exclusivity: Atlanta's mayor and corporate executives are counted among the residents, and the subdivision provides activities typically associated with middle-class lifestyles, such as golf courses and tennis leagues.

Even with its rich amenities, the Cascade area lost value during the Great Recession of 2007–2009. Indeed, due to the *racial* residential segregation dividing Atlanta, housing values in predominantly black neighborhoods across the class spectrum have been much slower to recover from the recession-led drop in assessed value compared to the similar housing of whites who live in Atlanta's northern suburbs.[84]

Although whites are no longer a majority of metro Atlanta's population, many are concentrated in predominantly white enclaves in the northern suburbs. College-educated Latine immigrants are settling close to these white neighborhoods rather than predominantly black neighborhoods such as the Cascade Corridor. Over half of metro Atlanta's Latine population with at least four years of college reside in just two northern counties—Cobb County and Gwinnett County (table 2.3). An additional 25 percent of college-educated Latine live in Fulton County, which extends into the northern and southern regions of the Atlanta metro area.[85] Yet, as the Latine population has grown in the northern suburbs, so has their residential segregation from their white neighbors. That is, Atlanta's Latine segregation from whites *increased* between 1980 and 2020.[86]

Table 2.3 relies on census data to show where Atlanta's Mexicans and Dominicans are settling and divides them by college education. The table suggests that Latine immigrant settlement patterns differ by social class and nationality. Well-educated Mexicans and Dominicans are more likely than their less-educated co-nationals to settle in whiter Cobb and Gwinnett Counties.

The interviews provide a window into day-to-day experiences of Atlanta's neighborhood segregation amid growing county diversity. María José described the area where she lived in Gwinnett County as racially diverse but also segregated:

> There are a lot of Latinos here. There's a bit of everything. I believe that there is everything. . . . We are exactly at the middle of [the city of] Norcross and [the city of] Duluth. Right there. And so, for example, in Norcross it's very interesting, because they have exactly two very different areas. It's incredible. (*laughs*) If you find yourself in Norcross, heading towards Beaver Road, it is completely Latino. And you see that . . . there are Latinos. If you go to the other side of Norcross, over by Peachtree Industrial and all that, there are . . . purely Americans. For example, that park that is here, where they play baseball, that . . . that is Norcross. The Norcross baseball team, although it is in Norcross . . . they are not . . . they are all Americans. All of them. They are from the other side.

María José, a Dominican, depicted the spatial and social divisions in terms of "us" (Latines) and "them" ("Americans"). Francisco talked about his neighborhood as more diverse without making an explicit "us" and "them" distinction. He clarified that there were "very few Hispanic families, like three, there are two hundred houses, and there are various: Hindus, Koreans, Vietnamese, African . . . African Americans, three or four Hispanic families, variety, multiracial."

Although respondents listed "diversity" as an attractive quality of their

Table 2.3 Distribution of Latine Immigrants across Atlanta Metro Counties by Nationality and Education Level, 2017–2021

County	Mexicans		Dominicans		Total Latine Foreign-Born		
	Percentage noncollege	Percentage college	Percentage noncollege	Percentage college	Percentage noncollege	Percentage college	Percentage total
North							
Cherokee	0.05	0.03	0.01	0.10	0.05	0.05	0.05
Cobb	0.20	0.28	0.09	0.17	0.20	0.21	0.20
DeKalb	0.04	0.06	0.03	0.02	0.05	0.07	0.05
Gwinnett	0.37	0.24	0.69	0.53	0.43	0.31	0.40
Subtotal	0.66	0.61	0.81	0.82	0.73	0.64	0.71
South							
Clayton	0.11	0.05	0.09	0.01	0.08	0.02	0.07
Douglas	0.02	0.03	0.03	0.01	0.02	0.02	0.02
Fayette	0.02	0.01	0.01	0.00	0.01	0.02	0.01
Fulton	0.13	0.23	0.06	0.13	0.11	0.26	0.14
Subtotal	0.27	0.33	0.18	0.16	0.22	0.31	0.24
Spanning North and South							
Henry	0.02	0.05	0.01	0.03	0.02	0.03	0.02
Rockdale	0.04	0.01	0.01	0.00	0.03	0.02	0.03
Total	1.00	1.000	1.000	1.000	1.000	1.000	1.000
N	16430		714		29610		

Source: American Community Survey 2017–2021 (U.S. Census Bureau 2022a) and Ruggles et al. 2022a.

neighborhood, the reasons they gave for choosing where to live were overwhelmingly based on two factors: good schools and proximity to work (see figure 2.3). These preferences brought respondents to Atlanta's predominantly white northern suburbs.[87]

Respondents selected their current neighborhood for reasons similar to those of native-born whites.[88] What was absent among respondents were reasons that pointed to a "minority culture of mobility." Especially noteworthy was that, while many middle-class blacks elect to live in a predominantly black neighborhood to shield their children from discrimination and to instill a sense of black pride, only one of our respondents mentioned that a concern with anti-Latine discrimination factored into her residential choices.[89]

Respondents also did not flag exclusive black neighborhoods, such as the Cascade Corridor, as one of their options. Instead, they pursued a path of "structural assimilation," that is, moving into white-dominated neighborhoods, schools, and workplaces in the northern suburbs. These spaces corresponded with the most highly ranked schools.

Figure 2.3 Dominican and Mexican Respondents' Reasons for Selecting Current Neighborhood

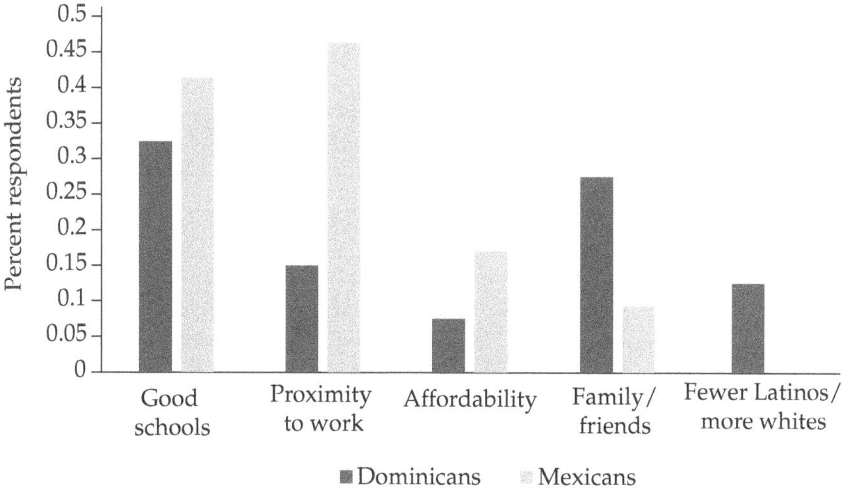

Source: Author's calculations from respondent interviews 2009–2016.

Children and Schools

Most of the respondents stressed the importance of education for their children and saw the U.S. education system as affording opportunities that the heritage schools did not provide. Yet some white parents, pushing against the influx of Latine into the schools, are now advocating redistricting to concentrate Latine schoolchildren in a few places.

Atlanta's schools have experienced a sea change in their demographic composition since 2000.[90] This change is part of a "diversity explosion" occurring in cities and towns throughout the United States. Following these trends, William Frey asserts that, because Latine and black populations are significantly younger than white populations, children and schools throughout the nation are at the forefront of the recent substantial demographic shifts; as a result, an increasing number of schools and communities are becoming majority-minority.[91]

The current demographics of public schools vary widely, and Atlanta's expanding number of low-income students of color still find themselves concentrated in low-performing schools.[92] Beth Tarasawa explains that, "for Latines and African Americans, public high schools in the metro Atlanta region are experiencing significant racial shifts with greater levels of segregation than integration." Ironically, the neighborhoods in Atlanta that would be expected to most strongly reflect racial diversity—those with the highest degree of diversity—have been the *least* likely to reflect this diversity in the student body of their local public schools.[93] This lack of diversity is largely attributable to the lower number of white children attending Atlanta's public schools compared to the white proportion of the population, since many wealthy white parents enroll their children in private or charter schools. For instance, over 80 percent of the students enrolled in Cross Keys High School in DeKalb County are Latine and only 1 percent are white, even though the census tract population of the two largest catchment areas (Chamblee and Doraville) is no higher than 55 percent Latine and no lower than 19 percent white.[94]

The concentration of black and Latine students in the relatively low-resourced schools is reflected in test scores. Only 30 percent of black children and 35 percent of Latine children in the Atlanta metro area are proficient in math, compared to 54 percent of white children.[95]

Monica, an attorney who migrated to the United States from Mexico as a child in the late 1980s, presented a vivid comparison of the uneven distribution of resources in Atlanta's high schools, in line with schools' racial composition. Transferring schools between ninth and tenth grade in the late 1990s, Monica moved from one difficult environment to another: from a well-resourced, predominantly white school where she felt "marginalized and alienated" to a poorly resourced school where she felt at home with her Latine peers:

> In Roswell [the predominantly white school], I finally felt that huge difference in how you're marginalized, and how you're alienated. But when I came back to our [predominantly Latine] school, you know . . . um, that's when I saw the huge differences in resources. [The building] is old. It's falling apart. Some, you know, lack of air conditioning. Broken windows. We have a couple of computers in the library. . . . But that was about it. And I remember in Roswell they had like all sorts of extracurricular and clubs and a lot of electives, with a lot of classes. Um, and here, I think that the only thing that was offered then is still probably . . . like . . . like a . . . tech electronic course?

As more and more middle-class individuals number among Atlanta's growing population of Latine immigrants, however, some schools are reflecting this demographic. Lourdes noted, for instance, that her son "has advanced classes, so I notice and the majority in the classrooms end up being Hispanics and before you didn't see that."

Well-Educated Mexican and Dominican Immigrants in Atlanta

The census data can answer several relevant questions: What time trends characterize the settlement of middle-class Latine immigrants in Atlanta? How has the population changed over time, not only in size but in education level? Has the settlement of middle-class Latines in Atlanta diverged from settlement patterns in traditional destinations? Is Atlanta's middle-class population more diverse in terms of national origin than the broader Latine population? Have they been in the Atlanta area longer? How many Latine migrants arrived in the 1990s?[96]

To follow the settlement of Mexican and Dominican immigrants in Atlanta since 1990, I took advantage of U.S. census data to contrast foreign-born Latines in the Atlanta metropolitan area with the nine metropolises identified as "major traditional immigrant destinations": Boston, Chicago, Dallas, Houston, Los Angeles, Miami, New York, Riverside (California), San Diego, San Francisco, and Washington, D.C.[97] Looking at figures 2.4 through 2.7, we see that the proportion of well-educated immigrants in Atlanta and traditional immigrant gateways alike seems to be lower among Mexicans than among other Latine immigrant groups. The proportion of Latine immigrants with a college degree is approximately the same across geographic areas for Mexicans. Dominicans in Atlanta have more college degrees than Dominicans in other immigrant destinations. This pattern

Figure 2.4 Proportion of All Foreign-Born Adults with a College Degree, 2000–2021

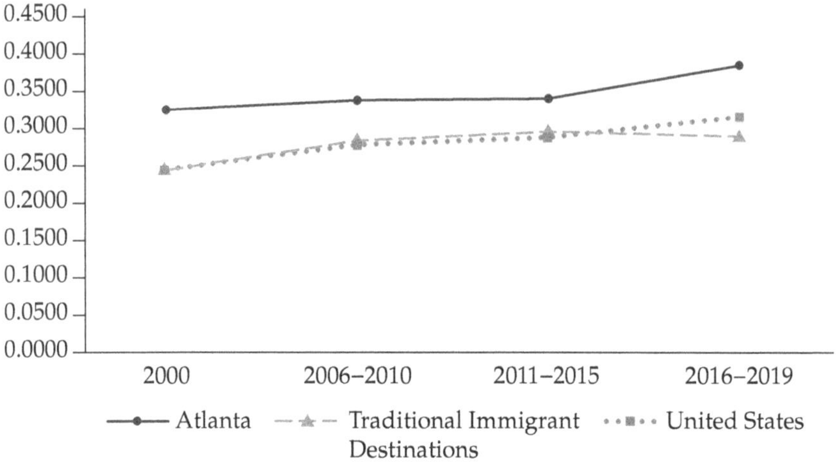

Source: U.S. Census Bureau 2001 and Ruggles et al. 2022a, 2022b, 2022c.

Figure 2.5 Proportion of Foreign-Born Latines with a College Degree, 2000–2021

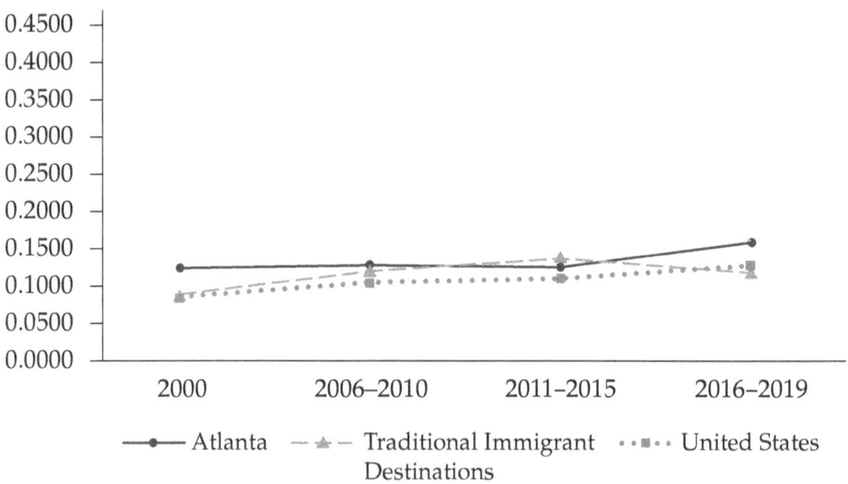

Source: U.S. Census Bureau 2001 and Ruggles et al. 2022a, 2022b, 2022c.

Figure 2.6 Proportion of Foreign-Born Mexicans with a College Degree, 2000–2021

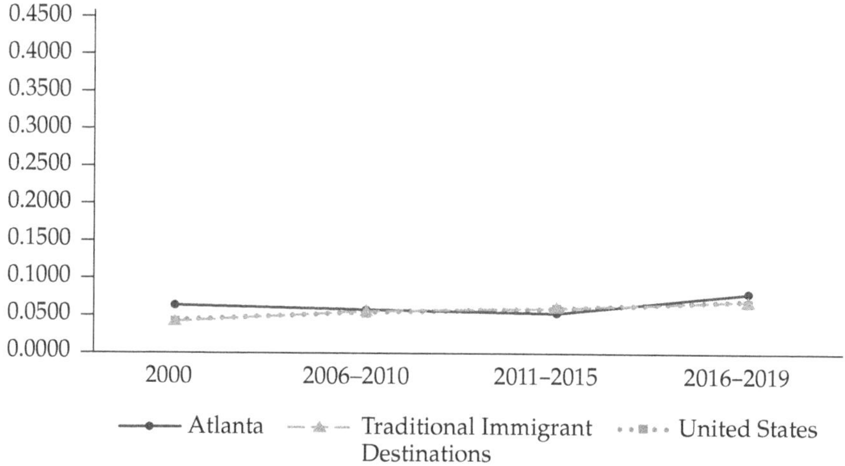

Source: U.S. Census Bureau 2001 and Ruggles et al. 2022a, 2022b, 2022c.

Figure 2.7 Proportion of Foreign-Born Dominicans with a College Degree, 2000–2021

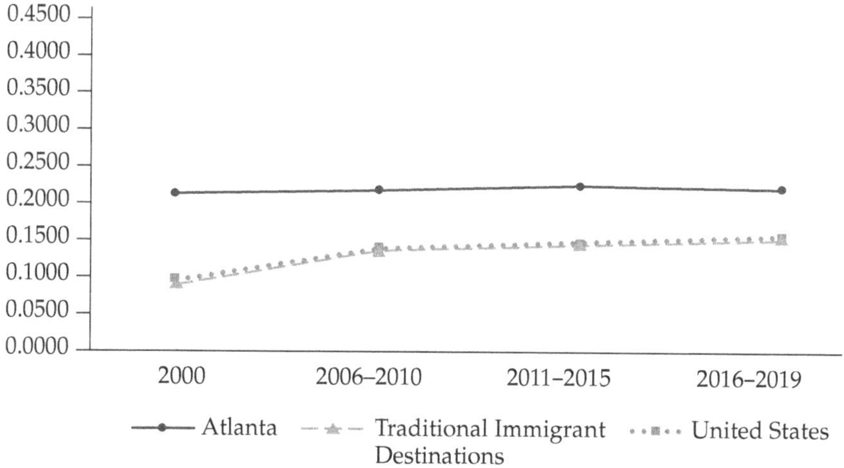

Source: U.S. Census Bureau 2001 and Ruggles et al. 2022a, 2022b, 2022c.

suggests that there has been a "selection effect" encouraging middle-class Dominicans to move to Atlanta.

In addition, middle-class Mexicans and Dominicans have been settling in Atlanta at approximately the same rates as their non-college-educated co-nationals. The overall proportion of Latine foreign-born and Mexicans has held steady since 2000, with a very slight increase in the Latine foreign-born between 2010 and 2021.

Relatively low rates of college completion among Mexicans and relatively higher rates among Dominicans translate into greater national diversity among Atlanta's Latine middle class. We can see this national diversity by examining contemporary patterns among Latine immigrants with a college degree or higher. As table 2.4 shows, Mexicans comprise 24 percent of Atlanta's college-educated foreign-born Latines in Atlanta, but they make up over 50 percent of the total Latine foreign-born population. In contrast, the proportion of Dominicans among the college-educated (5 percent) is similar to that among the total population of Latine foreign-born (4 percent). There are disproportionately more Argentinian, Brazilian, Colombian, Venezuelan, and other South American adults among the college-educated Latine foreign-born in Atlanta than there are among Atlanta's total Latine foreign-born.

With their college educations and advanced degrees, our respondents were members of an exclusive group both in Atlanta and in their heritage country, as table 2.5 illustrates. The benefits of a college education actually depend on the collective education level of the national-origin group. For immigrants, a college education takes on a different meaning and provides different levels of resources (financial and cultural capital) according to the average educational attainment in their heritage country compared to the United States.[98] Well-educated co-nationals import class-specific cultural institutions and practices from their countries of origin and re-create those that have the most utility in their new host country.[99] The difference in an immigrant group's stores of education not only is important for generating and accessing cultural and economic resources but also shapes how members of an immigrant group are perceived by the native-born.[100] The extremely low levels of education in the heritage countries are striking; over half of the adults in Mexico and the Dominican Republic do not have a high school diploma, and less than one-fifth hold a bachelor's degree. Thus, class inequality is high in Mexico and the Dominican Republic.

Because educated Mexican and Dominican immigrants from our sample originated from national immigrant groups with low average years of education, they experienced an especially wide class distance between themselves and other immigrants from Mexico and the Dominican Republic (table 2.4). For instance, high rates of poverty accompany low levels of education: "Mexico is one of the 12 countries where 80 percent of the

Table 2.4 Distribution of Nationalities of Latine Foreign-Born in the Atlanta Metro Area by Education, 2017–2021

Country of Birth	Percentage of Non-College-Educated Latine Foreign-Born	Percentage of Latine Foreign-Born College Graduates	Percentage of Total Latine Foreign-Born
Mexico	51.1	21.0	45.8
Dominican Republic	3.3	4.3	3.5
Cuba	2.1	5.1	2.6
Central America			
Belize/British Honduras	0.2	0.4	0.2
Costa Rica	0.7	1.8	0.9
El Salvador	7.3	2.4	6.4
Guatemala	8.6	2.8	7.6
Honduras	6.1	2.5	5.5
Nicaragua	1.2	1.5	1.2
Panama	1.6	2.2	1.7
South America			
Argentina	0.39	3.1	0.9
Bolivia	0.1	1.1	0.3
Brazil	3.8	11.8	5.2
Chile	0.3	1.0	0.43
Colombia	4.5	15.0	6.3
Ecuador	0.7	2.2	0.9
Guyana/British Guiana	2.8	3.8	3.0
Paraguay	0.0	0.2	0.1
Peru	1.6	3.6	2.0
Uruguay	0.6	0.5	0.6
Venezuela	2.8	13.4	4.6
Total	100	100	100
N (unweighted sample size)	8,360	1,779	10,139

Source: Ruggles et al. 2022a.
Note: Percents are weighted.

world's poor are concentrated."[101] Class inequality in the Dominican Republic is also substantial. Howard Wiarda and Michael Kryzanek observe:

> From a cold statistical viewpoint, the class differences in the Dominican Republic are stark. The bottom 50 percent of income earners receive 18.5 percent of the national income, while the top 10 percent receive 38.5 percent of the national income . . . per capita income has stagnated near the $1,000 level [since the 1980s and 1990s], keeping the nation poor and preventing it from

Table 2.5 Latines with a College Degree: Comparing Study Respondents with Immigrants in Atlanta and in the United States, 2017–2021

	Percentage Who Completed College Education			
	Heritage Country	Atlanta	United States	Study Respondents
Mexicans	17	8	8	95
Dominicans	18	22	16	80

Source: Ruggles et al. 2022a; USAID 2023.

> breaking out of its Third World status. . . . Although the 1980s and 1990s have not seen an improvement in the living standards of the poor, the situation of the Dominican middle and upper classes reveals a much different situation. They have done quite well.[102]

Not only did our Mexican and Dominican respondents occupy the top half of the class distribution through their own educational and professional accomplishments, but many of them grew up with college-educated parents who worked in prestigious professional occupations:

> SARA (Mexican, researcher): My father was the dean of a college.
>
> MONICA (Mexican, attorney): My father was a chef [in Mexico].
>
> JADE (Mexican, homemaker): My father is a public accountant, and my mom studied commerce.
>
> ELISA (Mexican, homemaker): My dad is a lawyer, and my mom is a pharmacologist.
>
> ALEXANDRA (Mexican, PhD student): My mother teaches chemistry at the university. My father is an engineer. My brothers are engineers.
>
> JUAN (Dominican, architect): [My father] . . . he's an accountant.
>
> SARITA (Dominican, administrator): My mother [is] a pharmacist. And my dad is an engineer.
>
> FELIPE (Dominican, physician): My parents, both were doctors in Santo Domingo and had come to do a specialty in the United States.

Several respondents described their privileged lives as children in middle-class households in their heritage country. For instance, unlike the

Mexican immigrants who are escaping violence and poverty in Mexico and who dominate the news, Juan Diego grew up in Mexico in a family that he described as "upper-middle-class." His educational experience reflected this background; as he explained, he "went to probably one of the best schools in Mexico . . . a [private European] school" where he made friends with children of diplomats. Juan Diego received a degree in the sciences in Mexico; when he moved to the United States, he entered a career in journalism and was especially valued in this profession for his multilingual skills.

Ignacia, whose father held a prestigious position as a judge, also described growing up in an upper-middle-class family in Mexico: "I lived with my family, you know very family-centered life. So we could be like middle-upper, upper-middle level. . . . And then [you] could [have] your own car. You could get to go visit different places, you know, go overseas for a short vacation, things like that, but it was good. It was a good life." That Ignacia's Mexican childhood, constituting what she called a "good life," included world travel suggests that her childhood was also characterized by comfort and privilege.

For the respondents who grew up in families that were working-class or poor and who earned a college degree in the United States, the collective meaning of an advanced degree still held. That is, as college graduates, these respondents enjoyed higher status compared to coethnics in their heritage country and in the United States. Francisco articulated the link between education and middle-class status: "Immediately after I graduated [from the university,] I passed as middle-class, becoming a part of it in the Dominican Republic."

Studies suggest that the benefits of a college degree may be lower for immigrants who are educated in their heritage country compared to conational immigrants educated in the United States.[103] These benefits include high earnings, high occupational prestige, and positive health outcomes. My respondents did not appear to differ according to where they attained their degree. The majority of my respondents were educated in Mexico ($n = 19$), in the Dominican Republic ($n = 18$), or in both their heritage country and the United States ($n = 9$). Many of them came to the United States with advantages such as English fluency, professional job connections, and familiarity with the United States based on their previous travels and experiences.

Implications for Identity Work

Respondents' status in Mexico and the Dominican Republic as members of the "privileged few" in their heritage country and in the United States could generate a self-concept that embraced a high-status position. A college education may create an incentive to resist stigmatization by reclaiming class privilege. At the same time, holding a college degree may also heighten vulnerability to stigmatization, since educated Latine immigrants are often found in predominantly white environments.[104] The more middle-class Latine immigrants interact in spaces with middle-class white native-borns the more they are at risk of being stereotyped as undocumented working-class Mexicans. (I discuss their experiences with discrimination in chapter 4.)[105]

College-educated Mexicans, Dominicans, and other Latine immigrants living in Atlanta in the twenty-first century encounter a metro with a confluence of rapidly changing demographics, a strong, growing economy, black and Latine poverty rates that are more than double the white rate, and enduring residential segregation by race and class.[106] These conditions not only facilitate successful economic integration but support a political climate that stokes the racialization of illegality.

GEORGIA'S ANTI-IMMIGRANT MOVEMENT AND THE RACIALIZATION OF ILLEGALITY

The rapidly changing demographics of Atlanta's schools, neighborhoods, and workplaces—including the fall of whites from majority to minority status—contribute to whites' experience of Latines as a threat. Native-born whites who view Latines as a racial-ethnic out-group that is lower on the social hierarchy will perceive the growing number of Latines as presenting greater competition for valued resources.[107] The pace of change in the Latine population, rather than the raw numbers, appears to determine white anti-immigrant sentiment. In Atlanta, the pace of change has been remarkable, particularly among Dominicans. As Maria Abascal explains, "Studies repeatedly show that members of dominant groups respond to group status threats by reaffirming both their commitment to the ingroup and their rejection of outgroups."[108]

These fears fit with the concept of "racist nativism," defined as the "assigning of values to real or imagined differences, in order to justify the superiority of the native, who is to be perceived white, over that of the nonnative, who is perceived to be People and Immigrants of Color."[109] Reinforcing the status hierarchy between white Americans and Latine immigrants, racist nativism toward Latine immigrants often appears as concerns with the problem of "Mexicans," who are assumed to be illegal.[110]

National polls indicate that between one-third and one-half of Americans believe that immigrants are hurting the United States.[111] Americans' rejection of immigrants differs dramatically, however, along party lines. Forty-six percent of Republicans and independents see immigrants as burdening the system and taking jobs, housing, and government benefits away from American citizens. Only 12 percent of Democrats view immigrants as a burden.[112]

Georgians have expressed more negative views on immigrants than others in the country as a whole. For instance, a 2006 poll of Georgia's adult population showed that 52 percent believed that immigrants take jobs from Georgians.[113] Of Georgians polled in 2013, 41 percent opposed any policy that gave undocumented immigrants a path to remain in the United States legally.[114] As I explained in chapter 1, Georgia also has been at the forefront in adopting omnibus legislation that imposes restrictions on immigrants and attempts to criminalize immigration.[115]

Although Georgia voters are split on their views of immigration, Georgia's state and local policymakers across the political spectrum have been taking anti-immigrant stances and shoring up restrictions on the state's undocumented immigrants. Georgia passed thirty-eight anti-immigrant policies from 2005 to 2012. Table 2.6, which summarizes counts for each bill by the topic (or provision) that the measure covers, shows "yea" votes for each of these categories of legislation. Republican state representatives voted almost unanimously in favor of each of the restrictive immigration bills.[116] The majority of white Democrats (62 percent) also supported restrictive immigration measures, with only two exceptions: the Democrats opposed HB 56, a punitive omnibus measure, and bills that restricted access to the ballot. Slightly over half (53 percent) of Georgia's black Democratic legislators voted in favor of restrictive immigration policies, but they opposed policies related to racialization and civil rights issues, such as policing and voting, and omnibus measures.[117]

Local and state-level support for the policies racializing illegality has galvanized some Georgia politicians to invoke the specter of the "dangerous immigrant" and to stress a need to "secure the border" against menacing Latine newcomers. As mentioned in chapter 1, when media pundits and political officials talk about "the border" they are often referring to the border with *Mexico*, not Canada.[118] Amplifying the perceived threat to life and limb that Mexican immigrants pose to white Atlantans, this rhetoric associates Mexicans with dangerous criminals.[119] For instance, in 2018 gubernatorial candidate Michael Williams campaigned on an "immigration bus" that racialized undocumented immigrants as Mexican with the banner: "Follow me to Mexico . . . Danger! Murderers, rapists, kidnappers, child molesters, and other criminals on board."[120] The "criminal" stereotype contributes to the racialization of illegality, reinforcing the stigma attached to the "typical Latine." It could be argued that the designation of "dangerous criminal" associates Latine immigrants with the lower classes.[121]

In tandem with the dual assaults of rhetoric casting Latine immigrants

Table 2.6 "Yea" Votes on Restrictive Immigration Legislation in Georgia by Bill Topic, Legislator Race, and Legislator Party, 2005–2019

Bill Topic	Black Democrats	White Democrats	White Republicans
Racialization			
Police	28%	50%	88%
Omnibus	13	29	94
Labor market			
Employment	50	62	89
Identity	83	84	86
Civil rights			
Education	69	70	92
Voting	26	46	87
Other topics			
Benefits	58	50	89
Budget	87	95	95
Miscellaneous	51	69	92
Total	53	62	91
N (total votes)	2,057	1,104	4,848

Source: Calculations by author on votes recorded for all enacted restrictive immigration legislation in Georgia from data at the Georgia state legislature website (legis.ga.gov); at the National Conference of State Legislators website (https://www.ncsl.org); in Browne, Reingold, and Kronberg 2018; and in Monogan 2018.

as a threat to public safety and the passage of restrictive immigration policy in Georgia, Atlanta has become home to a growing anti-immigrant movement. Founded in 2005, Georgia's Dustin Inman Society is a prominent anti-immigrant player among national anti-immigrant organizations whose leader, D. A. King, frequently referred to unauthorized immigrants as "criminals." Cautioning that Georgia is transforming into "Mexifornia," the Dustin Inman Society website pronounces: "Illegal aliens who demand the same driving privileges as U.S. citizens should migrate to California—the illegal immigration Capital of the world."[122]

The phrase "Mexifornia" equates undocumented immigration with Mexicans specifically. As I show throughout the subsequent chapters, this equivalence contains a class dimension. In their everyday interactions with non-Latine Atlantans, middle-class Latine immigrants are often assumed to be undocumented working-class Mexicans irrespective of their country of origin and privileged social class.

However, there are also pockets of immigrant acceptance in the Atlanta metro area. In the words of Mayor Kaseem Reed when the city of Atlanta joined the Welcoming Cities Initiative in 2013:

> As Atlanta positions itself to be a global leader, attracting and retaining talent is imperative. . . . The Welcoming Atlanta initiative builds upon the existing priorities for the city—public safety, welfare, economic development, civic engagement and education—and in so doing, will not only create an environment that is welcoming to new arrivals, but a stronger community for all Atlantans.[123]

Thus, amid the intensifying racialization of illegality, support for immigrants is being promoted by some local officials and state leaders and by many of Atlanta's voters.[124] How do Atlanta's middle-class Mexican and Dominican immigrants negotiate their identities in this climate? How do they reconcile the downplaying of race in their country of origin with the racialization of illegality in the United States? What role does social class play in these identities and negotiation strategies? The next chapter addresses these questions.

3 | Negotiating Racial Identities

ARCADIO, a Dominican engineer, described his annoyance the first time he was confronted with the question: "What is your race?"

> The term "Latino." I do not care. I do not care. To me that is a waste of time really. When I arrived [in the United States] [after] two weeks, with my fever to do new things, I said, "I'm going to join a gym," and went to the gym, and that was the first time, at twenty-three. . . . I had to answer the question: race. I swear the first thing that came to mind was: Doberman. (*laughs*) German Shepherd. What race am I? What do you mean what race I am? That's for dogs. And I asked the girl: "What race am I?" And she said: "Ehh, leave it blank." (*laughs*) . . . And from there I insisted on selecting "other." After "other" we move to "whatever." It does not matter.

Arcadio discredited the U.S. racial system through several maneuvers. He associated U.S. racial categorization with the classification of dog breeds, implying that racial categorization is not appropriate for classifying humans. He characterized the U.S. approach to racial categorization as an absurd waste of time and felt that "it does not matter" which racial category he selected for himself when forced to do so.

Caught within the dynamics of racialization despite assimilation, respondents like Arcadio faced an unrelenting pressure to claim a racial identity.[1] They experienced the expectation that they would racially identify across a myriad of social situations in the United States: when they joined a gym; when they were asked, "Where are you from?"; when they completed government forms; when they registered their children for school; and even when they participated in an academic study.

For many of my respondents, adapting to a U.S. racial system embedded in different social hierarchies than were found in their heritage country proved frustrating. My first-generation respondents explained that they did not fit into the U.S. census categories: white, black, Asian and Pacific

DOI: https://doi.org/10.7758/hvda9363.4954

Islander, or native American or Hawaiian.[2] Furthermore, in the Dominican Republic and Mexico, a racially and culturally "mixed" label is a proud marker of identity. For both nationalities, it is the "mix" of European with indigenous origins, rather than African origins, that is celebrated. In contrast, the sharply delineated U.S.-based white-black racial categories position whiteness at the top of a hierarchy and relegate blackness to the bottom, thus adding further complexity to the claiming of a racial identity in the U.S. context.

As I show in this chapter, respondents engaged in identity work to navigate the U.S. racial system and claim a socially valued racial identity by drawing on their heritage belief systems.[3] Some of my respondents, like Arcadio, harnessed Mexican or Dominican heritage ideas about race to reject the U.S. racial system wholesale. They overcame their precarious social status by discrediting race, the very basis on which they were judged in the United States. Rejecting the legitimacy of racial categorization became a rhetorical tool to negotiate the racialization of illegality. That is, respondents dismissed as irrelevant the racial categorization on which the racialization of illegality stands. Following heritage beliefs (*mestizaje*), they emphasized class hierarchies over race hierarchies to claim an identity and explain inequality.

Respondents also sometimes invoked heritage belief systems to claim racial identities that are unavailable in the United States. This approach provided a range of options, from creating distance from stigmatizing identities ("indigenous," "Latino," "black") to incorporating these identities into their heritage-based "mixed" racial category to cast them in a more positive light. In these cases, respondents were negotiating the racialization of illegality by resisting the preconceived categories of race in the United States and creating new hybrid categories by drawing on their own cultural approach to race. Finally, respondents often adopted a U.S.-based "Hispanic" or "Latino" identity and claimed it in tandem with non-U.S.-based racial identities.

My approach answers the call of Crystal Fleming, Michèle Lamont, and Jessica Welburn to understand stigmatizing processes beyond the realm of individual psychology. To do this, they urge researchers to consider how national belief systems ("cultural repertoires") combine with race-ethnic group attachments and individual perceptions to affect responses to stigma among marginalized groups.[4] While Fleming and her colleagues have used this approach to study stigma responses among African Americans in the United States, I add complexity to the picture by focusing on middle-class Latine immigrants. I compare two groups, Mexicans and Dominicans, whose class privilege both provides an additional source of frustration with the U.S. racial system and offers potential strategies to respond to that system. These complicating factors allow us to get a better handle on the relationship between class privilege, stigma, and the U.S. racial hierarchy.

In what follows, I first describe heritage categorization and beliefs in Mexico and the Dominican Republic and contrast them with the U.S. approach to racial categorization. I then unpack how respondents used these heritage beliefs to reject the U.S. racial system and construct their own identity categories, highlighting how social class comes into play.

MESTIZAJE RACIAL CATEGORIZATION

According to Edward Telles and Denia Garcia, Latin American belief systems about race have no U.S. corollary.[5] Mexican and Dominican belief systems about race and class inequality are called *mestizaje* ("mixture") ideologies.[6] Mestizaje beliefs provided my respondents with the means to negotiate the racialization of illegality by maintaining a positive identity and elevating their status in spite of the U.S. racial system.

Latin American mestizaje belief systems arose in the early twentieth century as part of state efforts to resist colonialism. Individual Latin American governments, including Mexico and the Dominican Republic, promoted an esteemed national identity based on embracing a mestizaje heritage that combined European and indigenous origins.[7] Elites in Latin American countries encouraged mestizaje beliefs among the general population through the education system, particularly children's history books, as well as through speeches and writings. These efforts included "tout[ing] their racial mixture as proof of their racial tolerance and *moral superiority over the United States* (emphasis added)."[8] Mestizaje ideology gave rise to a "myth of racial democracy" in Latin America that created a fluid and supposedly nonhierarchical continuum of racial categories and framed the existence of these European-indigenous "mixed" identities (*mestizaje/mestiçagem*) as indicators of racial harmony and as a bulwark against U.S.-style racism.[9]

Critics emphasize that mestizaje beliefs obscure the high degree of racial inequality and discrimination in Latin America. National mestizaje belief systems blame inequality on social class or "cultural differences" among indigenous groups.[10] According to its critics, the myth of a racial democracy in mestizaje ideology is harmful because it marginalizes or ignores indigenous group members (Mexico) and Afro-Latine individuals (Mexico and the Dominican Republic). The prominence of beliefs in a "racial democracy" reduces the chances that indigenous and Afro-Latine groups will mobilize to protest their disadvantage.[11]

In addition, mestizaje has been criticized for its implicit favoring of "whitening" (*blanqueamiento*). Mestizaje belief systems emphasize that members of indigenous populations are expected to "whiten" their line by marrying "mestizo" individuals with some European background.[12] In Latin America, skin color is an important marker of social worth, belying claims to a racial democracy.[13] As Telles explains, "Whites or lighter-skinned mestizos tend to be privileged, while indigenous peoples, Afrodescendants, and dark-skinned persons are often seen and treated as less deserving."[14] Evidence for the persistence of a "pigmentocracy" shows that in Latin America individuals with relatively light skin tone are more likely to work in professional occupations and to hold advanced degrees.[15] In addition, TV and magazines mostly feature light-skinned actors and models.[16]

While critics focus on the homogenizing and colorblind dimensions of the mestizaje belief system, some scholars argue that mestizaje beliefs are complex, ambiguous, fluid, and potentially progressive. These scholars propose that mestizaje belief systems hold the potential to support multicultural perspectives and social justice projects.[17] Peter Wade contends that while mestizaje erases difference as a dominant political ideology, individuals can experience mestizaje as inclusion through their relationships with family members who embody the full range of skin tones.[18]

Each Latin American nation has its own version of mestizaje based on its unique geography, demographics, and political history. Mexican mestizaje beliefs and practices are constructed by rendering existing members of indigenous groups as "other" and denying African heritage; Dominican mestizaje beliefs and practices are constructed against Haitians as the rejected "other." Both belief systems elevate a mestizo (mixed) racial identity as a national ideal while maintaining what they also deny—favored status for whites.

In Mexico, colonialism positioned the indigenous population as a denigrated category that faced profound disadvantage and repression. Anticolonialist struggles rebutted this categorization by incorporating indigenous origins into the construction of Mexican mestizaje identity.[19] Mexico's small Afro-Latine population became invisible in these constructions.[20] This provided incentive for many Afro-Mexicans to identify as mestizo and to negate or downplay their African origins.[21] According to Laura Gómez, "Mexico's nationalist, post-revolutionary ideology stands on a conception of Mexico as a nation without Blacks."[22] The erasure of Afro-Mexicans from popular descriptions of the Mexican population has been cited as a form of Mexican anti-blackness.[23]

Even though the majority of Mexicans identify as mestizo, there is evidence of preference for "whiter skin and European features" in Mexico.[24] Cristina Sue explains that "light-skinned individuals with European features dominate [Mexico's] top positions of society."[25] The value placed on lighter skin tones and the correspondence of skin tone and class suggest that, while Mexicans may espouse a racial democracy, their behavior favors lighter skin tones.[26] Yet, rather than acknowledging color-based discrimination and a national preference for lighter skin, Mexicans themselves attribute the unequal social hierarchy to educational (class) differences.[27]

Although Dominicans share with Mexicans a history of Spanish colonialism, there are important differences that have influenced the development of mestizaje identities in the Dominican Republic. Dominicans hail from an island shaped by a substantial African slave trade, years of dictatorship, and a shared border with Haiti.[28] Dominican mestizaje belief systems embrace a "mixture" of European and indigenous heritage. Yet, unlike Mexico, where indigenous groups maintain a presence, the Dominican indigenous population (the Taíno) was decimated by colonialism and no longer exists.[29]

Beginning in the early twentieth Century, Dominican elites constructed a distinctive Dominican identity in which "Dominican" was equated with "not Haitian," and they imposed this belief system on all Dominicans. The animosity toward Haiti and Haitians was built on years of political and social conflict between the two nations that share the island of Hispaniola. When the Dominican dictator Rafael Trujillo took charge of the country, he intensified the vilification of Haitians and ordered the 1937 massacre of "all Haitians in the Dominican Republic."[30] Through his policies, Trujillo converted an existing anti-Haitian stance into a "nationalist ideology" that forged a distinct separation between Dominicans and Haitians, marked Haitians as inferior, and built loyalty to Trujillo's regime.[31]

With "Haitian" associated with "black," Trujillo's efforts and subsequent Dominican state-sponsored racialization processes propagated anti-blackness through a distancing from the racialized category of "black."[32] In the Dominican Republic, Dominicans with strongly African skin tone, hair texture, and bone structure are more likely to refer to themselves, not as "black" (*prieto*), but as *Indio* ("indigenous").[33] As Perez remarked in his interview: "I laugh because the first time I had to fill out documentation was when my kid went to the school and when they [asked for] race. In the Dominican Republic we were always told we were white, black, and Indian. . . . Basically, 'Indian' was defined as not white and not black." Similar to belief systems in Mexico, the Dominican version of mestizaje defines social inequality through differences in social class—an ostensibly nonracial distinction.[34] That is, wealthy Dominicans are assumed to hold greater status as a function of their class position, and their overwhelmingly obvious whiteness is perceived as merely coincidental.[35]

Latin American mestizaje belief systems in both Mexico and the Dominican Republic hold appeal for identity work because they provide sources of social value that are absent in the United States. First, whereas racial categorization is preeminent in the United States and systemic class inequality is downplayed, mestizaje ideology explicitly promotes social class as the primary basis for Latin American social inequality and denies the salience of race. Second, while the U.S. racial system situated respondents as an out-group (Latine immigrants), they could utilize mestizaje belief systems to claim membership in the dominant heritage in-group (class-privileged Mexicans or Dominican). And third, although the United States positions itself as superior to the less developed countries of Latin America, the mestizaje status hierarchy casts the U.S. racial system as inferior to Latin American approaches to race.[36]

U.S.-BASED RACIAL CATEGORIZATION

In contrast to the emphasis on skin tone and class that is emblematic of Latin American mestizaje belief systems, the United States bases its racial system on ancestry. Under the ongoing legacy of the "one-drop rule" instituted in the early twentieth century, an individual with *any* African heritage is categorized as "black" and consigned to the bottom of the white-black racial status hierarchy in the United States, irrespective of skin tone.[37] Although there is a move in the United States toward categorizing race on the basis of physical appearance rather than ancestry, Latines who do not identify as black or white are still left outside of official U.S. race categories and defaulted to "other."[38] The U.S. census defines "Latino" as an ethnicity, not a race, meaning that Latines can select any race.[39] In practice, Latines often consider the "Latino" designation to be a race, and they are often treated as a nonwhite racial group.[40]

Rosa, who came to the United States from Mexico, expressed her frustration with the limits of U.S. racial categories:

> Not too long ago I filled out a form that had a check for race and it had "Oriental" and "European" and "white," and in parentheses it said "from western European country," and then it was "other." So I asked, "What do I put here?!" And it says "other" and in parentheses it says "unknown," and I said, "What do I put here?!" And [they said,] "Just put 'other.'" I said, "No, I am not unknown!" . . . That really bothered me, so I didn't fill it out. *I am not an unknown race!*

Rosa did more than simply remark that she didn't fit U.S. categories: saying that she was "really bothered" by the category of "other," which defined her racial identity as "unknown," she challenged that category. Her race was certainly known to her, she implied, even if it did not appear on the government form.

While the U.S.-based system of racial categorization departs from Latin

American mestizaje approaches, U.S.-based colorblind belief systems offer a parallel route to denying racism. Whites in the United States propagate a "colorblind" racial belief system that denies the role of racism in determining social outcomes.[41] Colorblind approaches attribute the persistence of racial inequality to differences in effort, to differences in culture, or to a disappearing vestige of the past rather than to systemic racial discrimination.[42]

When Latine immigrants espouse these mainstream racial beliefs to signal their integration into U.S. society, colorblind narratives can become an assimilation strategy.[43] Some scholars emphasize that by situating their belief system close to that of whites and denying systemic, race-based disadvantage, Latine newcomers deploy colorblind discourses to create social distance between themselves and low-status others, including undocumented immigrants.[44]

However, incorporating mestizaje beliefs into their accounts of identity work provided my first-generation respondents with a much more complex process behind "denying racism" than studies of U.S.-based colorblind strategies reveal. Some respondents were not attempting to move closer to the U.S. white majority when they invoked heritage mestizaje racial ideology.[45] Instead, they were emphasizing their national identity and reinforcing differences between Mexican or Dominican racial categories and those found in the United States.[46]

REJECTING THE U.S. RACIAL SYSTEM

In the interviews, we tried to capture the multiple dimensions of racial identity by asking each respondent three questions: how they identified; what race they indicated on government forms; and what race others perceived them to be.[47] My research team and I also coded skin tone for a subset of Dominican respondents.[48]

The interview questions about racial identity triggered frustration among a number of respondents, including Arcadio (quoted earlier). In reaction to these questions, some respondents invoked their heritage mestizaje belief systems to discredit the U.S. racial system and preempt racial categorization altogether. They often mentioned their social class within this identity work strategy. For instance, Michelle implied that concerns about racial identification are a uniquely U.S. problem, while emphasizing the importance of class stratification in the Dominican Republic:

> MICHELLE: So [my kids] put they are mixed.
>
> INTERVIEWER: And that's how they identify? That's how they describe themselves?

MICHELLE: I don't know. To be honest with you, I have never . . . we don't ever try to make an issue of race, so I have never really heard them refer to themselves one way or the other. They just say, "My mom's Dominican, my dad is white." So about themselves, I guess I'll have to see what they say. Because that's one thing. *In the Dominican, we don't have a race issue at all. We have a class issue, on the other hand.* (interviewee's emphasis)

Michelle revealed that she held a colorblind identity standard for her children (and herself). She contended that race was irrelevant in her children's lives and framed this irrelevance as a cultural distinction between the United States and the Dominican Republic, implicitly disparaging a U.S. race focus. Her use of the word "issue" to reference class stratification implies that she perceived systemic class inequality as a social problem in the Dominican Republic. Because she was a member of the middle class, her claim that "*we have a class issue*" (in the Dominican Republic) implicitly repositioned her from a lower U.S.-based status (Latine) to a higher Dominican status (middle-class).

Juan Diego communicated his unhappiness and frustration with the interviewer's questions about racial identity.

INTERVIEWER: How do you identify? Do you identify as Hispanic or Mexican?

JUAN DIEGO: Yes, not happily, but yes.

INTERVIEWER: What do you mean "not happily"?

JUAN DIEGO: Not happily because I just came back from Colombia and I grew up in Mexico and was well educated. I never saw race. I didn't really see race until I came to this country, where you are black, Hispanic, you are white, you are this, you are that, and I just don't like the way Americans insist on seeing people differently. *We don't ask if you are white or black or dark or brown in Mexico. I never heard that before coming to this country.* I don't see why that is relevant at all. Maybe in health issues, because some blacks are more prone to getting some types of illnesses and Hispanics for this and that, but other than that, I don't understand why even that question comes up. *The fact that you are asking me that question bothers me because I see this [as] completely irrelevant, and I think it should be irrelevant.* In Mexico we have blond people in the north, we have black, curly hair in the coast, and a lot of people look like me, white. I mean, people look like you. You could go for a Mexican, easily, and we never look at race or color or skin. We never describe them like that. We never ask

> that question, and I think it's a lot healthier for a society that way. So when they ask me, "la la la la Mexican," I mean, I just have to say it. Not that I don't know why they ask me that shit. I don't understand why that's important. (interviewee's emphasis)

Juan Diego inserted class in mestizaje ideology by linking the Mexican approach to race with being "well educated." He invoked the image of a racial democracy by asserting that Mexicans span the gamut of physical appearance ("In Mexico we have blond people in the north, we have black, curly hair in the coast, and a lot of people look like me, white"). He further delegitimized the U.S. racial system by insisting that race "*should be irrelevant.*" Claiming that the Mexican approach is "healthier," he inverted the U.S.-Mexico status hierarchy by suggesting that the Mexican system is "superior" to "that shit" (the racial categorization he encountered in the United States).

Luisa also expressed distaste for questions about her racial identification:

> I mean, I don't know. Yeah, I'm definitely Dominican, Hispanic, and . . . I know that, like I said, especially in the South, the perception is, okay, if you're Latin, there are all these stereotypes that may not necessarily apply. Do you speak English? Do you have documentation to work in this country? What's your education level? A lot of things are questioned. And I mean, from my perspective, it's a little sad, it's a little bit of ignorance. But I mean, it's just you're lumping a lot of groups into black. And you know, it's all these different countries and even within the countries all these different economic classes, social classes. So it's hard.

Luisa provided an especially vivid example of using class as an identity work strategy to reject the U.S. racial system. She highlighted class as one of the characteristics triggering the "typical Latine" image (uneducated, undocumented). She contrasted her educated social class with the stereotypical image of a Latine by attributing this U.S. perception to "ignorance" (a lack of education). She further emphasized that the U.S. tendency to "lump" a "lot of groups into black" ignores the class hierarchy. This observation that black homogenization pushes blacks to the bottom of the social ladder corresponds with the U.S. racial hierarchy.

Some respondents voiced a strong criticism of the U.S. racial system without referencing class. Although the intensity of their negative emotions varied, their common critique was that the U.S. perspective on race is inferior to their heritage perspective. Respondents perceived mestizaje approaches as fluid and nonhierarchical, allowing for a multitude of categories, which they juxtaposed to the rigid classification of U.S. racial identity options.[49] They drew a symbolic boundary based on their heritage nation as an identity work strategy that generated a positive identity, and they described the United States as deficient or backwards regarding race.

For instance, Perez, a Dominican, described "the American condition of race" as "very closed, very . . . how do you say . . . shortsighted. No more white or black, and they didn't understand that there were people who were in the middle. Basically, no Latino is white or black. There are some who are more white than others or more black than others." Perez positioned Latines "in the middle" of a black-white continuum and characterized "race" as fluid, advancing a mestizaje ideology superior to "shortsighted" American racial ideology. He echoed Dominican mestizaje beliefs about race when explaining that "no Latino is . . . black . . . some are more black than others." His declaration that "no Latino is black" hinted at the Dominican anti-black racial belief system. In this system, "Haitians" are categorized as "black," and there is a clear boundary between the "Latino" and "black" categories.[50]

Rubén also explicitly criticized the restrictiveness of U.S. racial categories and what he perceived as an overemphasis on race in the United States. Like many respondents, he was concerned about teaching his children Dominican or Latine approaches to identity, which he believed were not so racially focused:

> Well, what happens is, in the Dominican, kids grew up in a different way—in more freedom. With not a lot of things. . . . How do you say. . . . You know here . . . here you have the diversity thing. So African Americans go here, Hispanics go here . . . you know, different boxes for everything. When you look in the Latin culture, everybody's the same. . . . So I wonder if they grow up on their own in that way, thinking that everybody is the same. You don't have to classify people and grow up with that mentality. . . . So I would like that they grow up thinking that everybody's the same.

Rubén captured the frustration with poorly fitting categories when he referred to rigid "boxes." He also disliked the U.S. insistence on categorizing people (exemplified by a "mentality"). He compared the U.S. tendency to assign people to categories unfavorably with the Dominican Republic, where there is "more freedom." Rather than emphasizing the centrality of class differences among Latin Americans, as Juan Diego and Luisa did, Rubén referenced a Latin American racial democracy, proclaiming that "everybody's the same."

Table 3.1 Respondents' Selected Race Identity

	White	Black	Hispanic/ Latino/ Other	Dominican/ Mexican	*N*
Mexicans					
My sample	24%	0%	89%	71%	39
Dominicans					
My sample	13%	10%	22%	75%	36

Source: Author's compilation from respondent interviews, 2009–2016, 2021–2023.
Note: Atlanta metro percentages are weighted; *N*s are unweighted.

MESTIZAJE IDENTITY CATEGORIES AMONG RESPONDENTS

Mestizaje beliefs provide not only a basis on which to reject the U.S. racial system wholesale but also racial identity categories that are unavailable in the United States. The self-identification of the majority of my respondents as neither "white" nor "black" corresponded with their heritage mestizaje racial ideology and with published studies focusing on first-generation Latine immigrants.[51] Table 3.1 shows the racial identification categories that my respondents mentioned in response to the identity questions.[52]

Consistent with a mestizaje orientation, the majority of Mexican and Dominican respondents named a national identity when asked questions about racial identification.[53] Mexicans were much more likely than Dominicans to claim a Latine or Hispanic identity as well.[54] These pan-ethnic identities are part of the U.S. racial system; they are not used in heritage countries.[55] Only 20 percent of Dominicans claimed a Latine or Hispanic identity, and only a few of them in my sample (10 percent) identified as "black."[56] These racial labels that appear in the interviews are clues to how respondents drew upon mestizaje and U.S.-based categories to negotiate racialization.

Mexican Racial Identity: Engaging Whiteness

The majority of the Mexican respondents stated that they did not fit into any category on U.S. government forms. Alejandro overtly relied on the Mexican concept of "mixture" to define his "race" in the United States. Noting that government forms do not include a "mixed" option, he said that was "where I really belong." However, "it's never there." Claiming that his "true" racial identity does not appear on government forms, Alejandro concluded that there was no place for him in the U.S. system of classification.

As table 3.1 shows, Mexican respondents overwhelmingly preferred a national racial identity over the options offered by the U.S. categories, whether or not the interviewer used a "Mexican" prompt for the racial identity interview questions.[57] For instance, when asked to identify his race, José Marco responded: "I'm Mexican. That's my race, that's me, you know, so . . . (*laughs*), but yeah, ever since then I would always check 'other' and write in 'Mexican' [on government forms]."

Despite the status boost attached to a white racial identity, only 25 percent of the middle-class Mexican respondents and 13 percent of the Dominicans in my sample stated that they would select a "white" option.[58] This finding differs from other studies, which find a higher proportion of Mexicans selecting a white identity.[59] However, my interviews suggest that when the race question was asked in these other studies, Mexicans may have chosen "white" because that was what they assumed they were "supposed" to select, and not necessarily because it was a racial category with which they identified. For instance, interviews with Jade and Carla revealed these respondents' attachment to the white racial label:

> INTERVIEWER: If up to now you've had to write down at the dentist, hospitals . . . your nationality or your race where they label you as "white," "Hispanic," sometimes "Mexican," or "black Hispanic," or "Asian," or "other." What do you put down?
>
> JADE: Well, if they have it, "Hispanic." Obviously, I put "Hispanic," and if not, I put "Mexican."
>
> INTERVIEWER: "Black" or "white"?
>
> JADE: I put "white." Yes, I've had to put "white." Yes.

Jade's preferred racial identity was Mexican or Hispanic. She selected "white" only if her choices were between "white" and "black." A white identity would be something that she "had" to pick. Carla also described the external imposition of a white designation. "I think they kind of make you choose 'white.' I don't think you can click on 'black' because you are not black or Asian, so I think if there is no other option for most Hispanics, I think they just put 'white.' I think. I'm not 100 percent." According to Carla, the bureaucracy that forces people to choose between the limited categories of black and white creates distance from the "black" racial category ("You are not black").

Carla, from Mexico, rejected an emphasis on skin tone for assigning racial labels:

> [When] my husband was going to college . . . he got really upset with it because he had to put "Hispanic," and they have another category that says "white Hispanic" or "white non-Hispanic," something like that. He had just clicked "white," and I think they deleted [it] and said, "Uh, you're white, you have to put 'white Hispanic,'" though we kind of like try to stay away from that. We feel that they shouldn't be putting a color before their race, it should just be Hispanic.

Carla's denunciation of the category "white Hispanic" in favor of a "Hispanic" label departs from the U.S. categorization of "white" as a race and "Hispanic" as an ethnicity. Carla was joining the Latines who insist that "Hispanic" (or "Latino") should be included as a racial category in the United States.[60]

Beatriz went a step further and emphasized that she did not identify as white, even though that was how others perceived her in the United States:

> BEATRIZ: If they don't have the "Mexican" option [on government forms], I put "Hispanic." I don't consider myself white.
>
> INTERVIEWER: And if there is "Hispanic" or "Mexican," you put the "Mexican."
>
> BEATRIZ (*LAUGHS*): Yes. Forever. Always, I know that I am white, but I do not consider myself white.

The prestige that accompanies a white racial identity in the United States was not a draw for Beatriz. In fact, she repeated her claim that "I don't consider myself white" even though she could have used this option.[61] This move away from whiteness is consistent with mestizaje beliefs that the ideal national racial category is "mixed."

Dominican Racial Identity: Contending with the Black-White Color Line

While Mexican respondents most often wrestled with a white identity when asked the interview questions about their race, Dominicans engaged with a black identity. On the one side, their heritage mestizaje racial ideology sharply distinguished Dominicans from the racial category of "black," since "black" was equated with "Haitian."[62] On the other side, the cultural endurance of the U.S. one-drop rule, though it was legally outlawed in 1967, positions many Dominicans within the black racial category.[63]

Caribbean immigrants in other studies attempt to distance themselves from the perceived low status of an "African American" label.[64] For instance, first-generation Dominican immigrants may signal that they are not African American by speaking Spanish.[65] As Stephen Steinberg emphasizes, social class is central to the status differences that Afro-Latine immigrants perceive between themselves and African Americans. Traditionally in these other studies, middle-class black immigrants distinguish themselves from *poor* African Americans and the stereotypes associated with this lower-status group.[66] In contrast, my respondents described encountering *middle-class* blacks in their neighborhoods, schools, and workplaces. (I say more about this in chapter 5.) However, despite their exposure to Atlanta's black middle class, only four Dominican respondents in my sample (10 percent) identified as black—a lower rate than has been found among Dominicans in other cities.[67]

This discrepancy can be explained by several factors, including differences in how individuals describe their racial identity in an interview setting versus in a survey. Dominican respondents who identified as "black" or whose physical appearance could be read as "black" could also have been rare in my sample because Dominicans toward the top of the education and occupation hierarchy, as most of my respondents were, tend to have relatively light skin.[68] For instance, none of the scores of the respondents on our eleven-point skin tone scale—where ten equals the darkest skin tone and zero equals albinism—exceeded five (a "medium" skin tone).

The majority of our Dominican respondents (twenty-eight out of thirty-six) claimed a Dominican nation-based racial identity and reported categorizing themselves as "other" on official forms, a choice that did not appear to be related to skin tone. Respondents who were coded by interviewers as having quite light or medium dark skin tones favored a Dominican racial identity and explained that, as Dominicans, they were neither white nor black. For instance, interviewers rated skin tone as a one or two (very light) for eleven respondents, all of whom claimed "Dominican" as their primary racial identity and only one of whom also mentioned a "white" identity.[69] That is, racial identity among Dominicans was more likely to be based on nationality than on physical appearance. This finding is consistent with heritage beliefs, which emphasize national identity over racial differences.[70]

My interviews with Dominican respondents show that mestizaje ideology is flexible and can expand to incorporate U.S.-based categories.[71] The interviews resonate with Ginetta Candelario's findings from her study of Dominicans in Washington, D.C., and New York City:

> Operating in the context of both Latin American– and U.S.-framed white, African American and Latino conceptual practices of power, Dominicans engage in a sort of ideological "code switching" in which both the Dominican Republic's and the United States' race systems are engaged, rejected and sustained at various historical and biographical moments.[72]

Candelario acknowledges that racial identities emerge from structural processes in the heritage and host contexts—what she calls "practices of power." Similar to my respondents, Candelario's subjects took an active role in their identity construction, showing that Dominicans can form "hybrid identities" that not only creatively combine Dominican and U.S. racial systems but also can change with the situation.

Consistent with Dominican mestizaje ideology, several of my respondents explicitly claimed a "mixed" racial identity that included African, black, and/or Haitian. Some respondents even expanded the definition of mestizaje to include African Americans. For instance, Ana explained that

> I am Dominican, Latino, multiracial, African American. I . . . I don't know. I have so much behind. My great-grandfather was white from Spain. My great-grandmother was from Haiti, I think. I don't . . . I'm not even sure. But I know that we have a mix. You can see . . . my nose tells you that I'm from Africa. My hair tells you that I probably can be [*inaudible*] someone with white. So it's just a big mix. You can tell. I am everything. Latino, Dominican, African American, Hispanic all describe me.

In using the African American and Hispanic labels, Ana incorporated U.S.-based racial categories into a mestizaje characterization of her racial background as a "big mix." She also defied elite-generated Dominican racial ideology by embracing her Haitian background and African features.

Similarly, Federico adopted the U.S. racial categorization of "black" while describing his mix of backgrounds in terms of mestizaje ideology. Federico was coded by the interviewer as having very light skin (two on the eleven-point scale), but he was adamant that he and other Dominicans were "not white."

> We have everything in Dominican Republic. We have the black behind my ears. I am descendant. My grandmother, who is one hundred and two years old, she's black. Black black black. . . . I have Spaniards. I have white people, and I have black people. The only [people] I don't have in my nature, it is Indian aborigine blood, because Christopher Columbus killed all of them in thirty years, in the fifteen hundreds. So that is not in my blood. Even, I have Middle Eastern blood—I know that I have somebody behind that came from

> Lebanon, and I have three others that came from Spain. So I have a lot of things. Now, I have to check that I am Hispanic, because that's my culture, and I have to check that I'm white, because I don't qualify as a black here in the U.S. But I am black! . . . I am everything.

For Federico, a "black" racial identity could be a multicategory, *family-based* designation based on skin tone (his grandmother was "black black black").[73] Dominican and U.S.-based racial labels clashed when he asserted that he checked "white" on official forms despite believing that "I am black!" At the same time, he claimed, "I am everything." Further, his reference to "the black behind my ears" invoked the Dominican ideology of an African heritage as something to keep hidden.[74] This strategy is similar to Dowling's finding among Mexican Americans that claims of a "white" identity are often situationally based.[75] My interviews indicate that Dominicans also may assert a "white" identity situationally. (As Federico said, "I have to check that I'm white.")

The interviews with Ana and Federico show the mestizaje categories of "mixture" being expanded to include U.S.-based categories. Federico's interview further highlighted the complexity of racial identity when we asked him what ethnicity or race people thought he was when they met him: "I am an Iranian guy from the Caribbean," he responded. "Seriously. All people believe that I am from Iran." Federico epitomized the non-alignment of racial categorizations behind social identities. His skin tone code was scored a two (very light), he labeled himself as black within a "mix of everything," and people in Atlanta perceived him as Iranian.

Lio and Sofia adopted a specifically black racial identity in the United States for themselves and their children, though they expressed ambivalence toward this label. Lio explained that their son was "Dominican and dark, he's black," like his maternal grandfather, who was black, and his maternal grandmother was "white—blond white. So [his mother] is kind of mixed in between, and he's kind of then mixed again. So he's not exactly black, but he's not Indian either." Racializing his son using skin tone, Lio showed the distinction between a U.S.-based categorization ("dark" = "black") and a Dominican categorization ("not exactly black" but "not Indian either") that is consistent with Dominican mestizaje ideology, which recognizes a racially mixed heritage.

Pablo was one of the few respondents who identified as both Dominican and black. (His skin tone was coded as five on the eleven-point scale.) He described his efforts to assert a black identity among African Americans, who teased him by insisting that he was not "black" because he spoke Spanish.

> I tell them [African Americans] I'm Dominican. Then they ask: "Are you white?" And I say, "No, I'm black." So . . . it's weird. . . . I would always go to the court . . . I like basketball a lot, and I would go with some black guys. There was this short guy, I remember, who was joking a lot. He asked me and would say, "You speak Spanish, you're white." And I said: "What are you talking about? Why am I white? You see me? I'm black, like you!" And he said, "You ain't black."

Pablo's interview indicates that in Atlanta a "black" racialized category is not necessarily negative and can even be a net positive.

Oscar, who had a midrange score of four on the eleven-point skin tone scale, also explicitly embraced the African heritage of Dominicans and described an affinity with his African friends:

> When you talk about the Latin Caribbean countries—Cuba, Puerto Rico, and the Dominican Republic—it's a much more distinct type of culture. The African influence was so strong there that much of my food and music and . . . even hanging out with my African friends, even the way you raise your children are very similar to . . . to those strong African ties.

Oscar's emphasis on food and music and "strong African ties" brought the African influences to the fore, reworking a Dominican conception of "race."[76] Further, he connected Dominican identity geographically with "Latin Caribbean countries," which also include a large proportion of Afro-Latines.[77]

Oscar and Pablo resisted the U.S.-based status hierarchies and the negative connotations attached to a "black" racial identity.[78] Their preferred racial identity as "black" diverged from the identities of Caribbean immigrants in other studies who attempted to distance themselves from the perceived low status of an "African American" label by emphasizing that they were immigrants.[79] Oscar's and Pablo's incorporation of a black identity aligned with the perspective of the well-educated Dominicans interviewed by Roth, who attributes Dominicans' acceptance of black identities to the transnational lives that tie migrants to both the United States and their heritage country. "Better educated Dominicans," Roth notes, "may also be more influenced by messages from abroad, including those which define a mulatto, or mixed African and European identity, within a broader framework of blackness."[80]

While claiming a black identity, Teresa perceived that racism forced her into the black-white binary in Atlanta:

> I have to say, I didn't experience any racism until I moved here [to Atlanta]. . . . It feels totally different than New York. . . . Regardless of what you

> are, people [in New York] are so mixed. Everybody's . . . because even where I lived, it was predominantly Hispanic, but, you know, you have whites, you have blacks, you have, you know, Asians and. . . . Things just here [in Atlanta], it wasn't like that.
>
> [In Atlanta] it was either . . . black or white. There's no in between. Especially when I'm . . . nine years ago, yeah. And even today I would say, unless you're not going like downtown [Atlanta], where there's more so of a mixture. . . .
>
> There, particular interactions you had that kind of, you know, made you think, "Wow, this is serious, like, I really have to choose between my identity here and it's based on color and nothing else?" . . . If you found people from [New York], they would be more welcoming, but like [defining myself solely on color] . . . freaks me out.

Teresa perceived identity attributions as location-based. She "didn't experience any racism" and the rigid black-white dichotomy util she moved from New York to Atlanta. She also described her extreme discomfort with living within the confines of this dichotomy (which "freaks me out"). At the same time, Teresa used the Dominican criterion of skin tone as an indicator of race rather than the U.S.-based one-drop rule. Teresa placed herself in the "black" category and had moved into a predominantly black neighborhood.

Dominicans, such as Sofia and Teresa, who include an "African American" or "black" component in their identity can perceive that they share an identity with African Americans as marginalized minorities.[81] However, my respondents rarely expressed this perspective in the interviews. In fact, those who rejected the U.S. racial system protested their categorization as a "disadvantaged racial minority."

Although he defined his son's racial identity as "black," Lio was one of the few Dominicans who identified as white and positioned themselves at the top of the Dominican racial hierarchy. He presented a complicated understanding of racism in the Dominican Republic:

> The Dominican Republic is not . . . people are racist, but they don't know they are racists. And it's not much based on color of the skin because 90 percent of the people [are] all the same—mixed, brown, Latin. However, people of color like me, we're of Spanish descent. . . . We have this advantage that we didn't realize until we are not there. And I was telling, recently telling [my wife] how I was able to go into this private club [in the Dominican Republic] even though we were not members. And it's because I would go to the door, and the guard would say, "Let me see your ID." And I would say, "Oh, well, I forgot it." "Well, you can't come in." "Oh, come on. I can't . . . if you don't let me in, I'm gonna tell my dad." So I'm this blond and white kid saying

> "Dad," and the poor guy, you know, he's [*inaudible*] . . . he would not say no. If I were . . . if I looked like him and everybody else, he would just say no, right? And . . . so . . . the racism there is more based on social status. And . . . unless you are white. If you're white, then it doesn't matter.

At first, Lio seemed to contradict himself, asserting that Dominicans are racist, but that their racism is "not much based on color of the skin because 90 percent of the people [are] all the same—mixed, brown, Latin." He attributed this racism toward 90 percent of the Dominican population to status, which encompasses class in the Dominican context ("the racism there is more based on social status.") He then highlighted the race-based white privilege of the top tier of Dominicans who shared his blond hair and light-skinned features. "If you're white, then [status] doesn't matter."

Claiming a "Latino" Identity in Solidarity

The interviews also show the flexibility of the U.S.-based "Latino" category. Notably, some respondents identified as white and Latine while others identified as mixed or black and Latine. Given the wide variety of nationalities and backgrounds represented in the groups defined as "Latine," the "Hispanic" category has been "fuzzy" since its original inception.[82] In fact, the pan-ethnic category "Hispanic" was consciously forged and promoted by U.S.-based activists in the 1970s as an attempt to build collective political clout among Mexicans, Cubans, and Puerto Ricans.[83]

In embracing a Latine identity, some respondents saw commonalities with other Latines facing discrimination and racialization. As Sol (Dominican) pointed out:

> The majority, 80 percent, of the Hispanics come here to work. I can't negate that there are also people that come for delinquency, but 80 percent come to work. It's a race that throws themselves to the fields to work in the cold, or to work in the ranch mounting horses, to work in construction, to work in the chicken huts, and so I don't know, we move a lot in the case of Hispanics, we see each other, we, we come together.

Sol, who identified as white, expressed solidarity with undocumented immigrants through an identity that crosses class lines, stressing that "we come together." At the same time, Sol distinguished between "bad" Latines who come to the United States for nefarious reasons ("delinquency") and "good" Latines who throw themselves into work and comprise the majority of immigrants.[84]

Sol's encounters with a stigmatizing image of Latine immigrants and her selection of "Latine," national, and "other" racial identities fit within the concept of "reactive ethnicity"—defined as a response to discrimination by expressing ethnic solidarity and adopting collective identities such as Latine.[85] As we shall see in the next chapter, however, respondents did not often perceive discrimination as having a significant effect on their lives.

SUMMARY

Confronted with U.S. racialization processes, respondents frequently experienced the imposition of a racial identity that conflicted with the way they saw and described themselves.[86] To recapture a positive identity, they sometimes drew on Latin American mestizaje racial belief systems and categories. Following this route, they could reject U.S.-based racial classification or draw on hybrid identities that combined heritage and U.S. categories.

Invoking mestizaje belief systems does triple duty as a status-enhancing identity work strategy. First, adopting mestizaje identities distinguished respondents from the stigmatized groups in their heritage country—indigenous (Mexico), Afro-Latines (Mexico), and Haitians (Dominican Republic). Second, relying on mestizaje critiques of the U.S. racial system distanced respondents from the stigmatizing "typical Latine" image and from African Americans. Third, invoking a mestizaje framework provided a means to elevate the importance of class status. Through these maneuvers, respondents invalidated the terms of categorization as a "typical Latine," delegitimizing the relevance of race.

Contrary to studies that focus on U.S.-based colorblind perspectives, our interviews made clear that invoking mestizaje ideology was not an attempt to assimilate into the U.S. white middle class—the route most closely associated with assimilation—even when they perceived that a white identity was available to them. Respondents used mestizaje beliefs to emphasize the discrepancy between the heritage and host cultures and to place themselves squarely on the heritage side of the boundary. However, like U.S.-based colorblind racial ideologies that also deny racism, respondents' mestizaje-based identity work strategies failed to challenge the heritage and host racial hierarchies that position whites at the top. Instead, they reproduced those hierarchies.[87]

This chapter has explored how middle-class Mexican and Dominican immigrants subvert their potential precarity in how they respond to the question, "What race do you consider yourself to be?" But how did respondents signal a positive identity when they were treated as a "typical Latine" in social interactions? Under what circumstances did these middle-class Latine immigrants draw on their class resources to cue a high-status identity and dissociate themselves from an undocumented and working-class designation? Did they interpret erroneous assumptions that they were undocumented and working-class as "discrimination," or did they invoke colorblind explanations of their experiences? The next chapter addresses these questions.

4 | Stigma and the Image of the "Typical Latine"

We asked Pablo, a Dominican entrepreneur, "In general, how do you think that [Americans] treat Latinos here in Atlanta?"[1] He replied: "The American has a perception that Latino is Mexican. So the relationship between Mexico and the United States has never been good. When they say 'Latino,' it is with disgust."

For Pablo, "Mexican" was not simply a stereotype often applied to all Latines, but an identity marker that bred "disgust"—made palpable when Mexicans were publicly reviled as "crimmigrants" and "illegals."[2] Pablo's observation fits the classic definition of "stigma" as "an attribute that links a person to an undesirable stereotype, leading other people to reduce the bearer from a whole and usual person to a tainted, discounted one."[3] Stigma brings an emotional dimension to the racialization of illegality. Our respondents suffered frustration, annoyance, and bafflement when they were racialized and treated with revulsion.[4]

This chapter relies on the notion of the "typical Latine" to identify the ways in which respondents were racialized—and stigmatized—as unauthorized, working-class Mexican immigrants. The idea of "typicality" is much more flexible than the notion of a stereotype. Stereotypes are "beliefs about the features, opinions, and expected behaviors of a group that are generalized to individuals belonging to the group. . . . Stereotypes are problematic because they are often negative and are used to judge every member of a group in the same way."[5] As I discussed in chapter 1, the "typicality" concept allows for degrees of closeness from a constellation of stereotypes.[6] I use this concept to chart how respondents distanced themselves from the "typical Latine."

I employ the idea of typicality to explore three questions: How did respondents experience the racialization of illegality? How did they draw on class to negotiate these experiences? And how did they explain these ex-

DOI: https://doi.org/10.7758/hvda9363.7069

periences and resist racialization? The interviews show that respondents regularly encountered assumptions related to the "typical Latine." Their stigma-reducing maneuvers allowed them to maintain their elevated middle-class status and moved them away from an identity as a "racial minority." They invoked colorblind explanations of racialization and seldom acknowledged racism. By distancing themselves from the "typical Latine" and broadcasting their middle-class position, respondents may have converted their situational position from precarious to prestigious.

EXPERIENCING THE RACIALIZATION OF ILLEGALITY

The "Typical Latine"

I first inquire whether the "typical Latine" characteristics that middle-class Latine immigrants encountered correspond to the same nationality (Mexican), class (poor or working-class), and undocumented status that scholars have identified.[7] The interviews indicate that the answer is yes. Figure 4.1 presents a picture of how respondents discussed the "typical Dominican," the "typical Mexican," the "typical Latine," and the "typical immigrant." Each light-gray dot in the figure is a Mexican respondent, and each dark-gray dot is a Dominican respondent. I coded stereotypes that respondents described when they were asked how they thought others viewed Latines, Mexicans, or Dominicans ("reflected appraisals"). "Typicality" emerged when respondents elaborated on these major identities by describing additional stereotypes attached to being Latine, Mexican, or Dominican. For instance, among the twenty-two Dominicans who referred to stereotypes of the "typical Latine," fourteen pointed to a Mexican identity as part of the Latine stereotype.

Respondents described stereotypes most often when they were responding to the interview question that we asked Pablo: "In general, how do you think Latines are treated in Atlanta?" Typicality also arose when respondents were asked about how others perceived them and whether they had experienced negative encounters or discrimination because they were Mexican or Dominican.

Ten Mexican respondents discussed Latine typicality; some differences in Dominicans' responses were notable. Mexicans tended to discuss the stereotype that Latines are working-class. Dominicans overwhelmingly discussed the stereotype that all Latines are Mexican.

Looking at figure 4.1, we see that twenty-seven Mexican respondents and six Dominicans directly referenced the "typical Mexican."[8] Among these twenty-seven respondents, working-class status—that is, low socio-

Figure 4.1 The "Typical Latine": Content and Frequency of Stereotypes

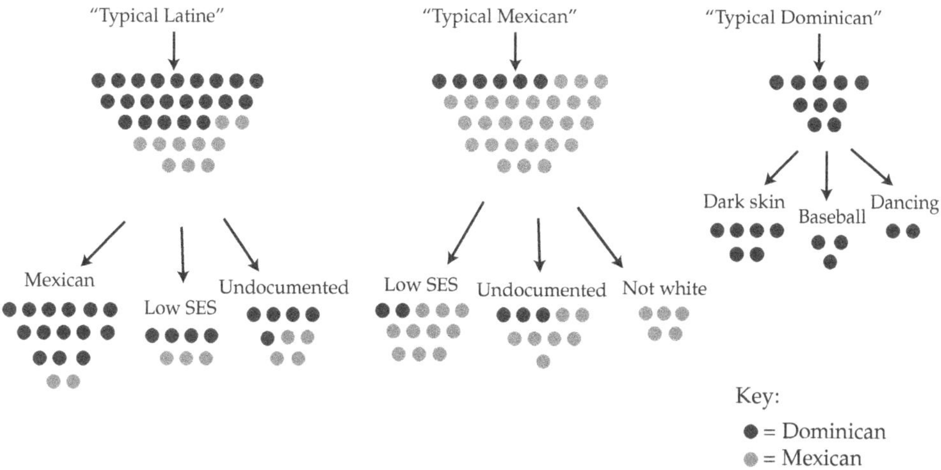

Source: Author's compilation from respondent interviews. Adapted from Browne, Tatum, and González 2021.

economic status (SES)—and being undocumented emerged as the most common characteristic associated with the typical Mexican.

Because Latine typicality includes the assumption of Mexican national origin, the low-status stereotypes that apply to Mexican typicality should carry over to Latine typicality. As explained by Felipe, the Dominican physician quoted in chapter 1, being perceived as Latine automatically triggers categorization as Mexican paired with being undocumented as well as "illiterate and uneducated." Miriam explained that, in the United States, "when you are asked where you are from? you say 'Mexico,' and for some that is automatically hav[ing] to say, slash legal, right? You can't just say 'Mexican.' . . . It's like right there the slash [illegal], and it [is] prevalent." The link between a Mexican nationality and undocumented legal status is so tight that Mexicans must engage in identity work signaling that they are legally present—or what Miriam described as "automatically [hav]ing to say, [Mexican] slash legal."

Rosa associated unauthorized status with negative stereotypes of Mexican immigrants: "Thank God I already have my papers, since everyone sees all of us as 'wet.'" The term "wet" references the term "wetback," a pejorative label that associates unauthorized status with Mexicans crossing the Rio Grande on foot. Rosa assumed that Americans ("everyone") apply this stereotype to all Mexican immigrants ("all of us"), without differentiating by social class.

Jade suggested that the "Mexican" label is not just attached to assumptions of undocumented legal status but also associated with a rural background ("on the plantation"), which could also imply working-class status: "I feel that Americans are a bit narrow-minded about the concept of being Mexican. To them it's the *typical* short, tan man with a mustache and a sombrero that's on the plantation." Jade described a long-standing Latine stereotype promoted by the U.S. media that, for instance, has appeared since 1959 in advertisements promoted by the National Federation of Coffee Growers of Colombia that feature "Juan Valdez."[9] Juan is depicted leading his trusty mule, Conchita, and wearing a sombrero on his head, a blanket over his shoulder, and a bag of coffee beans on his back. Although Juan is identified as a grower, the advertisements show him engaging in manual labor—washing the coffee beans "by hand" and raking the beans as they dry in the sun.[10] The Juan Valdez image conflates laborer and grower, erasing the high status that can accompany ownership of a plantation. Juan Valdez is Colombian, but as Jade explained, this stereotype spills over into assumptions about Mexicans.[11] Juan Valdez is one example of the kinds of stereotypes that Jade identified.

In contrast to the rural Juan Valdez image, respondents most often described the low SES characterizing the "typical Latine" by referencing an unskilled service job or a general lack of education. Ignacia's story illustrates the tenacity with which these characteristics are associated with Mexicans:

> I met a woman a long time ago. And I hate it when people ask where I am from the first thing when they hear me talk. Really? Like, there are so many things about me before you know where I am from. But she did that, and I was like, "Uhh, Mexico, why?" "Oh, because your accent." Blah blah. "And where do you work?" I told her CDC [Centers for Disease Control and Prevention], which is nearby and everyone should know. And she was like, "Arby's?" And I'm like, "No, CDC." And she kept thinking like, "I don't understand you." I told her I'm Mexican, so CDC is out of the picture.

Ignacia voiced frustration with being asked to racially identify as "the first thing" that Americans wanted to know about her. Her frustration was compounded when her response led to the erroneous perception that she was a fast-food worker at Arby's. Ignacia's reading of the conversation was that the association of Mexicans with professional credentials was so remote to her interlocutor that, even supplied with the correct information, she continued to perceive the CDC as "out of the picture" as a place where Ignacia would be employed.

Sofia recounted her son's experience when his peers assumed that his Dominican family was working-class:

> So [my son] used to be asked . . . "Where does your dad work?" And he would say, "[an international petroleum company]." They'd say, "Oh, he puts gasoline in cars." [My son] got really sad because my husband is a professional engineer, very successful. And he got hurt. He said, "Mom, why are they telling me that?" I said, "It's just your last name. Sorry. So you just have to . . . realize that . . . you're going to be teased." But my daughter was very strong; my son was kind of more sensitive, like I am, so we put him in private school—Catholic school—and he had to finish seventh, eighth [grade], and then high school.

Sofia attributed her son's difficulties to his sensitivity. However, she used her middle-class resources to transfer her son to a private Catholic school.

Once the typical Latine image has been activated, other stereotypes often follow. Illustrating the multiple stereotypes attached to the "typical Latine," Mexican respondent Juan Diego described a car incident in a Home Depot parking lot in which he assumed he was perceived, he assumed, as working-class. After he was accused of hitting a man's truck, the police came to investigate:

> You know I was not dressed like this [gesturing toward middle-class clothes]. I was working really hard. I was genuinely interested in the process, because they treated me like I was an undocumented migrant. I mean, I really looked like one. (*laughs*) *So I played along*. . . . The cops were there, and I didn't give all the information just so that I could kind of see what was happening. They brought dogs because I didn't allow them to get into my car because there was no reason. . . . But I was just going along to see, if I were an undocumented Mexican or just because I was Mexican, how would they [treat me]. . . . At the end they had to call one of their supervisors, and finally I said, "Look, this is who I am, my wife works for [government agency,] and you need to back off," and so they finally did. (emphasis added)

Juan Diego came across as a working-class Latine immigrant because of his clothes—he was dressed for "working really hard"—and his presence at Home Depot, a place where Latine day laborers congregated in search of jobs. These working-class cues quickly led to Juan Diego's perception that police officers believed him to be Mexican, to lack documentation, to have hit the car of the accusing man, and to be transporting drugs or participating in some other form of criminal activity. Criminality is one of the most common stereotypes associated with perceptions of undocumented status.[12] The mark of criminality moved Juan Diego's exchange from an encounter in which his social identity was simply not verified to possibly a serious engagement with the criminal justice system. Juan's perception that he could "play along" with these misattributions in encounters with the police reflected a type of middle-class privilege. He correctly assumed that he could manipulate others' assumptions that he was a "typical Latine."

Native-born Atlantans and local law enforcement are not the only groups that stigmatize Mexicans as "typical Latines." Respondents related that other Latine immigrants also placed Mexicans at the bottom of the status hierarchy and associated this position with class. For instance, Aracely encountered individuals from countries across the globe in her job as executive director of a human rights organization. She observed that immigrants from other Latin American countries looked down on Mexicans: "You are nothing; you're a bunch of dirty greasers . . . and *that has to do with class*, has to do with the part of the identity that they don't recognize" (emphasis added). The phrase "dirty greasers" illustrates stigmatization. Note that Aracely, consistent with mestizaje belief systems, interpreted this perception through the lens of class and downplayed the salience of race.

Like Pablo quoted at the beginning of this chapter, fourteen Dominican respondents indicated that Atlantans tended to assume that "all Latines" are Mexican (see figure 4.1). Sarita echoed Pablo's observation that a Mexican label was not simply a mistaken guess about nationality but rather an identity that carried stigma: "When people tell me, 'You speak Spanish, you're from Mexico,' I say 'No!' (*laughs*). . . . But I don't get offended. There are people that say (*showing sarcasm*), 'You didn't dare say I'm Mexican.' (*scoffing*) But for me it's not offensive." Presumably, the "people" taking offense at the Mexican label are other Dominicans. That is, they recognize a "Mexican" appellation as potentially stigmatizing. While acknowledging that a Mexican label could be and is considered offensive by other Dominicans, Sarita performed identity work in the interview by insisting that she was not offended.

Luisa described her frustration with Latin American friends' assumptions about the "typical Latine": "It's not just Dominicans," she said, who want people to understand that the Latino population is very diverse. "I have a lot of friends from Argentina and Venezuela. And there's a little sense of frustration that stems from some of them . . . you know, they think I'm Mexican just because I say I'm Latin."

In contrast to pervasive stereotypes that define the "typical Latine" as Mexican, working-class, and undocumented, respondents observed that Atlantans appeared to be unfamiliar with the characteristics of Dominicans. Only nine Dominican respondents encountered stereotypes of Dominicans: that they play baseball, they dance, and they have dark skin. The first two stereotypes are not necessarily stigmatizing, and the potentially negative dark skin stereotype emerged when some Americans perceived middle-class Dominican respondents as "too white" to be Dominican. When asked where people thought he was from when they met him, Alfredo said, "Yeah, I say . . . Dominican, and a lot of people say, 'So I never met a Dominican this white.'" That "a lot of people" were surprised by his light skin tone illustrates the pervasiveness of the stereotype that Dominicans have dark skin. That said, Alfredo did actually have a rare elite background: his father was a diplomat who had moved to the Dominican Republic from western Europe. He noted that he looked European, and the research team agreed. By eliciting comments that he was "too light" to be Dominican, Alfredo became "the exception that proves the rule" of Dominicans having dark skin.

Estefania's account shows that the stereotype of Dominicans dancing could lead to one of the very few overtly stigmatizing perceptions of Dominicans—by other Latines. When she arrived in Atlanta in 1999, she said, "it was embarrassing to say that you were Dominican, very embarrassing. . . . If you said that you were Dominican here, for the Central Americans, you were a prostitute." Estefania explained that Dominican women in Atlanta's Latine dance clubs charged Mexican and Central American men for dances, and that these women were assumed to charge men for sex as well. Once, when she got into a taxi, "the man said, 'Oh, you're Dominican, the ones that dance? . . . I'll put on a little bachata for you.' And I told him, 'I don't dance. I don't dance!'" The taxi driver was implying that Estefania was a sex worker, a perception that she attributed to Atlanta's demographics at the time:

> When I got here [in 1999], the Central American population was mostly men: like 80 percent men and 20 percent women. There weren't any women. And so, you went to a bar and all you saw was men. That's why the business formed of charging to dance. Because there were almost no women and the prostitutes also lived off that. . . . With the [economic] crisis, and with the immigration and all that, [the Dominican prostitutes] have all gone over to the upper side of Manhattan.

Estefania assumed that Dominicans were perceived negatively in the past and implied that, since all the Dominican prostitutes relocated to Manhattan, attitudes toward Dominicans in Atlanta had shifted in a more positive direction. As figure 4.1 shows, a Dominican identity is not stigmatized in Atlanta to the extent that a Mexican identity is.

NEGOTIATING RACIALIZATION BY SIGNALING CLASS

How did respondents negotiate being stereotyped as the "typical Latine"? While Estefania declared that she didn't dance, Juan Diego "played along" with the stereotypes that he encountered at Home Depot and also presumed that announcing his social class would neutralize the stigma associated with a Mexican identity and protect him from police apprehension and arrest. Indeed, unlike Ignacia's unsuccessful attempts to correct misperceptions about Mexicans, Juan Diego's expectations proved accurate. When he actively engaged in identity work to correct the false assumptions ("I said, 'Look, this is who I am'"), he was released. However, as Ignacia's story reveals, "playing along" with the stereotypes of the "typical Latine" can be risky. For instance, the police and Home Depot employees might not have seen or acknowledged Juan Diego's middle-class, law-abiding status.

The stereotype of the "typical Latine" as an undocumented working-class Mexican is so powerful that many U.S. natives assume that third-generation, middle-class, Mexican American citizens are newly arrived "illegal immigrants."[13] Tomás Jiménez identifies a range of strategies that U.S.-born Mexican Americans use to countermand this assumption: signaling that they are Mexican but that they are not immigrants; emphasizing their middle-class status; avoiding situations in which their identity could be challenged; and altering the negative connotations of "Mexican" by asserting their claim to a Mexican heritage.[14]

I find similar identity work strategies among first-generation, middle-class Latine immigrants in Atlanta and add to Jiménez's research by comparing how their nationality influences which strategies first-generation Mexican and Dominican immigrants employ. Middle-class Mexican respondents often distinguished themselves from the "typical Latine" by signaling that they were not working-class.[15] Middle-class Dominicans could counter the working-class and undocumented statuses associated with the "typical Latine" by simply communicating that they were not Mexican. These social class and national-origin signals may be sufficient to dispel assumptions of undocumented legal status.[16] Only a few members of both national-origin groups also asserted a positive identity by signaling that they were documented. These identity work strategies emerged in response to two types of interview questions: "Have you experienced neg-

Table 4.1 Identity Negotiation Strategies among Dominican and Mexican Respondents

	Emphasize Atypicality	Change Typical Characteristics
Mexicans	9 (25%)	21 (58%)
Dominicans	13 (33%)	7 (18%)

Source: Browne, Tatum, and González 2021.

ative treatment or discrimination because you are Mexican/Dominican?" and "What race do people tend to perceive you to be?"

"Not Working-Class": Changing Notions of the Typical

Some respondents negotiated the "typical Latine" image by attempting to change what they perceived as negative assumptions that Latines in general or Mexicans in particular are working-class (see table 4.1). Mexicans engaged in this strategy more often than Dominicans (58 percent versus 18 percent). Nobody described trying to change conceptions of the "typical Dominican," suggesting that perceptions of Dominican typicality have not taken hold in the Atlanta context or perhaps that they are less stigmatized.

Many Mexican and Dominican respondents reported conversations in which they corrected erroneous assumptions that they were working-class. Quoted in chapter 1, Mexican respondent Santiago described one such encounter. When his daughters contacted him because they were prevented from entering their community pool, Santiago confronted the neighbor who was barring the girls' pool access by equalizing their status, referencing his multiple diplomas and stating: "*We've* got a problem."

Santiago described an encounter in a public setting. Adrian, also Mexican, provided a workplace example of his response to frequently being labeled a "typical Latine." A practicing attorney, Adrian believed that he was perceived by colleagues as occupying a low-status position and being potentially dangerous. He would negotiate these stereotypes and put people at ease only after he had identified himself as an attorney (professional capital) and shown that he spoke English fluently (cultural capital).

> You can tell when I walk in a courtroom, especially if I'm in, like, Fayette County, or one of the southern counties, where the bar is predominantly white, not even a lot of African American attorneys. And you know, I'll walk in, and again the music stops until they hear me talking. I'm like, "Hi, every-

> body, calm down. You know, I'm one of you guys. It's gonna be okay. Nothing bad is gonna happen." You get that sort of sense of everybody's looking at you at least for the first three minutes or so until you start talking and they realize you can speak English and you're not going to hurt anybody. And then they appreciate you when they do have Hispanics, whether it be defendants or anybody else that needs help. And they're like, "Oh, we actually have a Spanish-speaking attorney here that could assist." So it's just that initial interaction or impression that people seem to be taken aback initially until they can, you know, get over it. . . . And *that's on a daily basis* where I've gotten used to it and I don't notice it. But if I pay attention to it when I walk in somewhere, you can just tell initially. It's not even just the other attorneys. It's the people that have cases there or the family members that are there for other people. "Oh, who's that guy going before the bar? He's about to get tasered by a deputy or something." It's that type of reaction that I get that's fairly noticeable.

Once Adrian demonstrated his middle-class status and bilingualism, his Spanish fluency took on a new meaning—shifting from a cultural threat to a professional asset. Adrian also noted that he had to undergo this identity test, proving his professional membership and repeatedly reclaiming his middle-class status, on a daily basis. That is, he confronted "precarious privilege" each day, but he also had the resources to rescue his identity from precarity.

Several Mexican respondents believed that in regularly emphasizing both their Mexican and class identity, they could help to change pervasive beliefs about the working-class status of the "typical Mexican"—and potentially of the "typical Latine" as well. For instance, Santiago mentioned his diplomas to negotiate the working-class stereotype of the "typical Mexican." Ignacia emphasized her Mexican identity in the workplace (CDC), where her professional status was already known.

> Every time in the office and every time I meet anybody, I'll say I'm Mexican. I like to because I think people have stereotypes about Mexicans that do not match reality. I know there are a lot of low-income Mexicans, but there's still a lot of middle-high-income Mexicans. I always say "Mexican" so that slowly, one by one, they're going to start changing their perspective of what Mexicans should look or be like.

Ignacia negotiated racial categorization by educating native-born Atlantans and persuading them to forgo the stigmatized stereotypes of Mexicans as "low-income" and to change their perception of Mexicans to encompass "middle-high-income Mexicans." Such a strategy, however, is not always successful beyond the workplace, as we learned from Ignacia's account of being mistaken for a fast-food worker at Arby's.

"Not Mexican": Dominicans Emphasizing Atypicality

The majority of Dominicans find that, unlike a Mexican national identity, their Dominican nationality does not carry stigma in Atlanta. In fact, many Dominican respondents emphasized the importance of clarifying that they were not Mexican to deflect potentially negative interactions. Respondents described situations in which they communicated their Dominican origins, shifting the tone of a conversation from one of potential hostility into something more pleasant. Pablo raised this concern explicitly when describing his relations with the customers who frequented his place of business: "When an American speaks to us, they ask us, 'Where are you from?' And I say, 'We are Dominicans.' And they say, 'Oh, you're Dominican. That's a pretty island.' And that changes the environment. If I say I'm from Mexico, they would immediately leave my business."

Pablo is not simply correcting neutral information about his country of origin; he is also responding to the "typical Latine" image triggered by customers' assumption that he is from Mexico. He explained that clarifying his national origin "changes the environment" in his enterprise, from a negative encounter ("they would immediately leave my business") to a positive exchange ("that's a pretty island"). Assuming that the stigma of being perceived as Mexican would eclipse the relatively high status of owning a business, he reclaimed that elevated status by communicating that he was Dominican.

For Esteban, clarifying his Dominican origins counteracted being perceived as undocumented and uneducated:

> I guess when we answer a form, we just say Hispanic. But when we talk to people, we immediately clarify that we're Dominican. We don't like, you know, I'm being very honest, we don't like to be confused with Mexicans. We make very clear that we're not Mexican because of the negative connotations that we have seen here in the Atlanta area. Because if they hear that, they think that you might be illegal or that you might not speak English or that you might not be educated.

Esteban not only named the constellation of stereotypes that surround the "typical Latine" stereotype—Mexican, "illegal," uneducated (working-class)—but saw this constellation as so prominent that he responded like other Dominicans: "we immediately clarify that we're Dominican."

Authorized Legal Status

One additional identity work strategy used by both Mexicans and Dominicans is notable for its relation to the racialization of illegality—signaling authorized legal status. Nine authorized respondents recounted instances of signaling their documented legal status during a negotiation of the "typical Latine" image. Carmen, a Dominican, explained:

> The way they see Hispanic here, you know, by the Anglo-Saxon community is . . . I don´t think we [are] valued . . . and maybe totally wrong; this is the sense when you read the newspaper, or when you watch the news, when you see that every day the police stopping people because they don't have the document. . . . [My] being here I have not faced that because, you know, because we have papers . . . it's easy for me to maneuver myself, and because I have education is another factor, so it's easy for me . . . because I know how to act for what I need, so, if I go to a place and I see that they treat me the wrong way, I will know how to approach the person and say: "Excuse me, I don't want you to treat me that way," and I don't care, the person could be black, Chinese, or whatever. . . . [I] feel free enough within myself to tell them: "No." . . . To me I could [not care less] how they see me, but I would demand that you respect me because I would respect you. I go . . . for that because I have the tools, you know, because I . . . I am an American citizen.

Carmen noted the anti-Latine atmosphere perpetuated in the media and in interactions with the "Anglo-Saxon community." She perceived her class and legal status advantages as "tools" that she could use to "maneuver" around negative treatment. That is, she consciously asserted her social class to negotiate the racialization of illegality. For Carmen, U.S. citizenship carried a legitimacy that allowed her to confront individuals who were treating her badly. She emphasized both her educated class status and her documented status, differentiating herself from Latine immigrants "without papers." Carmen also anticipated the need to ascertain her citizenship status when she was pulled over by police.

Dominican respondent Perez described being stopped by the police and ordered to "show his papers."

> PEREZ: But in the case of discrimination, I know it happens, and the police have stopped me after they have seen my face.
>
> INTERVIEWER: And how do you react in that moment when the police stop you? How do you act?
>
> PEREZ: What do I do? Show them the documents.

Perez showed his documented status not just as an identity work strategy but as a survival strategy in his encounter with police. Nevertheless, he still got extra police attention, which he attributed to discrimination against those guilty of "looking Latine."

Pedro, another Dominican respondent, created social distance from undocumented immigrants when he discussed the possibility of needing to rely on his citizenship status in the future:

> If the need presents itself [and] we have to identify ourselves as citizens and residents, we'll have to do that, of course, and I'm 100 percent sure that the benefits for a citizen and resident or for an illegal aren't the same. There are undoubtedly differences, there are steps, but, as of right now, we haven't needed to take them. (*laughs*)

Notably, Pedro used the pejorative term "illegal" and rhetorically distinguished himself and his wife from this group.

Including Pedro, five Mexican and four Dominican respondents separated themselves from undocumented immigrants during the interview by using the term "illegals." The documented-undocumented distinction was particularly acute in 2011 when we asked respondents about their views on the draconian immigration bill, HB 87, which had been recently passed. The majority responded that the law was unfair, emphasizing that most Latine immigrants were hard workers and were needed by the U.S. economy.[17] For instance, Marisol, a Dominican, told the interviewer:

> For me, when they talk about immigrants, and in all of these laws that they pass, and all of these things, they say that the abuses against the immigrants, I don't find it to be unjust. I am an immigrant, and I can tell you the amount of immigrants from other social statuses that have never had problems. The problem is not a problem of immigrants, the problem is the illegalness. That we can't take away from anybody. The world according to Jesus, if we can see things from the Christian form, is only one world and one people, but unfortunately each government has made its own constitution. And you were born into one, and I was born into another. You have to respect it. If we don't respect it, what are we going to do. . . . I believe that there is a need to respect the law. I believe that there is a need to stop the entrance of illegals. I think there needs to be a broader place given to immigrants that want to come legally from Hispano-America. Because yes, I tell you that the United States has been very unjust with them.

Marisol distinguished herself from undocumented immigrants by stressing that she had not found the laws to be "unjust" and by referring to the "entrance of illegals." She positioned herself outside the low-status position of undocumented immigrants by emphasizing that the "problem" was not immigrants per se (a group to which she belonged) but rather the undocumented newcomers (a group to which she did not belong). She further placed herself on the side of those supposedly sanctioned by the United States by insisting that "there is a need to respect the law." However, she left room for a critique of immigration law by stating her belief that the United States had been "very unjust" to Latine immigrants who "want to come legally."

Betty, also Dominican, expressed an equally ambivalent view toward undocumented immigrants in regard to HB 87:

> You know that in this country there are a lot of illegals. In that, I don't know if it's good . . . you know, because everything has its pros and its cons. . . . But I can't put myself to agree with the fact that they take them away as prisoners or that the police take them to prison or that kind of thing. But everything has its pros and its cons, as I told you.

Like Marisol, Betty referred to undocumented immigrants as "illegals." While she asserted that she did not condone imprisoning undocumented immigrants because of their legal status, she equivocated on this position by adding that "everything has its pros and its cons." That is, she suggested that there might be positive aspects of HB 87.

When unauthorized status combines with working-class human capital, job options and the ability to achieve upward mobility are severely constricted. Selma's situation provided a clear contrast to the advantages of authorized legal status and a middle-class background.[18] She described the pressure to stay in her current working-class job because her mother in Mexico relied on the remittances that she sent, even when officials began enforcing immigration laws that prohibited the hire of undocumented immigrants:

> Well, [there] came the situation of the papers, that they [employers] wanted to start checking them now. So after I was saying, if I leave this job, what am I going to do? I have always helped my mother. I send my mom money. . . . And I was afraid to change [jobs] because I didn't know English very well, I knew very little. I don't have the papers to look for whatever job I want.

The "situation of the papers" is a reference to the launching in Georgia of the E-Verify program, which required employers to begin checking documentation.

Yet the racialization of illegality also created situations in which authorized legal status went unrecognized. Sofia, for example, felt like an outsider, despite having lived in the United States for seventeen years and holding authorized legal status:

> I think we have been accepted pretty good [in my neighborhood], like, we're doing okay. But I do notice the neighborhood . . . talking about the influx of people and how [there are] . . . no jobs and how the neighborhood is changing. It's kind of, like, sad because in a way we have gone through so much to make it. . . . Then when you see this change in even your neighbors thinking, "Okay, you're also from outside," it makes you feel, after seventeen years, that's kind of sad.

Unlike the respondents who engaged in one-up assimilation strategies, Sofia had tried to dissolve Latine-American boundaries and blend with Americans. Nevertheless, seventeen years after she immigrated from the Dominican Republic, her (predominantly white) neighbors had come to see her as similar to Latine immigrants who were not assimilating—as "also from outside." Her disappointment was captured in her statement that the situation was "kind of sad."

In contrast to Sofia, the majority of respondents were much more likely to highlight their middle-class status or nationality rather than their legal status when anticipating or experiencing negative encounters with native-born Atlantans. Angela García finds that unauthorized immigrants in locales with especially severe immigrant restrictions consciously signal their authorized legal status by donning middle-class attire and comportment, a tactic she refers to as "legal passing."[19] Flores and Schachter's experiments also show that native-born whites are less likely to perceive a Latine immigrant as undocumented if the immigrant has a college education or middle-class profession, or if they are not Mexican. These authors suggest that undocumented immigrants who do not fit social stereotypes of illegality may be able to avoid some of the negative treatment associated with undocumented status.[20] My findings support this contention and suggest that asserting a middle-class or "not-Mexican" identity may be sufficient to dispel the stereotype of being undocumented.

ACCOUNTING FOR DISCRIMINATION AND RESISTING RACIALIZATION

Respondents often attributed misperceptions of their nationality, social class, or legal status to a lack of information ("ignorance") rather than to an unequal racial system. This is not surprising: attributing negative experiences to discrimination comes at a cost to stigmatized individuals.[21]

Claiming discrimination can lower status and diminish social self-esteem, so individuals are motivated to recast negative experiences as resulting from ignorance or personal fault rather than discrimination.[22]

I investigated the predilection to deny racism or discrimination in the face of negative experiences by broadening my inquiry beyond the "typical Latine" stereotype and focusing on "personal mistreatment." This concept combines two codings: (1) affirmative answers to the question, "Have you experienced negative treatment or discrimination because you are Mexican/Dominican?," and (2) experiences that, according to the research literature, were "negative events." Negative events can include negative stereotyping, racialization as an undocumented working-class Mexican, actions by others that express prejudice (a broad definition of "discrimination"), and institutional rules and procedures that create unequal opportunities (a narrow definition of "discrimination").[23] As I discuss later, casting a wide net allows us to identify how respondents explained contradictory information about their negative experiences.

I present findings for my combined personal mistreatment measure in table 4.2. The "recounted negative events" column reports the prevalence of negative events irrespective of whether the respondent categorized an event as mistreatment or discrimination. The "perceived personal mistreatment or discrimination" column reports answers to the question, "Have you had negative experiences or discrimination because you are Mexican/Dominican?" "Perceived group discrimination" reflects responses to the interview question about relations between Atlanta's Latines, whites, and blacks.

Ana, for example, asked whether she had experienced discrimination, replied: "No. Criticism, a lot because I am an educator and when students don't get good grades, they will [say] that it's my accent." Like other respondents who described negative treatment, Ana did not appear to perceive that she had experienced mistreatment or discrimination. Sarita was among those respondents who reported group discrimination when she stated, "I've seen [mistreatment] happen to other people, and I've jumped in and I defend them and I tell them that it's wrong and [in] bad taste." Overall, it was Mexicans—the group that most closely fit the stereotypes associated with the "typical Latine"—who most often reported perceptions of personal mistreatment and group discrimination.[24] As table 4.2 illustrates, 71 percent of Mexican respondents and 37 percent of Dominican respondents recounted negative events.[25]

Table 4.2 shows that a number of respondents gave answers that seemed contradictory. A higher proportion of Mexicans and Dominicans who told us about negative events also said that they themselves had not experi-

Table 4.2 Discrimination Experienced by Mexican and Dominican Respondents Personally and as a Group Member

	Recounted a Negative Event	Perceived Personal Mistreatment or Discrimination "yes"	Perceived Group Discrimination	*N*
Mexican	71%	30%	30%	33
Dominican	37%	0%	26%	35

Source: Author's compilation from respondent interviews, 2009–2016.
Note: Respondents could discuss both types of discrimination in the interview. Totals of 100 percent are coincidental.

enced negative treatment or discrimination. As I discuss later, respondents reconciled this discrepancy through several identity work strategies.

Mexicans also reported instances of personal mistreatment more frequently than they reported perceptions of group discrimination. Pablo, whose comments on the poor relations between the United States and Mexico are quoted in the beginning of this chapter, was answering the question about how Americans treat Latine immigrants in general. This study's group discrimination numbers suggest that respondents' own negative experiences did not necessarily lead them to believe that they lived in an environment that was generally hostile to Latines.[26]

Over 40 percent of Mexicans and 25 percent of Dominicans who described adverse treatment experienced these incidents in public spaces such as restaurants and stores. For both groups, about 12 percent of the negative events reported occurred in the workplace. These patterns suggest that respondents from both countries were most likely to experience or perceive mistreatment from strangers in public places rather than from coworkers or customers in their workplace.

The worsening political climate for Latine immigrants during the study period (2009–2016) did not significantly affect perceptions of discrimination toward Latines. These perceptions held steady even though stories of mistreatment increased in prevalence after 2012, when the momentous anti-immigration law, HB 87, was passed.[27]

Beyond uncovering basic patterns, the interviews can reveal the meanings that respondents attributed to negative experiences. Specifically, I can delve into questions of how respondents interpreted and explained mistreatment in light of the U.S. racial system, and I can explore how social class was integrated into these identity work strategies.

Reclaiming Class, Resisting Racialization: Uneducated Perpetrators

A number of respondents who described mistreatment downplayed systemic racism as an explanation by recasting anti-Latine experiences as the result of the perpetrator's lack of education. For instance, Horacio referred to the U.S. racial hierarchy as the "color code system" and described common conditions under which he was stereotyped and treated as an out-group member or as a Mexican. Yet he also explicitly claimed that this was "not discrimination":

> When I enter a room where the group is, whether it is African Americans or all Anglo English speaking, there is a change in the dynamic of the group about how they behave and react and talk to me. It changes the dynamic. They become very aware that you are not part of the "we," that you are outside of the "we," but that's not completely negative. They are very aware that you are not "we." So in that sense I could be Serbian, I could be Slovak, or I could be Mexican. . . . Now, when I say "Mexican," then a whole range of information in their heads comes forth about Mexico, and they begin to talk about—guess what—drugs, crimes, immigration. The questions revolve around that. I don't feel that I'm being rejected or discriminated. I just think that they don't know what else to talk about. Instead of just talking about what they would with anybody. Like what would happen if I were just a white, a white person, what would you be thinking about? Golf, or baseball, or business, stocks, but it becomes about Mexico and Mexicanity.

Horacio explained that every group is at risk of being confronted with stereotypical topics of conversation, and that for Latines this is linked to falling outside the "we" (the dominant group). He pointed out, however, that some stereotypes and conversation topics that are attached to white persons and maintain them in the high-status dominant group are neutral (baseball) or associated with the middle class (golf, business, stocks). Horacio implied that the stigmatizing stereotypes applied to Mexicans (drugs, crime, immigration) resulted from the perpetrators' limited knowledge, not an intention to discriminate: "I don't feel that I'm being rejected or discriminated. I just think that they don't know what else to talk about."

Like Horacio, Brisa offered an interpretation of negative interactions through the lens of education (class). She attributed this kind of interaction to a lack of information about Latines:

> Americans that treat you badly are the ones that aren't very educated, because someone who is educated knows about Latino countries. They know

> about the riches of those countries, and those who are ignorant about it are the ones that see you as lesser. That's what made me feel okay when I realized that this is a matter of education, not race. Right? So as someone who is educated, I am not going to treat you badly. I want to show you that the country isn't still riding donkeys! Haha, right? I have an education! I have a bachelor's degree from a good university in Mexico.

Brisa explicitly attributed the poor treatment of Latines by some Americans as a matter of low education rather than race. Invoking the image of the "typical Latine" as riding a donkey, she debunked this image by citing her university degree.

Oscar also viewed discrimination as tightly associated with the education level of the perpetrator. Once he entered graduate school, he said, he did not experience the type of discrimination that he experienced in New York as a child.

> I do believe when you're in a more educated setting, the probability of you running across [negative treatment] is less. You know, and I think it's well known that, you know, that is very, you know, just comes from ignorance really. So the more educated you are, the less likely you are to be ignorant and, you know, I didn't really run across that because I was in more [situations with] everybody seeking to be a professional in one shape or another. So people didn't really come across that way.

Attributing discrimination to the education level of those around him, Oscar perceived individuals with professional aspirations as less likely to practice discrimination. Through this maneuver, Oscar differentiated himself from working-class immigrants.

Middle-class Latine immigrants may have encountered a clear opportunity to recognize racism in the United States when Donald Trump repeatedly maintained during his 2016 presidential campaign that Mexicans were "rapists and criminals." However, some respondents insisted that these remarks were not discriminatory; Carla, for instance, asserted that Trump's remarks had "nothing to do with . . . race":

> You know, the candidate Donald Trump, he has said horrible things. I do hate it because you do hear on the news all the time or you hear on the newspaper, you know. So it's sad, it's really sad. I think it's more of an issue with [Trump's] education than with [discrimination]. I think that people [like Trump] are just not educated enough to know the difference between . . . [Mexicans] being bad because you are just a bad person, but it has nothing to do with . . . race.

Carla emphasized that Trump's negative depiction of Latine immigrants was not about discrimination but was "more of an issue" with his education—that is, social class. She explained that those who are poorly educated have no knowledge about differences among Mexicans, particularly the distinction between Mexicans in general and individual Mexicans who are "bad people."[28]

It is unclear how Carla defined being poorly educated. In the United States, "poor education" implies a lack of schooling or a general ignorance, but Trump is wealthy and holds a college degree. In Mexico, the term *mal educado* is associated with being rude or ill-mannered. (Carla's interview was conducted in English, so she did not use the term *mal educado*. However, she still may have been using a Mexican-derived definition of "educated.")

Like Carla, Alejandro reframed white prejudice against those who speak Spanish—another aspect of the racialization of illegality—in terms of the perpetrator's lack of education. Alejandro was asked in his interview what he saw in his community's attitude about migrants:

> Well, you just have to see how it's been with Trump, or how it's going, to know that quite a few Americans who are middle-class white have views that are very retrograde about immigrants, no? And just, for example, for speaking Spanish, I mean . . . you can see that also education in the U.S. hasn't been, like, very good.

Alejandro noted the race of the perpetrators (white) and attributed their negative views toward Spanish speakers to the poor education that U.S. natives receive—even middle-class whites. He alluded to adverse treatment by referencing Trump and "very retrograde" views, thus elevating his own status above that of middle-class whites.

Dismissing or Downplaying Racism: Colorblind Narratives

In addition to stressing low education or "ignorance" (class), respondents also commonly relied on colorblind frameworks to explain experiences of mistreatment. As I discussed in chapter 3, colorblind perspectives point to "nonracial" reasons for racial inequality.[29] In particular, my respondents claimed that individuals, not the system, are responsible for perpetrating discrimination, and that individuals can choose whether or not to interpret their experiences as discrimination.[30] This perspective aligns these respondents with both the core tenets of the American dream, which posits that anybody who works hard can make it, and heritage mestizaje beliefs, which downplay racial inequality.[31] Colorblind discourse also provides respondents with a way to maintain privileged middle-class status in a climate hostile toward Latine immigrants.[32]

For instance, Juan explained that discrimination is the result of personal weakness. When asked whether he felt he had faced any barriers in terms of opportunities for his children, he replied: "I didn't have a culture shock. I just came in and just blended into the society. I think . . . but my experience was like that. I'm sure not everybody had that experience. But I didn't come . . .with those rough edges, you know. I didn't find any excuses not to be able to fit in." Juan suggested that an individual's focus on discrimination in claiming such treatment reflects their own shortcoming: they are making "excuses not to be able to fit in." His own middle-class education in the Dominican Republic, where he attended an American school and spoke English, had removed any "rough edges" he might have otherwise had on arriving in the United States. He explained:

> [My parents] placed me in an American school . . . in Santo Domingo. And I've been speaking English ever since, you know, both languages obviously. But, when I graduated university, I was exposed to the U.S. culture. We had cable; we had all that stuff. So I was very in tune with the U.S. Besides, I grew up with American teachers, you know, in school. So it wasn't like . . . for some people, culture shock or any of that. I was already very accustomed to it all.

Note that for Juan being "very in tune with the U.S." did not encompass a perception of racial inequality. His account transformed racialization despite assimilation into assimilation ("I . . . just blended into the society").

Like Juan, and consistent with a colorblind belief system, many of my respondents expressed the view that discrimination comes to those who "dwell" on it.[33] Dario, also Dominican, made this point quite clearly:

> Well, I don't know . . . I never felt discriminated against that I know of. . . . I just never gave [this topic] much attention. . . . The people that are looking for that type of attention, I believe, to feel discriminated against. . . . I never put that much attention on that experience, what I have to do is focus on my own responsibilities and see them through to the limits that I can . . . to invest myself in something.

Although Dario claimed to have never experienced discrimination, he invoked the notion of coping mechanisms. He tried to "focus on my own responsibilities," which he perceived as attempts to "invest myself in something." Later in the interview, Dario spoke about American views that could be considered systemic and prejudicial:

> Americans . . . definitely want you to adapt to their culture, the way of being, very very quickly, and for us that's not easy. . . . They want you to . . . be American . . . that you're here, you're living in America, you are obligated to speak English, and if you don't like it, go to your country. . . . Not everyone is like this, but there are those people that think that you should assume their culture . . . and that's not easy.

Being told to return to your heritage country if you don't speak English could be interpreted as a form of mistreatment. The systemic aspect of Dario's experiences arose when he admitted that attempting to conform to American expectations of Latine immigrants was "not easy."

Sofia, a college professor, also mentioned the importance of staying positive, even though being "looked at differently," as a Latine, when engaged in public activities, such as shopping, could be trying. She offered me this advice about my daughter: "It's really important that [she knows] ahead of time, sometimes you're going to be looked at differently."

> But you . . . need to know, like, I always value myself for who I am and what I have given and not because of what other people think. I try . . . never ever . . . I don't think I have lost my temper once. I don't . . . I try not to.
>
> And [customers in a store] start to talk to you. So, "Could you tell me where I can find this?" "Oh, okay, ma'am. So what do you do? Do you clean homes too?" And I don't mind. . . . So you go through things like that, but I don't really care. Honestly, it doesn't bother me. I just go where they tell me to go, and it's fine. I just know inside who I am. But it's . . . it's getting tough.

The contrast between Sofia's experience of being taken for a "typical Latine" looking for a cleaning job and her insistence that "it doesn't bother me" illustrates what Eileen O'Brien calls the "sunny" spin that many immigrants give to stories of mistreatment and discrimination.[34] Sofia reinforced a positive social identity by stating, "I always value myself for who I am and what I have given and not because of what other people think." Yet Sofia also alluded to the ongoing pressure exerted by outsider status and racialization despite assimilation with her contradictory statements that "it doesn't bother me" and "it's getting tough."

Sofia mentioned that managing her emotions ("I don't think that I lost my temper once") had been part of her effort to maintain a positive attitude.[35] Such efforts could be seen as a form of "resistance" to racialization. This strategy is similar to the emotion work described in Evans and Moore's study of minorities in predominantly white institutions. The professional people of color in their study faced a conflict with a high emotional cost.

They experienced the negative stereotypes and racialized narratives woven into their workplaces in tandem with colorblind discourses that denied racism. To reap the rewards of their position, they needed to keep their emotions "in check" and appear professional. As a coping mechanism and a strategy to achieve mobility and success, emotion management was a critical element of their cultural arsenal.[36]

In my study, Rubén (who was interviewed in English) navigated racialization by asserting that the experience of discrimination is linked to an individual "mentality" or "complex":

> I don't feel discrimination or something like that. No. The first instance, I never put in my head discrimination. You know, I don't feel that complex. You don't have to classify the people. Grow up with that mentality. . . . So I would like that [my children] grow up thinking that everybody's the same.

Often associated with an obsession or considered a negative attribute, the term "complex" is used in psychology to connote "a group or system of related ideas or impulses that have a common emotional tone."[37] By refusing to "put . . . discrimination [in his head]," Rubén suggested that this negative frame of mind could be avoided at will.

Mexican respondent Marta downplayed anti-Latine discrimination by relegating it to "isolated cases":

> I've heard of very isolated cases [of discrimination]. But not like that where they've discriminated against me, no. I haven't had that experience. . . . Well, one time my son had an issue with another boy. . . . He didn't like [that] they we [were] speaking poorly about Hispanics, and he even wanted to push him, but [my son] defended himself, they sent him to detention, they called his attention, and it all ended with that. Things didn't escalate.

Marta's perception of discrimination as "isolated cases" she had heard about was tempered by her son's experience. When her son was targeted with anti-Hispanic slurs at school, he retaliated and landed in detention. Marta perceived this incident as an "isolated case" too, however, and did not attribute it to systemic race-based discrimination.

Some respondents put more distance between themselves and characterizations of Latines as a disadvantaged minority group by emphasizing the welcoming reception that they had experienced in Atlanta. Mexican respondent Eduardo called his reception in the city "absolutely the contrary [of discrimination]. I say, I feel that the kind of American people . . . they are very open . . . they want to learn much about your culture." Insisting that his experience was the *opposite* of discrimination, Eduardo interpreted the questions of native-born Atlantans as expressions of curiosity and a desire to "learn more" about Mexican culture.

Denouncing U.S. Racism

Not all respondents described their reception as welcoming or offered colorblind explanations of racial inequality. Some—including Betty, Federico, Santiago, Pablo, and Ignacia—called out U.S. racism when describing their experiences of being categorized as a "typical Latine" as racial discrimination.[38] They pointed to a general climate of racism as well as to specific instances of racism experienced in institutional settings, such as their workplace or their children's school.

For instance, Aracely referred to anti-Latine hostility in terms of the U.S. racial hierarchy: "At this point the climate is so bad that if you are not conscious about that . . . somebody else is going to let you know that you are not white, you know." The "bad climate" for Latine immigrants that she mentioned is characteristic of the racialization of illegality. She connected this climate to prejudice toward Latines who are "not white." As we saw in the previous chapter, such a racial categorization applies to the majority of middle-class Mexican and Dominican immigrants.

Federico discussed the racism in his workplace, a national company in the finance, insurance, and real estate industry:

> FEDERICO: [In] general, United States is racist. . . . Okay, so where anybody that it is not white. Now, second, one thing is to allow me to be here. Other thing is to let me do business. . . . Many people have no other way to behave, but lots of the people want those Latins in general as consumer or as a second-class citizen. But other thing is, try to compete in the business industry, whatever the area, that's another story. At this moment, it is hell for us, in this office, to do business. The vast majority of our customers are Hispanics because White people don't want to deal with us . . . because we are Hispanic.
>
> INTERVIEWER: Interesting.
>
> FRANCISCO: Well, you say "interesting." I say painful.

Federico differentiated between acceptance of Latines "as consumer or as a second-class citizen," on the one hand, and the complete rejection he had experienced in the professional workplace ("that's another story"), on the other. For Federico, both the company and the white clientele rebuffed agents who were Hispanic. Labeling this mistreatment as racism, he pointedly emphasized its emotional toll by terming it "painful."

Betty recounted her son's experience of mistreatment at school, which she attributed to racism. Her son "has had his small [problems] at school, but nothing out of control. . . .So everything, they've called him Mexican, you know . . . that kind of thing. . . . With other students . . . it's the racism, you know." By interpreting being called "Mexican" as an example of mistreatment, Betty reinforced the idea that this is a stigmatized identity. Further, although Betty recognized the racism behind an attribution of a Mexican identity, she focused her identity work strategies on handling stigmatization in experiences she considered "small" and "nothing out of control."

Mexican respondent Agustín was one of the few respondents who highlighted parallels between white racism against Latine immigrants and the treatment of African Americans. His narrative was consistent with studies suggesting that black-Latine solidarity emerges from Latines who recognize discrimination as part of a larger system of racial inequality.[39]

INTERVIEWER: How is the relation between Hispanics and whites at school? Are there tensions?

AGUSTÍN (Mexican): Yes, there are tensions. There are tensions because the white isolates himself, he leaves the group of African Americans and Latines on the other side. . . . I have seen [that] it is easier for the children to integrate as a minority between African Americans and Latinos, and my problem is that sometimes they do not integrate for positive things, honestly, and the American remains distant. Well, it costs them . . . that this is another thing. Georgia is a special state, it is not . . . we are not talking about California.

Agustín described the distinction he made between "us" (Latines and African Americans) and "them" (white Georgians) as perpetrated by Anglos as "natural"; thus, "the white isolates himself" and "remains distant." Class enters Agustín's account in two ways. He referred to native-born white Georgians without designating their class. In contrast, the African Americans with whom his family interacted were well educated. Further, he explicitly stated that Latines and African Americans are in a common position as minorities: "It is easier for the children to integrate as a minority between African Americans and Latinos." However, Agustín perceived the Latine-black connection as a problem: "Sometimes they do not integrate for positive things."

Perez also recounted an example of the hostile climate of immigrant reception—police discrimination against him as a Latine. He connected this to African American experiences.

> Honestly, it has happened to me twice. [The police] will block off the street and stop the whole world, and at night they put the flashlight on people and say, "Move on, move on," but they will stop me. . . . I have documents . . . I give it all to them, and they still tell me to get out of the car. . . . Comparatively . . . I know that black people complain about the same treatment. (*laughs*)

Recognizing that African Americans also experience heightened police surveillance, Perez appeared to perceive grounds for Latines' common identity with them. Later in the interview, however, Perez distinguished himself from blacks when he suggested that his discrimination experiences were due to looking "Latine," not to looking "black":

> INTERVIEWER: Have your children had those experiences? Or have they had [them] since they've been here?
>
> PEREZ: They know that . . . they have told me about some things but never anything serious. . . . But yes, because when something happens, they first look at every Latino face.

Sergio, a Mexican, took a historical perspective, drawing parallels with discrimination against Chinese immigrants:

> It's basically going back to the Chinese, going back to the 1924 exclusionary law, that . . . threw all Chinese out of the United States, and it's the Irish being told, don't even come to apply for a job, don't even try to apply. And sometimes when the Chinese were being thrown out, the Mexicans were white, were considered to be white so that they wouldn't be thrown out, because they were labor. If the Chinese were [not] meant to be here, then who else was going to do the cheap labor? The Mexicans. But we are talking about a nation and color and things, but no no, they are white, so somehow the sense of them became white. So it's a game, but it's a very dangerous game, and it's a very cruel game, but it's the game we live in.

Sergio interpreted the designation of Mexicans as "white" not as an upward bump in status but rather as part of "a very dangerous game . . . a very cruel game" through which Mexican labor could be exploited. By placing Latine immigrants in the "white" category, however, he also was positioning Latines as separate from blacks. As an undocumented Latine immigrant, he was part of the "cruel game" that he described. Sergio would explain that he had been "radicalized" in response to circumstances that scholars associate with the racialization of illegality, including the events of September 11, 2001, the Arizona anti-immigrant bill SB 1070, and what he described as the fascist news media coverage of Latine immigrants.

Finally, the most forceful recognition of discrimination was expressed by Ignacia, the CDC professional discussed earlier. Unlike Sergio, Ignacia was documented, so she was able to engage the legal system to combat workplace discrimination:

> I tried to sue one of my employers before I worked at CDC, and I thought I had the strongest case ever. That's when I was a teacher, but I went to see several lawyers, and they all wanted for [bringing a] discrimination [case,] like $5,000 in front that I was gonna lose if I lose the case. . . . I mean, that was really a very strong case that I had discrimination in front of my face often. Like . . . when you . . . apply for a job and then you learn somebody else got it and you're like, "Wait a minute, I think I have more experience." . . . You kind of get the hint like, and people will tell you maybe you didn't interview as well and it's like, "But I thought I interviewed really good." So I think that happens way more often than it should, but we [are] working on that. . . . That's why I keep saying I'm Mexican—[to] help change perspectives—but I think discrimination happens on a daily basis.

Ignacia perceived that discrimination "happens on a daily basis." She described in detail how anti-Latine discrimination could create barriers to employment and taint a workplace environment. Although she decided not to pursue her lawsuit, given the amount of money that losing the case could cost her, she continued to pursue the identity work strategy of changing people's views of the "typical Mexican."

SUMMARY

The interviews show how class infuses the stigmatization experiences and identity work strategies described by Atlanta's middle-class Latine respondents. Their experiences illustrate the three concepts underlying this study: racialization despite assimilation, the "typical Latine," and identity work. Even in middle-class settings where they had achieved structural assimilation, respondents were racialized. Often stereotyped as "typical Latines," they responded by drawing on their national and class resources to distinguish themselves from this stereotype. Mexicans engaged in identity work to signal that they were middle-class, with the aim of "teaching the ignorant" American and changing the stereotype of the "typical Latine" to a more positive and nuanced image.[40] Dominicans engaged in identity work to signal that they were "not Mexican." This national designation appears to have been sufficient to correct others' assumptions that they were working-class and undocumented.

Tellingly, it was primarily in encounters with police that documented Dominican and Mexican respondents flagged their legal status to negotiate racialization. Beyond dealing with law enforcement, respondents were much more likely to rely on their middle-class status than their legal status to confront negative assumptions. In a vivid example, Rosa's children countered a racial slur by making invidious class comparisons:

> One time we were leaving Walmart, and eh . . . they yelled at us. . . . My youngest son said: "Mom, he called us beaners." And I say to him: "And what did you say back?," because my son, the oldest, [had] yelled [something] back, and the middle one was laughing. I ask him: "What did you say back?" He said to me this is what [they] answered: "Yes, you might be winning, but look at that [clunker of a] car you're driving . . . the filth. . . . But we have a house and a new car, things you don't have," and they flew into fits of rage.

Although Rosa was documented and her children were citizens, her oldest son responded to being called a "beaner" by mentioning the caliber of car they drove and the homes they could afford. This response positioned Rosa and her family as middle-class and the Americans taunting them as working-class. Further, Rosa's son stigmatized the Americans as Walmart customers who drove a "clunker," and in associating their car with "filth," he gave their lower class position a moral valence.

In my interviews with middle-class Atlantan Dominicans, they resisted categorization as Mexican more often than they resisted categorization as African American. While my findings on Dominicans depart from patterns described in other cities where Dominicans are plentiful, this pattern is consistent with Jiménez's theory of "replenishment."[41] Unlike their presence in those other cities where Dominicans predominate, Mexicans in Atlanta are the numerically dominant Latine group and Dominicans are a relatively tiny and new group of newcomers.[42]

When Dominican and Mexican respondents interpreted their experiences of negative treatment and discrimination, most of them avoided casting themselves as a disadvantaged minority. One of their class-based responses turned on its head the perception that, as immigrants, they had little education by attributing the perpetrator's discriminatory behavior to poor education. Another approach was to cite nonracial reasons for patterns of racism. That is, they offered colorblind explanations. In contrast to the colorblind approach, one small group of respondents interpreted their experiences as discrimination arising from the U.S. racial system. However, even those who perceived their mistreatment as resembling African American experiences frequently drew a distinction between Latines and U.S.-born blacks.

The identity work strategies that foreground middle-class status and dismiss experiences of mistreatment could be reflecting a "politics of respectability." This concept was first developed to explain African Americans' public adherence to white middle-class norms as one of the few routes to reclaiming dignity in the face of Jim Crow racism.[43] The concept of respectability politics has been applied to Latines in various circumstances, from presenting middle-class plaintiffs in court cases to organizing for social change.[44] I build on these studies by looking at the politics of respectability in relation to how middle-class Latine immigrants negotiate the racialization of illegality. Many of my respondents broadcast characteristics associated with white middle-class norms, including a middle-class status and attainment of the American dream, as they positioned themselves away from discrimination experiences. These strategies moved respondents closer to whiteness while allowing them to remain deeply rooted in their Mexican or Dominican national identity.

Critics accuse respectability politics of being problematic and even "reactionary." When minority group members engage in identity work strategies that rely on the politics of respectability, they harden distinctions between working-class and middle-class coethnics and do not challenge the position of the white middle class as the standard of social worth.[45] Yet my interviews show that respondents also sometimes engaged in class-based identity work to *undermine* the white middle-class standard and the U.S. racial hierarchy. The next chapter examines how they accomplished this—specifically, how moving strategically between and beyond the "two worlds" of their heritage and host social norms, categories, and expectations rescued their class privilege from situational precarity and resolved the racialization-despite-assimilation dilemma.

5 | Leveraging Cosmopolitan Orientations and Resources

THE RACIALIZATION of illegality frames Latine immigrant characteristics—such as having a Mexican or Dominican identity, maintaining ties to Mexico or the Dominican Republic, and speaking Spanish—as emblems of foreignness and a failure to assimilate.[1] Recall Juan from chapter 1, who encountered stigmatization when a restaurant customer admonished his table for speaking Spanish. Juan's friend retorted that they spoke three languages—English, French, and Spanish—and challenged the American harasser by asking, "What do you speak?" Through this maneuver, Juan's friend took charge of a situation in which the Dominican group's middle-class privilege was rendered situationally precarious. His identity work strategy turned the American-Latine immigrant status hierarchy on its head by highlighting the American's limited language skills.

The ability of Juan and his friends to speak French did not simply connote one additional language they could speak but also gestured toward a familiarity with refined European tastes and lifestyles—that is, "highbrow culture."[2] As this example illustrates, cultural symbols that signal middle-class membership can be as important to resisting the stereotypes associated with the racialization of illegality as the resources provided by a professional occupation, a high income, or a college degree.

Juan's story also illuminates a key idea in understanding middle-class advantages—Pierre Bourdieu's concept of "cultural capital," which encompasses culturally valued aptitudes such as speaking French, knowing how to navigate social institutions and situations (especially the education system), and using a vocabulary that demonstrates comfort with and mastery over cultural objects and activities.[3] Bourdieu termed these symbolic resources "cultural capital" because actors can convert these cultural resources into other advantages, such as access to well-resourced schools and professional jobs.[4]

DOI: https://doi.org/10.7758/hvda9363.7280

The idea of "cosmopolitan cultural capital" extends Bourdieu's original concept to take into account globalization, or the movement of labor, capital, and worldviews across national borders.[5] There are debates over how to define "cosmopolitanism"; here I use the prevalent definition, which provides a lens on cultural capital formation and identity work.[6] Specifically, a cosmopolitan orientation harbors an openness to foreign others and cultures, the ability to navigate a broad range of cross-national experiences, and the finesse to interact with people from a wide variety of nationalities and backgrounds.[7] Individuals with a capital-generating cosmopolitan orientation also have the visas and credit cards to facilitate international study and travel.[8] Cosmopolitan cultural capital highlights the "privilege" side of "precarious privilege."

Scholars argue that cosmopolitan cultural capital is tied to class advantage and is concentrated within the upper and middle classes.[9] In fact, Don Weenink maintains that when parents convey cosmopolitan cultural capital to their children, they are engaging in a social reproduction strategy of the upper-middle class.[10] That is, children acquire cosmopolitan cultural capital that they can use to maintain their middle-class position in school and in their chosen occupation.[11] Although working-class immigrants navigate two nationalities, they are less likely to possess the social mobility–enhancing resources and global orientations toward work and education that members of the upper and middle classes enjoy.[12] Claire Maxwell and Miri Yemini highlight the cosmopolitan leanings of the immigrant middle class by emphasizing that cosmopolitanism includes "the confidence to imagine oneself as having the credentials and skills to apply for professional positions that may be located almost anywhere around the globe."[13]

Alfredo, a financial planner, displayed this confidence when he described his advantages working for a global firm: "I think this is a perfect place for me to work. I had to use my language skills here and we got . . . we manage funds from Europe, from Australia, South America. [We have] . . . companies in Chili and Mexico and Brazil. We've got people from all the place coming and going. . . . So there are opportunities around the globe." Alfredo's confidence that he was working in the "perfect place" for his skills and perception of "opportunities around the globe" from working for his firm fit Maxwell and Yemini's definition of cosmopolitanism. His class-based professional expertise was reflected in his position as a funds manager.

This chapter shows how Alfredo, Juan, and our other middle-class Latine respondents leveraged cosmopolitan cultural capital to negotiate the racialization of illegality. Specifically, I illustrate how respondents' cosmopolitanism allowed them to affirm a positive identity as they drew social boundaries with respect to themselves, Americans, and African Americans.

Even as they used cosmopolitan cultural capital to reinforce *distinctions* between Americans and themselves, they emphasized *inclusion* with Americans for their children. In addition, respondents maintained a selective association with middle-class African Americans by invoking a cosmopolitan notion of "diversity."[14]

DISTINCTION FROM "AMERICANS"

Our interviews reveal that respondents did not simply mobilize their cosmopolitan cultural capital to maintain their middle-class status in the face of potential stigmatization; they also sometimes invoked these forms of capital strategically to raise their status *above* that of U.S. native-born whites.[15] My colleagues Katharine Tatum, Belisa González, and I use the term "one-up assimilation" for identity work strategies that flip the position of a Latine immigrant in the U.S. status hierarchy, which has native-born whites at the top; this strategy puts the immigrant at the top of the status hierarchy instead of at the bottom.[16] The response of Juan's friend to the taunts from an American in the restaurant provides an example of the sort of "one-up" identity work strategy that recurred in the interviews.

Middle-class status is key to achieving a one-up social position. Respondents were already on par with white middle-class Americans with respect to social class. When respondents inverted the migrant-American status hierarchy through identity work, they lifted themselves above Americans on the basis of nationality ("race"). In contrast, when working-class immigrants engaged in tactics that flipped the migrant-American status hierarchy, their working-class social status still kept them below Americans on the dimension of class. As such, they were still seen as a "typical Latine."

One-up assimilation identity work strategies replace the "typical Latine" stereotype with an image of the "typical American." (Research shows that the "typical American" is assumed to be white.)[17] Respondents drew on a globally circulating image of an ignorant, uncouth American who is unaware of the world outside the United States.[18] One common means through which respondents engaged in one-up assimilation was by ridiculing many Americans' assumptions about Latines and Latin America. For example, respondents combined criticism of the homogenized image of the Latine with their own cosmopolitan understanding of the diversity within the United States. Oscar, for instance, showed his fluency in both the American and Latin American worlds:

> If you go to Mexico City, Buenos Aires, and Santo Domingo, Dominican Republic, they're three very, very different places. Even though we may speak the same language, you may not understand it from one place to another. It's

> like your accent from the South here in the United States as opposed to a Brooklyn accent as opposed to somebody from Wisconsin. The accents are different; some of the words may not even mean the same thing. And, you know, you can make an analogy for Latine countries, South American countries. But I think Americans, especially from the South, just think that basically it's all the same.

As Oscar's comment reveals, respondents often moved beyond heritage-host biculturalism to achieve a broader cosmopolitanism. In responding to Americans' one-dimensional perception of Latines, Mexican and Dominican immigrants mentioned the richness and diversity within Latin America, referencing the European, indigenous, and African influences. They connected their Mexican or Dominican heritage with a cosmopolitan appreciation for and familiarity with Latin American heritage.

Like Oscar, many respondents generalized about Americans' limited understanding of Latin America, often pointing out their geographical or cultural gaffes. Dominicans in particular were very aware of Atlantans' limited knowledge of geography: "The experience that I have had with many North Americans," Felipe said, "[is] they ask you, 'What country are you from?' You are Dominican. 'Ah . . . in which part of Mexico is that?'" It is a complete ignorance." By associating Atlantans' "complete ignorance" of geography with "many North Americans," Felipe implied that this ignorance was "typical" of Americans.

Luisa also perceived that Americans lack knowledge about Dominicans and the Dominican Republic. She was surprised to learn that this was true of her coworkers, given that they were "highly educated."

> INTERVIEWER: When you tell someone that you are Dominican in the area where you live, do they know what the Dominican Republic is, or do they know what you are referring to, or . . . how do they react?
>
> LUISA: The American in general doesn't know, no, at least if I tell them that . . . including, including, I, well, you know I work in a high class of studies, with people that are supposedly highly educated, and a lot of them don't know, no. At least that people say, well, they more or less know . . . but some don't, but that more or less is the common response. People who follow baseball a lot might know, the country is identified by its ballplayers, but they probably couldn't identify it in the map.

Both Luisa's reference to her coworkers as "supposedly highly educated" and Felipe's invoking of "ignorance" engage class-based criteria to lower the social status of their American clients and coworkers. Luisa decoupled Americans' educational capital from their cultural capital.

Americans may be able to identify Mexico on a map, but "many Americans" show their "ignorance," Alfredo said, in their assumptions about his heritage country:

> Many Americans . . . while talking say: "Hey, listen to me, where are you from? From Mexico? . . . From what part?" I responded: "From Guadalajara . . .," and there are people . . . well, I think, they are a little ignorant because, sometimes, they asked things like: "Hey, are things over there like . . .? Or are [there] cars over there? Are malls over there?" . . . [These are] *people who have not traveled, who do not know*. (emphasis added)

The characterization of Mexico as lacking cars and malls reflects a homogenized view of Mexico as a "third world" (underdeveloped) country. Alfredo associated Americans' misperceptions about Mexico with their provincialism by characterizing them as "people who have not traveled" and who therefore lack knowledge ("do not know") about Mexico.

As Marisol's situation illustrates, cosmopolitan-oriented immigrants can sometimes glean occupational benefits from their coworkers' perception that they more easily navigate cross-cultural contexts. She used the stereotype of the monolingual U.S. native to explain how her cosmopolitan resources provide occupational advantages: "You know, with the education that the American [has], there is no need to deny it, when they saw a German last name, they would send it to the Hispanic. Because it wasn't American. They sent us everything that wasn't English (*laughs*)." Marisol attributed her colleagues' assumption that she could handle "foreign" documents to their general lack of familiarity with non-U.S. cultures, alluding to their deficient education ("with the education that the American [has]"). Notably, Marisol remarked that she was expected to deal with not just anything bearing a Hispanic-sounding name but everything that "wasn't English."

Although scholars often situate a cosmopolitan orientation within the upper and middle classes, working-class Latine immigrants may also engage in one-up identity work strategies, such as ridiculing Americans' limited knowledge of geography.[19] In fact, portraying one's in-group as superior to the out-group is a common practice that stigmatized individuals use to neutralize stigma.[20] However, beyond neutralizing stigma, these identity work strategies do not necessarily generate more resources for working-class Latine immigrants, such as (professional) occupational advantages. As I show here, raising children provides opportunities for respondents to describe specifically middle-class forms of cosmopolitan cultural capital.

Raising Cosmopolitan Children

For Bourdieu, the home was foundational for cultivating middle-class dispositions and generating cultural capital in the next generation.[21] The parents among our interviewees described their efforts to instill a cosmopolitan orientation in their children by encouraging their bilingualism, traveling, and teaching them to maneuver in situations with individuals from a wide range of backgrounds. Our findings suggest that respondents looked beyond maintaining bicultural heritage-host ties and instead saw bilingualism and transnationalism as a path to a broadly cosmopolitan lifestyle that could serve their children well later on in life.

Many of our middle-class respondents highlighted bilingualism in particular as a trait that would help their children surpass their native-born U.S. counterparts. Respondents who spoke English at home were especially keen to provide resources to enable their children to remain fluent in Spanish. Barbara (interviewed in English) said, "We've always encouraged, like, if you speak two languages, most Americans only speak one language." Teresa (also interviewed in English) felt that her son would "have a leg up on people" by being bilingual.

In stressing mastery of Spanish and promoting bilingualism, middle-class immigrant parents hoped to provide their children with an occupational advantage over monolingual middle-class Americans. Respondents were demonstrating their greater levels of cultural capital compared to U.S. natives, whom they read as largely provincial. Middle-class financial resources also can come into play to facilitate bilingualism. For instance, Eduardo's middle-class resources allowed him to send his two children to a private school (with annual tuition of close to $20,000) where all students became fluent in at least two languages. The family also took frequent trips to Mexico as part of the concerted efforts of Eduardo and his wife to develop their children's cultural capital:

> INTERVIEWER: Have you taken [your children] to Mexico?
>
> EDUARDO: Yes. All the time. If we travel for at least three times a year, two times per year we go to Mexico.
>
> INTERVIEWER: Oh, to visit family and all that?
>
> EDUARDO: To visit family, and we are well soaked in the culture all the time . . . all the time we are trying to see how it is there.

Parents like Eduardo believed that family trips to Mexico or the Dominican Republic provided opportunities to improve their Spanish-language skills as well as to ensure that their children were closely familiar with ("well soaked in") Latin American culture. These parents often described travel to heritage destinations as a cosmopolitan endeavor, an attempt to tie Mexico or the Dominican Republic to a broader Latin American culture rather than just a bicultural experience for the family. For instance, Juan Diego also took his family on many trips throughout the world.

> We, my family and I . . . we pretty much like to go all over the world. We try to have two to three trips a year. So we've been to a lot of countries and we just enjoy doing that.
>
> . . . My kids were having fun about six months ago counting the countries, and I think that we were up to twenty-five countries or somewhere around there. Mostly Europe and Latin America. We've been to a couple of countries in Africa, and [my son] has gone to Thailand and some places in Asia, but yeah, there are a lot of other countries that I would like to explore.

Juan Diego and his family had a middle-class cosmopolitan lifestyle. Their middle-class resources and authorized legal status enabled them to become "world travelers," embarking on global travel two or three times per year.

Ignacia also encouraged global travel combined with visiting her heritage country. She took her children on trips to Mexico to instill pride in their Mexican background, to perfect their Spanish, and to visit relatives. Her family traveled to other countries as part of a larger educational endeavor:

> IGNACIA: [My children] are very well integrated, but at the same time I taught them from the beginning to be very proud of their background, uh, that they're Spanish-fluent—writing, reading, speaking, no accents allowed. (*laughs*) You know, no "I didn't get you, can you repeat that." (*laughs*) And I would be like, "No, that sounds funny. You sound like a gringo speaking Spanish. . . . I try to bring them [to Mexico] often, as often as possible, so they can experience [speaking Spanish] with their cousins . . .
>
> INTERVIEWER: And where else have you traveled?
>
> IGNACIA: Mmm, well, um, we went to a few countries in Europe. We have been to France, Britain, Belgium, and Turkey. And here we just [went to] Canada, of course, United States some travel, and Mexico some travel.

Ignacia's rule that her children speak Spanish without accents facilitated their ability to move smoothly between the two worlds of the United States and Mexico. At the same time, she expanded their frame of reference beyond Mexico by taking trips with them to Europe.

Encouraging children's global travels often produces a cosmopolitanism that lasts into adulthood, when adult children, with their parents' encouragement, make forays to places in Europe and Canada. Sofia told her daughter, "'If you like French, go to Paris.' And she went three months to Paris and then to Quebec. And she just . . . in college you can do that." Sofia described the opportunity to live in Paris and Quebec as part of the "college experience." That is, she associated cosmopolitanism with her daughter's membership in the middle class.

Sofia also took pride in her daughter's cosmopolitan life beyond the United States:

> Besides her normal engineering job, [my daughter] teaches meringue and salsa. . . . She went to [eastern Europe] to a salsa festival. And I'm like, "Where are you?" "Oh, I took a train from [Spain]." She went to [Spain] for a year. "And I'm in [eastern Europe] in a salsa." And I'm like, "What?" Couldn't believe it. . . . My daughter was really Latin American. But at the same time she lives in New York, she works in Manhattan, she has a nice apartment in Astoria. It's not all Dominicans.

Working and living in Spain and the United States, Sofia's daughter gained labor market advantages by crossing geographic and cultural boundaries, a hallmark of elite cosmopolitanism. She could also exercise an eclectic range of competencies—from working as an engineer to teaching salsa. Sofia also stressed that, while her daughter maintained a Latin American identity, she lived in a New York neighborhood, Astoria in Queens, that is "not all Dominicans." That is, Sofia's daughter lived in two worlds, one Dominican and one not Dominican, in a city where she had the option of living in an almost exclusively Dominican neighborhood.

Rather than focus on frequent travel, Ana emphasized that living in the United States provided opportunities for appreciating "diversity" and achieving a cosmopolitan orientation:

> I believe that it is a great opportunity to accept my own roots, for my son to learn his own roots while he adjusts to the world because I believe that diversity is important in teaching. If he's in Dominican, he will be Dominican and everybody else is going to be Dominican. . . . But if he's in the United States, you have the world around you. And for me that is great opportunity.

Unlike those respondents who used a one-up assimilation strategy, Ana saw the United States as having a cosmopolitan advantage ("you have the world around you") over the Dominican Republic. From this perspective, a cosmopolitan identity was complemented by an "American" identity that included exposure to and "openness to diversity."[22] At the same time, Ana encouraged her son to "accept" his Dominican heritage ("roots").

Indeed, many of our respondents encouraged their families to travel the world, to have an elite cosmopolitan orientation, and to take pride in both their American and Mexican or Dominican identities. As Francisco remarked: "[My children are] American, yes. I have insisted that they are world citizens, and I have insisted to them that there is only one race, and that's humanity. Nationality is what one chooses."

Consistent with the colorblind narratives that I discussed in chapter 4, Francisco was promoting a cosmopolitan orientation ("world citizenship") that erased racial differences (and a racial hierarchy). Two of his children had parlayed their cosmopolitan cultural capital into educational benefits by obtaining master's degrees, one in international business and the other in international education. Note that later in the interview Francisco departed from a colorblind perspective and discussed the racial inequality in the United States that favors Latines over African Americans:

> I think [Hispanics and African Americans] live peacefully, although there's always . . . sometimes there are problems with relationships at work. I have been told that when . . . if there are two people looking for work from . . . that are down on . . . that are low income, low salary, and they see a Hispanic can do it, versus an African American, in whatever, normally, normally they prefer the Hispanic . . . here.

Francisco relegated the Latine–African American competition to the working class, stressing that he was referring to "low income, low salary" workers. Through this maneuver, he differentiated middle-class immigrants such as himself from working-class immigrants.

Besides parents, peers can also instill cosmopolitan orientations in children. Alejandra explained that among her (middle-class) friends in Mexico, it was expected that she would travel abroad to obtain an advanced degree.

ALEJANDRA: I got my MBA in France . . .

INTERVIEWER: Why France?

ALEJANDRA: I grew up in this environment, you know, uh, professional—professional, middle-class. . . . I hung out with the smart kids. . . . And there was this idea—there was an idea that . . . people would go get there master's somewhere else. So most people were finishing their . . . bachelor's degrees in Mexico . . . and then they

> would go get their—an MBA, or a master in arts in the U.S., or a lot of people went to Spain. So I still had this idea that your MBA or your master's was a chance to go somewhere else. And I was already in the U.S.

Because she was "already in the U.S." after obtaining her BA degree, Alejandra expanded her cosmopolitan cultural capital still further by studying in France. She explicitly tied these expectations that she would have a highly educated, cosmopolitan lifestyle to a professional, middle-class environment.

The payoff to a middle-class cosmopolitan upbringing that carries lifelong class advantages can be seen in Alfredo's experience as a teenager in the Dominican Republic. With a European diplomat father, Alfredo grew up as a member of the global middle class.[23] He investigated U.S. college programs that would fit his specific interests (and the interests of a friend):

> I selected three [U.S.] universities for aerospace engineering, which is what I wanted to study. I had done bottle rockets when I was a kid, and . . . I enjoyed that, so . . . I had a buddy of mine [in] New York moved back to Dominican Republic. He wanted to study industrial engineering. So I wanted to find out . . . what colleges have both industrial and aerospace. . . . I selected three schools in the U.S. . . . I ended up at [a major U.S. state university].

Although playing with bottle rockets may not be considered a childhood pastime limited to the middle class, Alfredo's association of this activity with a career in aerospace engineering is an example of a middle-class orientation (or, in Bourdieu's theory, "habitus").[24] Note that Alfredo possessed Maxwell and Yemini's "cosmopolitan confidence" that he could study in the United States. He drew on middle-class cultural capital to navigate information about the U.S. educational system as he considered a range of programs in his chosen field. Given that he was accepted into a major U.S. university, it would seem that he also possessed a healthy store of educational capital to realize his aspirations. Once he graduated, Alfredo's educational attainment itself then became a form of capital; for Alfredo and the other well-educated respondents we interviewed, a college degree opened the door to professional employment opportunities, signaled middle-class status, and differentiated the college-educated from those without a college degree.

My interviews with middle-class Mexican and Dominican immigrants add to our understanding of how cosmopolitan cultural capital can be used as a resource to negotiate racialization. With their cosmopolitan cultural capital, our middle-class respondents could benefit from professional employment in multinational firms and secure rich (diverse) educational environments for their children that included world travel.[25] They could cultivate Spanish-language skills in the home as advantageous cultural capital. They could successfully gain authorized status. Augmenting these material benefits was the symbolic capital that accrued to respondents from a cosmopolitan orientation. Specifically, they could counter racialization by engaging in one-up assimilation strategies. Because the literature on the racialization of illegality tends to focus on working-class immigrants, it often misses these forms of cultural capital associated with the middle and upper classes.

In addition to a cosmopolitan approach to racial socialization ("we are citizens of the world"), respondents took both a colorblind approach ("I teach them not to look at race") and a racialization approach ("I teach them to demand respect"). These approaches map onto the two dimensions of racial socialization that Diane Hughes identifies: (1) teaching about history, culture, ethnic pride, and diversity; and (2) discussing unfair treatment and bias based on ethnicity or race.[26]

Teresa responded to her son's experiences of being teased at school because he was Latine by having frequent conversations with him:

> Think about, you know, when you were ten and eleven. I don't . . . you don't remember how cruel and how . . . what . . . how kids say things. . . . So that's moreso a conversation every other month. I'm, like, "Don't let the kid bother you," you know. "You're the best, and you have a leg up on people. As soon as you can say you wanna learn Spanish, you're gonna be bilingual. You're a man, so you need to be up on your game all the time. It doesn't matter what you are."

Teresa was one of the few respondents who spoke about ongoing racism in her child's life. Specifically, children said cruel things based on his last name. She responded by emphasizing the cosmopolitan cultural capital benefit of being bilingual. Teresa's son was also teased at school for not being sufficiently dark. He was called "vanilla boy." Rather than embracing the white identity implied by this moniker, he adopted his mother's identity as "half Dominican and half Puerto Rican." This is an example of a "reactive ethnicity," or adherence to a heritage identity as a response to racism.[27]

Overall, parents reported that their children's racial identities resulted from the richness of their cultural and class backgrounds rather than as direct responses to discrimination experiences. One-fourth of both Mexican-origin and Dominican-origin children were described as expressing a "dual identity" that included both their parents' heritage and an American identity. Children's heritage-host identities could even vary within the same family, illustrating the flexibility of ethnic and racial identities within the second generation. This was especially likely when parents were from different countries.

The lessons that Teresa and the other parents taught their children about race in the United States had "important consequences for youth's identity development and well-being."[28] Racial socialization prepares members of racial minority groups, including Latines, through "adaptive and protective practices" that maintain high self-esteem in the face of frequent experiences of racism.[29]

Implications for Theories of Assimilation

Rather than following the path of straight-line assimilation, the middle-class Latine immigrants in my study engaged in "selective acculturation" of their children.[30] Scholars describe selective acculturation as the retention of heritage language, customs, and beliefs as an upward mobility strategy when racism prevents straight-line assimilation.[31] However, my respondents described these efforts as inculcation into the global middle class rather than as a bulwark against racial discrimination. For instance, many studies of assimilation measure mobility by comparing the improvement in English fluency among parents and children.[32] What happens when parents are already fluent in English? My interviews suggest that they engage in efforts to develop bilingualism in their children as a form of cosmopolitan cultural capital. Further, the parents in my study not only encouraged connections to heritage customs and "global culture" but also used their resources to select environments that cultivated cosmopolitan identities and social connections in their children.

As part of their cultivation of cosmopolitan cultural capital, Latine immigrant parents encouraged diverse friendship networks that reached beyond Latine and non-Latine native-born friends. That is, while straight-line assimilation theory stresses the predominance of white middle-class American friends and segmented assimilation theory stresses the predominance of Latine friends, our respondents offered a third option: having friends from a range of countries and backgrounds in order to become cosmopolitan "world citizens."[33]

Diverse friendships and fluid, multivalent ethnic identities also reflect a type of "ordinary cosmopolitanism" that has been found among working-class second-generation immigrants.[34] The specifically middle-class orientations of my respondents were reflected in their expectations that they and their children would engage in global travel, attend private secondary schools, achieve an elite college education, and work in a professional job.

SELECTIVE ASSOCIATION WITH AFRICAN AMERICANS

In addition to drawing boundaries that excluded Americans, respondents also revealed in their interviews the salience of cosmopolitan cultural capital in shaping Latine-black divisions in Atlanta. As Zamora summarizes: "Immigrant groups may place themselves above blacks by certain measures such as race or intermarriage with whites, alongside blacks as fellow subordinates to whites, yet below them along the axes of citizenship and national belonging."[35] At the same time, African Americans also participate in racialization processes, either rejecting Latine immigrants as competitors or welcoming them as fellow minorities.[36]

Local circumstances shape whether Latine-black relations follow a "competition" route or a "commonalities" route.[37] A competition orientation occurs when Latine immigrants and blacks perceive the other group as a threat to their social position and access to resources.[38] A commonalities orientation arises when Latine immigrants and blacks perceive their shared status as minorities disadvantaged by white racism. Studies of Latine-black relations in new immigrant destinations report that competition and African American perceptions of a "Latine threat" dominate Latine-black relations.[39] However, in her investigation of a North Carolina community, Jennifer Jones finds a strong commonalities situation, with blacks and Latines working together on what they see as common ground (having a "sense of group fate") because each group perceives a shared racial discrimination.[40] Linda Tropp and her colleagues also find that frequent opportunities for blacks and Latines to interact can lead to familiarity and cultivate warm intergroup relations.[41]

Beyond the competition and commonalities frameworks, our interviews reveal a third approach to relations between Latine immigrants and blacks; based on cosmopolitan cultural capital, this approach adds a middle-class spin to the familiarity thesis. Specifically, some of our middle-class Dominicans and Mexican respondents perceived common social positions and solidarity with African Americans not through the lens of competition or similar experiences of discrimination, *but through the lens of cosmopolitan cultural capital and shared middle-class status.*

Agustín's interview provides a clear example of the class-based social world that shaped his interactions with African Americans and with whites:

> We arrive with a visa, we arrive directly, and we insert ourselves very rapidly into the American community. And at best we go to church, we get together regularly, and, and . . . and . . . see? My theory is that we get together with whites, and that we get together with African Americans, they are the top

> African Americans, educated. . . . We go to the white churches, eh . . . eh . . . it is not like when you are an undocumented immigrant.

Agustín made several moves here in the class and race positioning of middle-class Latine immigrants. First, he distinguished between "us"—documented immigrants who "arrive with a visa"—and "them"—undocumented immigrants. Second, he aligned himself with the upper- and middle-class African Americans and whites with whom his family socialized. Consistent with assimilation theory, Agustín described rapidly integrating into the American community ("we insert ourselves"). Third, Agustín equated African Americans at the "top" of the social hierarchy specifically with education. A college degree holder, Agustín was engaging in middle-class distinctions that maintained his own class status.

Indeed, their children's school was one of the important spaces where respondents described positive relations with African Americans. Many of the Mexican and Dominican respondents discussed their children's African American schoolmates appreciatively as part of a "diverse" environment. Speaking about the composition of his child's charter school, Reinaldo described it as "like the UN there. African Americans, they connect a lot with African Americans, our children." The comparison to the United Nations, a prestigious international organization, reinforced the cosmopolitan dimension of the school's racial composition, further reinforcing the middle-class standing of the school's diverse student body. Reinaldo included African Americans in particular within his praise of the school's racial and ethnic makeup.

Marisol also viewed the diverse population of her children's school as a positive quality, saying that it was a "marvelous" community:

> When my children were in school in Stone Mountain, there were black, white, and Hispanic people. There was a little bit of everything. But it was like a good essence. That I can tell you. Maybe, I can tell you that maybe more than half was white, and the other half was 80 percent black and 20 percent Hispanic. It was a marvelous community. It was marvelous.

Marisol included black students in her depiction of the school's diversity. Moreover, in providing concrete evidence for diversity in her evaluation of the school by quantifying the proportion of students in each of three racialized groups, she reinforced her own educational credentials.

Sonia discussed the educational environment that she was seeking for her preschool-age child and mentioned the appeal of a diversity that went "beyond black and white." Comparing her neighborhood school with a school that, she said, had a "large African American group," she explained:

> The people have been very nice, and I have never had a problem here [in Atlanta] and everybody's ultra-sweet here. I don't know, I would like [my children] to experience something more than black and white. . . . I think that [school], it's very, just in everything . . . it has more multicultural diversity in the families. [It's] going to be the [school] that is a little of everything.

Sonia invoked a cosmopolitan orientation when she explicitly tied diversity to multiculturalism that was "more than black and white." She presented such diversity as a positive quality by explaining that "everybody's ultra-sweet here." That is, there was no racial discrimination at the school.

Francisco framed the diversity of his children's friend groups in superlatives, using the phrase "a grand experience." That is, he moved beyond simply describing the diverse friendship groups and including African Americans by praising the rich environment these groups provided for his children:

> There weren't differences among relations among races; they had African American friends, Koreans . . . friends of theirs; it was a grand . . . grand experience, they tell me, the diversity that they lived. . . . [My daughter] says she feels appreciative to have studied [in public school] because there you struggle with all humble classes: poorer people . . . Asians, African Americans, Russians, Bosnians, Koreans, Vietnamese, a great diversity of classes. This gave her a good experience.

Francisco combined a colorblind perspective ("there weren't differences . . . among races") with a cosmopolitan orientation toward diversity. He maintained class distinctions within this orientation when he mentioned "struggl[ing] with all humble classes: poorer people."

Horacio's daughter enjoyed a cosmopolitan experience in elementary school by singing in an international children's chorus. He valued her participation in the group as "very fostering for her appreciation for subtle differences in culture." He elaborated: "Many kids were from Africa, or Latin America, there were kids from Asia, Arab countries, of course several Jewish kids, um, so a very diverse group. That was her activity that she enjoyed after class." An after-school activity such as participating in a chorus cultivates middle-class cultural capital.[42] Horacio put a cosmopolitan spin on this children's chorus by praising its composition as a "very diverse group," with kids from countries around the globe.

It is possible that these respondents were expressing a form of social desirability by describing the diversity of their child's school in glowing terms. However, their invoking of the term "diversity" is meaningful because it is associated with cosmopolitan cultural capital and is made possible by a school's demographics.[43] That is, diversity language provides a window into the available "cultural repertoires" to frame race relations.[44] As part of this cultural repertoire, respondents tied "diversity" to specific educational outcomes, such as cultivating a rich learning environment. Tellingly, none of these parents described situations in which the majority of their children's schoolmates or friends were African American or Latine. Parents valued a "diverse" environment with just a modicum of African Americans among children from a wide array of backgrounds.[45]

These preferences gesture toward Shani Evans's finding that white middle-class parents "want diversity but not so much." Although white middle-class white parents perceive racially diverse environments as an important form of cultural capital, they avoid majority-black schools. Instead, they enroll their children in majority-white schools with a relatively low number of black students.[46] Ellen Berrey also shows that, in prestigious colleges and workplaces, diversity discourse "affirms inclusiveness," yet it does not fundamentally challenge the institutional arrangements and practices that undergird racial inequality.[47]

The picture of a diverse environment that includes African Americans as one of multiple groups also became clear in my study when respondents discussed their neighborhoods—the majority lived in predominantly white or mixed Latine-white neighborhoods—and their adult friendship networks. For instance, Francisco described a diverse neighborhood and friendship network that included African Americans:

> INTERVIEWER: In the area where you live, what is the cultural makeup?
>
> FRANCISCO (Dominican): Culturally, we are mixed. There are black, there are white, I have a Chinese or Asian. There are Hispanics close too. . . . We have no problems.
>
> INTERVIEWER: Your circle of friends . . . are they Dominicans or other nationalities too?
>
> FRANCISCO: Different, different—Mexicans, Peruvians, Argentinians, Hondurans, Salvadoreans, African Americans, Vietnamese . . . Haitians . . . *diverse* (emphasis added).

To indicate the diversity of his circles, Francisco listed the multiple nationalities of his friends and neighbors, spanning Latin America, Asia, and the Caribbean. Contrary to the anti-Haitianism embedded in the Dominican racial system, Francisco also included Haitians among his friends.

Lina and Pablo explained relations with African Americans in terms of distinctions between social spaces:

INTERVIEWER: How do [you see] community relations between . . . white Americans and African Americans?

LINA (Dominican): Here there are no clashes. . . .

PABLO (Dominican): This is because of the area. The area where we live is a very quiet area, you don't hear about any of that here. For us, we spend the day working and we're not involved in the bars or the clubs. We don't get into that kind of trouble where other people can get.

When asked about African Americans, Pablo made a morally based distinction between his "very quiet" location and activities ("we spend the day working") and being "involved in the bars or the clubs," which were sites for "trouble." Although Pablo did not tie this distinction specifically to the middle class (since working-class individuals are also hardworking), both Lina and Pablo were business owners, and the specific activities in which they engaged did entail class-based pursuits. In addition, frequenting "bars and clubs" could be considered a "lowbrow" cultural activity geared toward mass consumption and engaged in by lower- and working-class adults.

Evoking the concept of diversity to describe interactions with African Americans is a way to discuss race without acknowledging racial *inequality*. That is, this strategy fits with both mestizaje-based strategies (discussed in chapter 3) and colorblind strategies (discussed in chapter 4). Since cultivating diversity is promoted by schools and some workplaces, diversity discourse could be seen as a form of assimilation.[48]

Through a diversity discourse, respondents could maintain cordial links to *middle-class* African Americans, whose presence in their (diverse) social circles they explicitly noted; they did not see themselves as sharing status with disadvantaged African Americans. Further, they sometimes tempered their appreciation of the rich cosmopolitan environment generated by middle-class African American schoolmates and friends with a desire for these circles to reach "beyond black and white."

Cosmopolitan cultural capital and its middle-class diversity discourse underscore the relevance of class to Latine-black political and social relations. Incorporating the concept of cosmopolitan cultural capital into an investigation of Latine-black relations contributes to recent theorizing beyond the competition-commonalities dichotomy. These studies reveal that Latines and African Americans may experience parallel lives in which they peacefully coexist.[49] In my study, I find a new route to peaceful coexistence: a diversity discourse that allows authorized middle-class Latine immigrants to express warm relations with middle-class African Americans without claiming "commonalities" as oppressed minorities.

In contrast to embracing diversity, a minority of respondents described tensions in encounters with African Americans. Nine respondents stated that they felt bias or discrimination from African Americans more often than from whites. For instance, in Perez's experience, "the black person from here is more of a discriminator than the white. . . . That is my experience that I have here. . . . I have found that a lot with black people here that are . . . they give us dirty looks." Yet the interviews also illustrate that a perception of Latine-black conflict can accompany a diversity discourse. Irma, a Dominican, discussed African Americans as a collective group that attempts to suppress Latines:

INTERVIEWER: And do you have negative experiences about any race in particular, like white Americans or African Americans?

IRMA: Well . . . in general . . . for example, blacks here think that Hispanics are below them, but Hispanics never will think like that, do you understand? And there is a conflict there. More or less there is a conflict, but one tries to keep these things calm because we have been here for a long time (*laughs*), because who wants a war?

Irma's interview shows classic in-group–out-group distinctions. She positioned blacks as an out-group and criticized them for believing that they were "above" Hispanics. Interpreted through the lens of mestizaje belief systems, her insistence that Hispanics "never will think like that" discursively gave Hispanics a status higher than blacks. Yet, Irma emphasized that this was her perception of Latine-black relations "in general." When asked about her daughters' friendship groups, and her African American friends in particular, she painted a different picture, reflecting a cosmopolitan openness and evoking a colorblind ideology:

> The oldest one has friends; near our home one lives, and his father is a reverend. They are black. . . . All of them have friends, but they do not see differences; they grew up thinking that there not differences between races. . . . We have never taught them to make any difference among people regarding races.

Public versus private spaces allowed Irma to simultaneously perceive negative relations with blacks "in general" and maintain a colorblind philosophy that her daughters could be taught to "not see" racial differences in their everyday encounters. Irma established the middle-class "respectability" of her daughter's "black friend" by explaining that the friend's father was a minister.

IMPLICATIONS

Cosmopolitan cultural capital—along with one-up status positioning and diversity language—provides Mexicans and Dominicans with a symbolic resource that they can use to navigate or preempt the racialization of illegality. My interviews raised the question of whether and how these maneuvers have any immediate or long-lasting impact. Three traditions offer different answers: theories of class reproduction; theories of a "shared humanity"; and theories of status and stigma.

Advocates of class reproduction theories would contend that given the connection between globalization and cosmopolitanism, there may be far-reaching effects of one-up assimilation strategies and cosmopolitan orientations. Specifically, cosmopolitan cultural capital may be contributing to globalization's "class reproduction machinery."[50] As Maxwell explains, "It is argued by many that such forms of cosmopolitanism are aligned with current geo-political relations of power, neo-colonial North-South divides, and local socio-economic inequalities. . . . Within this latter conceptualisation, cosmopolitanism can therefore be understood as part of the class reproduction machinery."[51] Put simply, by reestablishing their esteemed status as middle-class through deployment of cosmopolitan cultural capital, middle-class Latine immigrants could be reinforcing the distinction between middle-class and working-class.

In contrast to viewing cosmopolitanism as a mechanism for increasing inequality on a global scale, some scholars argue that cosmopolitanism could bridge differences and dismantle hierarchies.[52] These perspectives see cosmopolitanism as a philosophy centered on ideas of a shared humanity that working-class individuals can also promote.[53] For instance, Michèle Lamont and Sada Aksartova show that working-class men in the United States and France mobilize the discourse of cosmopolitan universalism ("we are all part of the human family") to engage in antiracism, drawing on a different set of discourses to articulate their claims. American men use language about the market and socioeconomic success; French men invoke "solidaristic and egalitarian themes that are part of the socialist and republican traditions."[54]

Lamont and Aksartova's study suggests that different social and national conditions produce divergent cosmopolitan understandings of race. If this is the case, we could find differences between Mexican and Dominican immigrants in their cosmopolitan identity work strategies. The one distinction that stands out among our respondents is Dominicans' experience of encountering Americans who "can't find the Dominican Republic on a map," while Americans do tend to know where Mexico lies. Beyond this difference, Mexican and Dominican respondents were quite similar in their reliance on one-up assimilation strategies and diversity discourse. They used their cosmopolitan cultural capital to create multiple boundaries while appearing to hold an antiracist stance. Respondents' claims that we are all part of a "shared humanity" dovetailed with the mestizaje and colorblind discourses, which reinforce the U.S. racial hierarchy.

Indeed, social psychologists would tell us that when respondents relied on cosmopolitan cultural capital to deploy one-up strategies during social interactions, they had little or no effect on the race- and class-based perceptions of their U.S.-born white interlocutors because of the inherent power relations between the groups. As the dominant group, U.S.-born whites could rebuff their stigmatization by Latine immigrants as "ignorant, uncouth" Americans. Bruce Link and Jo Phelan contend that stigmatization is embedded in a wide range of situations as a "persistent dilemma": "As long as dominant groups sustain their view of stigmatized persons, decreasing the use of one mechanism through which disadvantage can be accomplished simultaneously creates the impetus to increase the use of another."[55] In other words, even as middle-class Latine make it more challenging for dominant groups (native-born whites) to paint all Latine as uneducated, dominant group members may intensify their persecution of less-educated Latine migrants. Link and Phelan suggest that stigmatization stemming from the racialization of illegality can be dismantled only by challenging the hold of powerful groups in multiple arenas. For these scholars, combating the racialization of illegality and the resulting stigma is part of a larger project of dismantling the U.S. racial system.

Although the impact of respondents' identity work strategies on the beliefs and perceptions of U.S.-born whites may be limited, deploying cosmopolitan cultural capital may add meaningfully to respondents' well-being.[56] That is, seen through an immigrant-centered perspective, my findings make an important contribution to our understanding of Latine immigrant incorporation and resilience in the face of the racialization of illegality. The advantages of cosmopolitan cultural capital, coupled with abundant financial resources, led respondents to speak with appreciation of the middle-class lifestyle that they enjoyed in the United States and to disavow race-based precariousness. I explore this appreciation and disavowal in the next chapter, which summarizes my key findings.

6 | Understanding the Racialization of Illegality through a Middle-Class Lens

As LATINE purchasing power approaches $1.7 trillion and "Hispanic [market] influence reaches new heights," my study holds increasingly greater relevance for understanding the Latine population in the United States.[1] The presence of middle-class Latines in all new immigrant destinations is growing as the population of college-educated Latine immigrants increases and the number of individuals with advanced degrees expands worldwide.[2]

Focusing on Atlanta, I have argued that the racialization of illegality has made these growing groups of middle-class Latines susceptible to stigma and put them in a position of "precarious privilege." Yet many of my respondents vehemently rejected this characterization, insisting that racialization and stigmatization did *not* play a significant role in their daily lives. Instead, secure in their middle-class status, they spoke about their experiences in Atlanta as overwhelmingly positive.[3] This chapter explores this conundrum, highlighting the implications of my findings for theories of race, class, and immigration.

Recall that I told the stories of Santiago, Felipe, and Juan in chapter 1 to illustrate the dimensions of the racialization of illegality. Felipe lamented that North Americans perceive all Latine as undocumented and uneducated Mexicans. Yet later in the interview he asserted, "I am also very patriotic towards the United States. . . . I am a person who completely defends the United States. . . . This is the country that has given me opportunity, and I, ah, if they send me to fight a war . . . I will go." Felipe, a U.S. citizen, was willing to put his life on the line for the United States, the ultimate attachment to a nation. His U.S. patriotism was anchored by the class-based opportunities that he had experienced in Atlanta as a physician.

Like Felipe, the majority of our respondents took pride in their connec-

DOI: https://doi.org/10.7758/hvda9363.3836

tion to the United States, and many expressed "love" for their life in Atlanta. Alfredo appreciated the friendliness of the Americans he met in Georgia:

> We came to Atlanta, (a) because I went to school here, (b) I love this place because of the forest . . . it reminds me of Dominican Republic in the mountains. . . . I knew how people in Georgia are very friendly. Even outside of Atlanta, even though it's a different country outside of Atlanta, they're still very down to earth.

Far from having anti-Latine encounters emblematic of the racialization of illegality, Alfredo found native-born Georgians to be "very friendly." His mention of his Atlanta-based advanced educational training made clear that class figured into his positive outlook. Alfredo also demonstrated his ties to the Dominican Republic when he said that he loved Atlanta because its forest reminded him of his heritage island.

Other respondents praised the opportunity in the United States to purchase a home and live a middle-class lifestyle:

> SOLEDAD (Mexican): We now have bought a house, where before we were in an apartment.
>
> INTERVIEWER: Oh, and how did you find your community? Was it open? Did you feel welcome, or . . .?
>
> SOLEDAD: Oh yes! The community, I love! I quickly got involved with the PTA of my daughter's school.

Soledad not only prized owning a house in Atlanta and the benefits of consumption but also loved the community and enjoyed her involvement with other parents and teachers in the PTA. These middle-class spaces provided Soledad with the types of opportunities for positive interactions—or "intergroup contact"—that are conducive to friendly intergroup relations.[4]

Sofia took her appreciation of the United States an extra step, distinguishing herself from immigrants who seek better opportunities in the United States. She explained that when she migrated from the Dominican Republic,

> I didn't come looking for opportunities. I needed to study hard to give something to the states. I wasn't going to come for welfare or to get money. . . . I really made sure I had my degree. So we went straight to [western U.S. state] because, I said, "I have to be as big as I can be so I can give back a lot." Be-

> cause it wasn't going to be like needing something. I wanted to give to the country.

Sofia contrasted herself with immigrants who arrive "needing something" from the United States, such as a job or welfare benefits, because their lower socioeconomic status has put them in the greatest need. Sofia's middle-class position, by contrast, allowed her to avoid this situation. Grateful for the opportunities available to her in Atlanta, Sofia wanted to "give back" to the United States—as her middle-class status ("I really made sure I had my degree") enabled her to do.

EXPLANATIONS: RACIALIZATION AND CLASS PRIVILEGE

How can we make sense of the views of Felipe, Sofia, and other respondents when they extolled the benefits of living in Atlanta while downplaying or dismissing the salience of race as a factor in their lives? There are at least three possibilities: (1) they may have been successful in deploying their class resources to avoid negative experiences of racialization; (2) they may have adopted a social comparison view of race-based discrimination; or (3) they may have been experiencing racialization and engaging in defensive identity work strategies that maintained their class privilege. I explore each of these motivations here, understanding that more than one may explain the actions of some respondents.

Taking the interviews at face value, we might conclude that for many respondents the benefits of middle-class status overwhelmingly outweighed scattered incidences of anti-Latine immigrant treatment. Rather than assimilation despite racialization, they mainly experienced assimilation, reinforced by the absence of middle-class Latine immigrants who had moved out of Georgia after meeting with blocked opportunities and frequently having race-related negative experiences. Fifty-seven respondents claimed that they had "never" encountered negative treatment or discrimination. Importantly, they did not consider assumptions that they were undocumented, working-class, and Mexican as discriminatory. That is, what social theories consider stereotypes that reinforce the U.S. racial hierarchy these respondents understood to be minor issues.

Respondents' assertions that race did not matter in their lives aligned with assimilation theories that stress the diminishing impact of racialization over time. Emily Greenman and Yu Xie summarize this position:

> Alba and Nee (1997, 2003) and Perlmann and Waldinger (1997) are . . . skeptical of the idea that the racial distinctiveness of contemporary immigrants

> will be a long-term disadvantage. Because racial boundaries in the United States proved to be fluid for past "white" immigrants (such as Irish, Italians, and Jews), they propose that contemporary Asian and Latin American immigrants may not be considered racially distinct in the long term.[5]

This perspective suggests that children of Latine immigrants and possibly Latine respondents who were longtime residents in Atlanta were not experiencing race-related disadvantage. The "diminishing disadvantage of race" interpretation resonates with the classic theory of straight-line assimilation articulated by Milton Gordon, who posits that "immigrant group[s] gradually adopt the cultural habits of the core society." He defines "core society" as the white middle class.[6] Throughout Gordon's rendering, assimilation follows generations: the children of immigrants (the second generation) become more "Americanized" than their parents, and subsequent generations strengthen their ties to American ways as they increasingly lose customs and beliefs from the first generation's heritage culture. This depiction of assimilation—particularly assumptions that race will lose salience for immigrants of color over generations—has been widely criticized and even disproven for some groups.[7]

A second way to interpret the views of respondents who "loved" Atlanta even when they recounted negative experiences focuses on their efforts to make social comparisons. Respondents' middle-class status enabled them to live comfortably, work in fulfilling jobs, and establish rewarding relationships with professional friends and neighbors. They may have perceived that these amenities had a much greater impact on their lives than any experiences of racialization. In addition, opportunities in the United States for upward mobility may have been even more deeply treasured when compared with a relative lack of opportunities in their heritage country.

For instance, recollect Santiago's story in the beginning of the book about encountering anti-Latine bias in an Atlanta community pool. Despite this experience, racialization and stigmatization did not dominate Santiago's views about living in Atlanta. Instead, he focused on his middle-class status and the improvement in that status he had achieved by moving to the United States, even though he was not documented:

> The middle class [in Mexico] is almost disappearing because we are on the struggle all the time [to not] fall to the poor class, and the wealthy class is so high. Now when we came here and realized that the majority of the people in the life of the middle class is so wide, we fit perfect in the middle class because it is like a dream come true. You can buy your home, you can buy a car with credit as long as you keep a good credit grade, you can do whatever you want to do with material stuff. In Mexico it is so complicated.

Santiago was expressing a "social comparison" view of racialization.[8] He compared his abundant class-based opportunities in the United States with what he perceived as inferior economic prospects in Mexico. In light of this comparison, race disadvantage and undocumented status seemed to be minor influences in his life.

Despite racialization and the potential stigma attached to Latine identities, many of the middle-class Dominican and Mexican immigrants we interviewed shared Santiago's viewpoint. For instance, recall that, in chapter 3, Pablo said, "When they [Americans] say 'Latino' it is with disgust." He elaborated later in the interview: "You could say that there is a rejection amongst [the] American population . . . of the Latino." Yet Pablo also greatly appreciated his opportunities in Atlanta, which he compared to New York:

> I love Atlanta, and I would recommend it to any family in those states where fourteen people live in a shack the size of a shoe, as we say, in a low-life apartment in New York or places like that. I am proof that you can make it here. There are opportunities to work, to grow, to do business, to buy your house . . . we bought this house and we are paying for it. Here people live comfortably. The cost of living is also not high. . . . So I recommend this state, I recommend this place to live. And we have the connections to the entire world. It is the busiest airport with the most international connections.

Pablo's comments reflected a cosmopolitan orientation by highlighting the "connections to the entire world" in Atlanta.

In describing his positive views on immigrants, Pablo made a distinction between "good immigrants," who have a strong work ethic and a family, and "bad immigrants, who by implication do not have these attributes:

> There have also been people who have come here that we don't want, and we don't like them, but they are gone, thank God. But the families who have come to work and have establish[ed] a family life are good, because this is a good place, for study, for work, for housing . . . and yes, the people . . . I love living here.

Like Soledad, Pablo not only praised the advantageous opportunities but also flagged "the people" as a reason why he "loves Atlanta."

Federico offered a clear example of how middle-class Latine immigrants reconcile their class advantage with ongoing racialization by comparing opportunities. As a business owner with a college degree, Federico elucidated the "problems" that he perceived as an immigrant living in the United States: "If you really try to . . . fulfill what the forefathers of this country said, this is a free country for all, with justice, equality, and you have that in your mind—it's going to be hell. Maybe you will make it, but you will leave your blood and your soul down the road." Federico painted a vivid picture of the struggles that immigrants face in the United States, describing the toll taken by success as "leav[ing] your blood and your soul down the road." However, rather than being critical of the United States, Federico went on to emphasize U.S. advantages:

> I still believe that this country is the beacon of light in the entire planet for human progress. Even with all the problems, I really believe that. Every time that I see that, and you can come here, you can fall, but there is always a possibility of going up. Take, for example, when we close our restaurant [in] 2008. If that would happen in Dominican Republic, who would tell that in less than four years you would have been thinking [to] establish another business?

Despite recognizing the profound difficulties in the United States that immigrants encounter as they achieve economic success, Federico emphasized the chances for upward economic mobility (structural assimilation). That is, the United States provides opportunities for reversing declining fortunes, opportunities he perceived as unavailable in the Dominican Republic. Pointedly, Federico saw that these opportunities are restricted to middle-class Latine immigrants.

Sarita also acknowledged anti-Latine discrimination even as she praised living in Atlanta: "Even if right now, you feel tension because of migration policies when you speak Spanish, it's perceivable. But besides this, it has been a good experience." Sarita offered a window into the racialization of illegality by attributing to U.S. immigration policies the "tensions" that arose when she spoke Spanish. Despite this stigmatization, Sarita described her life in Atlanta as a "good experience."

It is not surprising that respondents maintained positive outlooks on the United States. Our respondents came to Atlanta precisely to improve their lives. Importantly, their middle-class status allowed them to realize this goal, even during years when the racialization of illegality was intensifying and solidifying. Their experience runs counter to that of many undocumented immigrants who describe a "hope turned sour" and the reversal of economic mobility generated by the racialization of illegality.[9]

Stigma theory offers a third way to understand respondents' experiences. Theories of stigma predict that respondents will be motivated to use their heritage belief systems to "save face" by denying or downplaying racism.[10] This situation suggests that some middle-class Latine respondents and their children may have suffered racialization and negative treatment in their day-to-day activities more often than they related.[11] For instance,

Evans and Moore, describing regular occurrences of racism and dignity-retaining responses among middle-class people of color in white-dominated workplaces, find that

> people of color in white institutional spaces negotiate their responses to racist institutional practices in such a way that creates avenues to resist racial objectification and degradation and emotionally protect themselves from the damaging consequences of racism. These everyday micro-resistances, as we call them, represent an important aspect of racial resilience and resistance, enabling people of color to participate in racially oppressive institutions while maintaining and valuing their human dignity.[12]

In my interviews, the stigmatizing assumptions attached to the image of the "typical Latine" clashed with respondents' perceptions of their relatively privileged social class status and their mestizaje belief systems. In response, some of these middle-class respondents may have engaged in strategies to reconcile these conflicting social identities and to downplay or ignore experiences of racism.[13] These respondents can be seen as "active challengers" of stigmatization processes.[14] Resonant with Evans and Moore's study, my respondents may have been practicing resistance to racism in ways that retained their dignity. However, what Evans and Moore sidestep is that these "everyday micro-resistances" can reinforce systems of inequality—particularly class inequality.

Juan Diego, for example, had a class-based favored status that shielded him from most experiences of discrimination:

> I think that it happens with African Americans as well. If you are well educated, if you have a good job and stuff like that, people think people are less discriminatory against you. I think that in this country it has a lot to do with your social status, independently of your race, but I also think that if you are low-income, whether you are Mexican or African American, you are more prone to be discriminated against. Whereas, you know, people that I . . . my neighbors are highly educated people, well-to-do, and I never felt that they treat me any different than anybody else or at work or anywhere else.
>
> *I think that the issue is not race.* I really don't think, at least in Cobb County and the circles where I move, I don't think that this is discrimination based on your race or your origin, but on your social status. (interviewee's emphasis)

Juan Diego's account shifted the focus away from a stigmatized identity category (Latine immigrant) and toward his privileged class position. He doubled down on the advantages of his class status by emphasizing that he was surrounded by middle-class neighbors and colleagues who were "highly educated people" unlikely to discriminate. Juan Diego also drew parallels between Latines and African Americans, interpreting negative treatment of both groups as class-based. He explicitly stated that anti-Latine and anti-black discrimination is not about race.

When respondents such as Juan Diego signaled that they were not a "typical Latine"—that is, when Mexicans signaled that they were not working-class, and when Dominicans signaled that they were not Mexican—they reinforced the lower status of these depreciated groups. When respondents distinguished themselves from immigrants who "take welfare," they reinscribed the line between "bad immigrants" and "good immigrants."[15] When respondents displayed their cosmopolitan capital and emphasized the benefits of their trips to Europe, they fortified the hierarchy that keeps the middle class above the working class. These maneuvers were not necessarily a bid for Anglo-conformity. Indeed, some respondents used one-up identity work strategies that upended the immigrant–native-born status hierarchy, setting themselves apart from "Americans."

Racialization and Identity Work in the Post-Trump Era

Respondents' identity work strategies and the types of experiences that engendered them were consistent across the original interview time frame (2009 to 2016), a period when the racialization of illegality intensified. Supplementary interviews conducted in 2021 through 2023 reveal that the patterns found among the original respondents appear to have carried over through the Trump era and beyond, including a disdain for U.S.-based racial categories and a disregard for personal experiences of discrimination. At the same time, the more recent respondents recognized that anti-immigrant hatred increased under Trump. For instance, Matías, a Dominican physician interviewed in 2022, remarked:

> The whole Hispanic terminology is kind of a hot mess for me. I think it's a big bag to hide a lot of ignorance. Overall, I obviously identify myself as a Dominican. In the United States I am Hispanic, and that's what I click on everything that gives me that choice. I identified with Latin America, which is, I think, where they are trying to go, although "Hispanic" is a term that mainly refers to Mexican immigrants here.

Matías described the identity category of "Hispanic" as highly problematic ("a hot mess"). Consistent with the typical Latine image, "Hispanic" is equated with "Mexican." His implication that it is Americans whose views on "Hispanics" carry a "big bag of ignorance" reflects a one-up assimilation strategy.

Matías also intuited an increase in discrimination against undocumented Latines during the Trump era but claimed that he had been unaffected:

> Trump being in power does not affect me individually. I have kept the same job, I kept the same house, kind of the same environment, and so on. I think that it does greatly damaged . . . or really sent back the immigrants. Which is a group that I belong to. Now I am very clear in understanding the status of me as an immigrant because of my education. The great majority of immigrants into any country, and specifically in the United States, is socioeconomic. But I'm not an immigrant for socioeconomic reasons. In that regard, although I'm not affected directly in my day-to-day basis, it brings back an ugly face or racism and marginalization and supremacy that might not affect me directly but affects the group that I feel like I belong to.

Matías recognized the "racism and marginalization and supremacy" that many Latine immigrants experienced under Trump, but also believed that his class status (education) had protected him from these difficulties. Matías had been a successful physician in the Dominican Republic, and he did not move to the United States "for socioeconomic reasons" but rather, presumably, to improve his material position. Later in the interview, Matías expressed a deep appreciation for the United States. Other respondents interviewed between 2021 and 2023 echoed these themes.

These patterns speak to the growing literature on high-skilled immigrants. In these studies, migrants whose college degrees were earned in the heritage country find that their credentials and skills are not necessarily transferable to the U.S. labor market.[16] They are often overeducated for their U.S. jobs. In my study, twenty-two Mexican respondents and twenty-four Dominican respondents came to the United States with college degrees in hand. The majority of these respondents found employment befitting their credentials, did not report a skills mismatch, and retained their class privilege as they settled in Atlanta.

RACE, CLASS, AND THE POLITICS OF IMMIGRATION

My respondents' perspectives on living in Atlanta provided a window into understanding Latine public opinion across the political spectrum.[17] Their gratitude for U.S.-based opportunities combined with their heritage-inspired belief that race "does not" and "should not" matter enabled them to hold a wide range of political stances. As a *New Yorker* article covering Latine supporters of Trump explains: "[Immigrants] come to the United States . . . to find economic and religious freedom, and because they believe in America's promise of equal opportunity and inclusion. They see themselves . . . not as members of a minority group but as individuals and families who left Latin America to look for something better in the United States."[18]

In Georgia, it appears that Latine voters are becoming more conservative. Although Joe Biden won the majority of the Latine vote in the 2020 presidential election, Donald Trump increased his base of Latine supporters in Georgia from 27 percent in 2016 to 37 percent in 2020.[19] Our interviews provide insight into this shift toward conservatism. Many middle-class Latine respondents perceived economic opportunities rather than barriers, and they did not see race and racism as entrenched problems in the United States.

Hana Brown looks at political engagement in new immigrant destinations from the opposite end of the political spectrum, focusing on the potential for left-leaning coalition-building. Brown contends that the racialization of illegality opens up possibilities for producing political alliances across groups of Latines and between Latine immigrants and African Americans.[20] Some respondents expressed a common identity or a sense of "linked fate" with Latines, a necessary condition for political coalition-building. For instance, Teresa discussed Latine unity in the face of discrimination: "[Americans at work] were making fun of us. And we're like, we don't care what country we're from. Understand this. She's from Venezuela, I'm from Dominican. But when it comes to us . . . to being united, we don't care what we are." Several respondents translated their sense of linked fate into political activism. Monica recounted:

> [In college] I started working a lot with committee-based organization, Latino community-based organizations. So I got involved with Latino Coordinating Council, which now is GLAHR [Georgia Latino Alliance for Human Rights]. And I started . . . participating with GALEO [Georgia Association of Latino Elected Officials]. . . . And at that time, there was a Latino, Mexican-American Georgia senator. The first and last so far in our senate—in state senate. [My Latino mentor] introduced me to him initially and introduced me to a lot of people in the university.

Notably, Monica, a Mexican attorney, became involved in these organizations when she was introduced to leaders by a Latine mentor in college. That is, her participation was the result of her "social capital" within a middle-class framework. She currently worked as an attorney litigating immigration cases for undocumented immigrants, and she mentored Latine students.

IMPLICATIONS

My interviews point to productive avenues for future research on race and immigration and offer important new information to combat the racialization of illegality in new and traditional immigrant destinations throughout the United States. My study has specifically considered the intersection of race, class, and migration status, recognizing the agency and relative privilege of middle-class Latine immigrants.[21] In particular, my interviews illuminate the opportunities and barriers attached to class privilege within growing Latine national groups. I have explored how that privilege can reproduce social hierarchies, and how status bound up with heritage and U.S. racial systems complicates attempts to bridge the class divide.

These complications raise questions about the impact of identity work strategies on the beliefs and perceptions of U.S.-born whites. Stigma theory suggests that the effects on whites may be limited, since they are the dominant group and one-up assimilation does not threaten their dominant position in the racial hierarchy. Seen from an immigrant-centered perspective, however, identity work strategies may be important to respondents' well-being.[22]

Relying on heritage racial belief systems that emphasize class over race-based distinctions not only fortifies respondents' well-being and national identity but may also provide important resources for their children. Patricia Fernández-Kelly calls these heritage ideologies and identities a "back pocket map"—that is, stores of knowledge from [the] heritage country that facilitates upward mobility and shores up resilience against discrimination, and in which "cognitive and behavioral elements attached to class position are transposed across borders as invisible but precious assets."[23] Fernández-Kelly shows that the "back pocket map" benefits the children of immigrants by providing them with social and cultural tools to achieve mobility and thwart discrimination.

How much did respondents' children need to rely on their back pocket maps as they navigated the U.S. racial system? Did the racialization of illegality fade across generations, as straight-line assimilation theory would predict? Tomás Jiménez's theory of replenishment suggests that the answer to the latter question is no. Stigmatization as a "typical Latine" may have continued to affect respondents' children and grandchildren through the constant inflow of working-class Mexicans, many of them undocumented. Jiménez argues that as long as the working-class Mexican population is "replenished" by ongoing in-migration into locales such as Atlanta, it may be difficult for middle-class Latine immigrants to avoid being stereotyped as a "typical Latine" any less frequently.[24]

My interviews with Dominicans allow us to see how Jiménez's theory of the effects of Mexican replenishment can extend beyond Mexicans. Atlanta's middle-class Dominicans are assumed to be members of the largest local Latine immigrant group—Mexicans. Given the continual demand for working-class Latine immigrant labor, the replenishment of the Mexican immigrant population in Atlanta should continue to promote this assumption, influencing how middle-class Dominicans are perceived by the non-Latine native-born. Mexicans predominate in Atlanta's demographic landscape, unlike other cities where Dominicans predominate and are often assumed to be African American. We may expect to find similar patterns in other new immigrant destinations with a preponderance of Mexicans in their Latine immigrant population.

My study population takes on increasing importance given that the number of middle-class Latine immigrants is growing throughout the nation, with an increasing proportion receiving a college or graduate education in the United States.[25] This increase has important implications for the integration of this group into the political, economic, and social domains. While a U.S.-based education may facilitate their assimilation, increases in experiences and recognition of stigmatization may heighten their awareness of racism and give them a needed impetus for political engagement.

Atlanta may be an especially fertile place to target efforts challenging the racialization of illegality, given the city's storied role in the civil rights movement. Atlanta's sister city in the Dominican Republic is the home of the three Mirabal sisters, Dominican revolutionaries who helped to overthrow the Trujillo dictatorship. As Samuel (Dominican) notes, Atlanta and Salcedo "are the home to great leaders. From one great North American leader that is Martin Luther King and the three women who gave their lives for the Dominican Republic. What better ones than that. . . . They are leaders who fought for similar ideals and they have had an huge international impact."

With their educational credentials, secure economic status, and cosmopolitan cultural capital, Atlanta's middle-class Latine immigrants are especially well positioned to assume key leadership roles in achieving Latine civil and human rights. Research on stigma shows that when individual efforts to reclaim social status do not target the institutional foundations of stigmatization, "they are insufficient to eliminate prejudice and the predisposition [of dominant group members] to discriminate."[26]

State-sponsored institutional solutions must be applied to systemic problems such as the racialization of illegality, including the dismantling of "structural stigma" by repealing harsh anti-immigration policies.[27] Reducing the policy-induced stigmatization of undocumented Latine immigrants will not only ease the lives of the undocumented but send a message that affects all Latines "about who belongs [in the United States], who matters, and who is worthy."[28]

Appendix A |

Table A.1 Number of Deportations in Georgia, 2003–2019

Year	Mexico	Dominican Republic
2003	164	7
2004	193	34
2005	155	17
2006	449	69
2007	1,217	132
2008	915	110
2009	1,263	92
2010	2,176	150
2011	1,635	85
2012	1,270	130
2013	1311	112
2014	907	119
2015	781	140
2016	413	124
2017	570	83
2018	473	89
2019	1,318	15

Source: TRACImmigration 2021. "Latest Data: Immigration and Customs Enforcement Removals."
Note: Data for figure 1.1.

DOI: https://doi.org/10.7758/hvda9363.7699

Appendix B | Coding for Georgia Immigration Bills, 2005–2019

As MY COLLEAGUES and I explain elsewhere, the data in table 2.6 include "final votes on all proposed restrictive immigration legislation that received a roll call vote in at least one full chamber for 2005–2012, combining 182 bills that were enacted with 14 bills that were vetoed by the Governor, died in committee, or failed to pass in at least one chamber." Using the enacted bills from the National Conference of State Legislators (NCSL) and bills that were not passed, we collected voting data for each of these bills from the individual state legislature websites. We coded bills as "restrictive" if they "aim to exclude or restrict immigrants from access to resources (jobs, education, housing, etc.), increase surveillance of immigrants and enforcement of immigration laws (expanding police authority), or reinforce the exclusion of immigrants from the polity (voter ID)."[1] Bills that refine, clarify, or provide funds for existing restrictive laws were also included in our sample (for example, participating in the E-Verify program or specifying the type of ID that is valid for voting).

BILL TOPICS

We coded bill topics using the NCSL's eleven topic codes, then recoded further to test our hypotheses about whether bills would evoke a response from African American state legislators grounded in a perception of black-Latine common interests ("commonalities") or a "competition" response.[2] Specifically, we subdivided the "ID/licenses" bills into three categories: (1) licenses and IDs related to employment (driver's licenses, professional licenses, and business licenses); (2) driver's licenses not specifically related to employment; and (3) firearms licenses (public safety). The few licenses that did not fall into these categories (for example, fishing licenses) were included among the "miscellaneous" topics. Bills pertaining to budget items were coded according to the activity targeted by the budget bill. For instance, a bill allocating funds to support the E-Verify program was coded under the employment topic. For each restrictive immigration bill in our data set, we recorded the roll call vote of each state legislator.

We sorted the bill topics into four groups according to their relevance for competition or commonalities issues. The first group of topics ("competition") encompassed labor market bills that restricted the employment of undocumented immigrants. These included bills that both explicitly targeted the labor market practices of employers or workers and bills that increased the difficulty of working by prohibiting work-related driver's licenses, professional licenses, and business licenses.

We categorized proposals regarding voter identification, expansion of police powers, education, and omnibus restrictions as "civil rights" bills. In addition to the continued struggles of civil rights groups to renew and implement the Voting Rights Act of 1965, poor African American voters are overrepresented among those without identification to vote. Similarly, concerns about police brutality and racial profiling remain central for African American civil rights organizations.[3] Education emerged as the most salient concern for African American state legislators across all issues listed on the NAACP scorecard.[4]

The final set of topics (other") included bills concerning welfare benefits and health benefits, budget bills, and miscellaneous bills (for example, fishing licenses and refugee settlement). We also classified public safety bills under "other." This topic operates differently than the labor market threat bills, in that whites depict immigrants as a "threat to public safety" but blacks do not.

Appendix C | Methods

THE INTERVIEWS

The interview data used in this book are based on a qualitative study investigating social mobility strategies used by middle-class Dominican and Mexican parents in the metropolitan Atlanta area. The project was supported by two grants from the National Science Foundation (NSF)—a pilot study grant and an award to conduct the full study. I received additional funds from the Russell Sage Foundation to conduct follow-up interviews between 2021 and 2023.

We focused our study on middle-class Latine immigrants because these families had the resources to exercise their preferences in the midst of Atlanta's "Latino backlash."[1] Between 2009 and 2016, we conducted semistructured interviews that yielded a total of thirty-three college-educated Dominican and thirty-five Mexican immigrant respondents for this book.[2]

Sample

Our original plan was to obtain a stratified probability sample of Mexican and Dominican respondents. We used census data to identify tracts with high concentrations of Latine and visited establishments in these neighborhoods. We visited restaurants and asked to speak to the proprietor, and we visited Dominican hair salons. This approach yielded very few interviews; no hair salon owners, for instance, agreed to be interviewed. It seems that potential respondents were unwilling to spend time being interviewed by a "stranger."

We next recruited Dominican and Mexican respondents through organizations in order to achieve a broad sample. Our strategies included:

Making an announcement over a local Spanish radio station

Establishing contacts with the Latin American Association

Distributing flyers at a Dominican restaurant

Making an announcement at the annual Spanish-language service for the Dominican patron saint, the "Virgen de Altagracia"

These efforts yielded several more respondents, but our numbers were still far below our target sample size. Therefore, we turned to a purposive snowball sampling design with multiple starting points. To recruit Mexicans, our starting points included a Latina graduate student with ties to multiple organizations (such as a Spanish-language Catholic church, a Mexican dance ensemble, and a Latine parent organization); an instructor in a university Spanish department; a Latina CDC employee; a Peruvian graduate student conducting research on Mexican immigrants in Atlanta; and previous respondents.

For our sample of middle-class Dominicans, the starting points included a Dominican higher education administrator, a software engineer with Dominican coworkers, an Argentinian attorney, a Dominican community leader, a Dominican elementary school administrator, and previous respondents.[3]

In recruiting respondents, we followed Lacy by operationalizing "middle-class" as immigrants who met at least one of these criteria: holding a postsecondary degree, working in a professional occupation, or being self-employed. Lacy also uses family income as a criterion for defining middle-class status.[4] We believed that asking individuals their income would greatly reduce our response rate, so we did not include an income threshold in our recruitment materials.[5]

Data Collection

We conducted interviews in Spanish or English, depending on the respondent's preference. Following the directive of one of our NSF grant reviewers, most of the interviews were conducted by bilingual Latine graduate students. Several interviews were conducted by an Argentinian attorney we trained for the project. I conducted fourteen interviews (in English).

Interviewers had an interview guide and asked a series of questions regarding childrearing practices, including choices about raising children as bilingual, involvement in extracurricular activities, and selection of neighborhoods and schools, as well as a series of questions on racial-ethnic identification, categorization by others, and experiences of discrimination.

Analytic Strategy

To analyze the transcripts, we completed multiple phases of coding using MaxQDA v.12. During our first round, we coded for the original foci of our project—experiences of racial discrimination and racial identity.[6] This process yielded two published papers, which form the building blocks for this book. The first round of coding revealed a pervasive theme in the interviews: respondents described experiences that the literature would classify as discrimination, but they asserted that they did not experience discrimination in their day-to-day encounters with Atlantans. Additional themes arose inductively during the initial rounds of coding that indicated certain identity management strategies ("identity work") to negotiate this seeming contradiction. We conducted additional rounds of coding (separately for each paper) to take a deep dive into each of these themes.

Our coding yielded several key concepts, including: racialization and the clash between heritage and U.S. identities (chapters 1 and 3);[7] responses to the stigma of being seen as a "typical Latine" (chapters 1, 4, 5, and 6);[8] and one-up assimilation strategies (chapter 5).[9] We also coded the specific strategies that respondents used to reproduce or assert their middle-class status, from responses to the question "where are you from?" to decisions about where to live to commitments to raising children as bilingual. For each of these concepts, we conducted an additional round of coding that identified subthemes.

For the book, I conducted additional rounds of coding to investigate how cosmopolitan cultural capital was reflected in the lives of the respondents. These codes included respondent discussions of education and of other markers of cosmopolitan cultural capital (such as diversity) (chapter 5). I also coded for their relations with African Americans (chapter 5).[10]

MY POSITIONALITY AS A WHITE, NON-LATINE CISGENDER FEMALE RESEARCHER

Given my position in the research enterprise as a white, non-Latine professor, it is possible that some respondents I interviewed did not feel comfortable discussing negative experiences with me. We conducted checks for this possibility by comparing responses across interviewers. These comparisons indicated that the interviews conducted by Latine graduate students did not appear to differ from my interviews, particularly in stories of negative treatment or in the extent to which their narratives were pervaded by the theme of whether race mattered or should matter.

In addition to the methodological issues that arose from my outsider standing, the literature on race and positionality suggests that a power dynamic was at work in which I, as a white, non-Latine professor, occupied an advantaged position with respect to my respondents, even though, occupationally, my social status was similar to theirs.[11]

To address the power relations in my study, I rely on the argument of

Jody Mellor and colleagues that "power relations in qualitative research are multidirectional, with the various stages of research—from recruitment to dissemination—involving differing power distribution between the researchers and researched."[12] As a researcher, I had a high degree of control in the interview, since I selected the study theme, formulated the interview guide, steered the conversation toward particular topics, and could stop the interview at will. But respondents also could exercise ownership and control over the data, since they decided what information to share.[13]

Ultimately, the balance of power rested with me when I interpreted the findings and wrote up the results.[14] I could impose my interpretation on respondent experiences and perceptions, and both the methods literature and the ethics literature acknowledge that my interpretations were likely to be influenced by my social position as a white non-Latine professor.[15] I relied on the literature and BIPOC readers and collaborators to move away from a white-centered perspective. These checks on my interpretations are especially important given my argument that respondents experienced stigmatization that they were unaware of or were downplaying. I bring an interpretation, informed by the literature and my colleagues, that challenges the view of the many respondents who claimed that "race doesn't matter" and that they "don't experience discrimination." I try to do justice to their perceptions of the world in chapter 6, where I explore explanations that would most resonate with the worldview of some respondents that their middle-class status protected them from negative treatment and experiences of racism.

TERMS

"Hispanic," "Latino," "Latino/a," "Latinx," "Latine"

I also am mindful of the debate over what terms to use in describing immigrants from Latin America and the Spanish-speaking Caribbean.[16] As the term most familiar to the respondents, we used "Latino" in our interview questions. My respondents used the terms "Hispanic" or "Latino" to describe themselves when they were discussing pan-ethnic labels, and we used these terms in the interviews. Both of these pan-ethnic labels are U.S.-based constructions, and my use of them in the book raises questions.

The "Hispanic" label was introduced by the U.S. Census Bureau.[17] According to Suzanne Oboler, "the term, 'Hispanic' effectively racialized all immigrants, exiles, refugees, and U.S. citizens from sovereign Latin American nations and from Spain, and it homogenized them into a faceless statistical category."[18]

The "Latino" designation originally was promoted by U.S.-based activists endeavoring to create political solidarity among individuals from Mexico, Cuba, and Puerto Rico.[19] The term "Latino" raises equity problems, however, because it is gendered masculine and connotes the generic "he." Some scholars use "Latino/a" to include women. However, this term reproduces a binary approach to gender (Latino = male; Latina = female) and therefore excludes individuals who place themselves outside the binary (such as transgender individuals).[20]

The terms "Latinx" and "Latine" provide a gender-neutral alternative. The "Latinx" term has been critiqued as an English-language imperialist construction with no corollary in Spanish.[21] That is, no Spanish words end in "x." In contrast, an "e" ending, as in "Latine," does occur in Spanish (for example, *estudiante*, or "student").

Some argue that, because the Spanish language itself is the result of colonialism, there is little difference between using "Latino," "Latinx," or "Latine." Further, none of these terms show widespread use among the individuals they aim to describe.[22] Given that there is no ideal solution, I use the term "Latine" throughout the book.

Terms: "Unauthorized," "Undocumented," "Illegal"

Scholars, policymakers, and activists also debate the terms used to describe individuals who are in the United States without authorization. I follow Helen Marrow and use "undocumented" and "unauthorized" interchangeably to denote individuals who were not born in the United States, are not citizens or permanent residents, and are currently living in the United States without an official temporary status that would enable them to work and live in the country lawfully. This group can include individuals who entered the United States without authorization as well as those who entered with a visa that has expired.[23]

Notes |

CHAPTER 1: MIDDLE-CLASS LATINE IMMIGRANTS, THE RACIALIZATION OF ILLEGALITY, AND PRECARIOUS PRIVILEGE

1. Chacón and Coutin 2018; Lee and Bean 2010; Oboler 2021; Agius Vallejo 2020.
2. Heiman et al. 2012. For a discussion of similar strategies used by middle-class African Americans to combat negative stereotyping, see Fleming, Lamont, and Welburn 2012.
3. For a discussion of the racialization of Spanish, see Davis and Moore 2014.
4. Bourdieu 1984; Toribio 2000. Almeida Toribio (2000, 1135) argues that Dominicans are "fiercely loyal to their native dialect, which serves as an immutable marker of Dominican identity. Thus, while there exist a number of markers of identity, such as social group, geography, cultural traditions, and race, for many Dominicans, language is the most significant criterion of self-identification."
5. Cobas and Feagin 2008; Davis and Moore 2014; Oboler 2021.
6. Bailey 2000; Browne, Tatum, and González 2021. As I discuss in greater detail in this book, Dominicans in other parts of the United States often focus their energies on emphasizing their Latine identity and distancing themselves from a "black" identity.
7. Flores and Schachter 2018.
8. Asad and Clair 2018; Brown, Jones, and Becker 2018; De Genova 2004; García 2017; Menjívar 2021; Romero 2008. I thank Helen Marrow for pointing out links between my interviews and the racialization of illegality.
9. These arguments build on the work of scholars who discuss middle-class Latine immigrants and identify the centrality of social class in conditioning immigrant experiences in traditional destinations. See Agius Vallejo 2020; Callister, Galbraith, and Galbraith 2019; Clark 2003; Duany 1998; Fernández-Kelly 2008; Itzigsohn 2009; Kim 2018; Portes and Zhou 1993; Roth 2008. I also develop these arguments in greater depth in Browne and Odem 2012; Browne,

Reingold, and Kronberg 2018; Browne, Tatum, and González 2021; Odem and Browne 2011; Tatum and Browne 2019.

10. Ebert, Estrada, and Lore 2014; Kim 2018.
11. Race matters for my daughter in complicated ways beyond her Guatemalan heritage, of course, including, especially, my positionality as a white heterosexual single mother and her status as adopted, which shape how she experiences race in the United States.
12. Jonsson 2006; Lovato 2008. More recent scholarship critiques the term "Juan Crow" as detaching the history of Latine immigrants in the United States from the history of racism against blacks. As I show in chapter 3, these two histories are intertwined. See Márquez 2019.
13. Jones 2019; López-Sanders 2011; Marrow 2011, 2020; McDermott 2011.
14. Jones 2019; Marrow 2020; Massey 2008; Odem and Lacy 2009; Schleef and Cavalcanti 2010; Smith and Furuseth 2006; Winders 2005.
15. For instance, the number of immigration-related bills passed by states increased from 38 in 2005 to 346 in 2010 (Bohn and Lofstrom 2012; see also Brown, Jones, and Dow 2016).
16. Marrow 2020.
17. My use of the term "precarious" in this book departs from the concept of precarity discussed by Pierre Bourdieu (1998) and others in the literature (for example, Millar 2017), which focuses on marginalization and labor market precarity. I am focusing on social precarity within privileged economic status.
18. Jiménez 2010; Jones 2019; Landgrave and Weller 2022; Winders 2011; Yarbrough 2010.
19. For an overview of the repertoire of responses to stigma used by African Americans, see Lamont et al. 2016.
20. More specifically, I am using Bourdieu's theory of social class as encompassing a position in a social hierarchy as well as a set of dispositions, worldviews, discourses, and resources that middle-class immigrants can mobilize to create distance from other groups. See chapter 5 for an in-depth discussion of middle-class resources.
21. Berger, Ridgeway, and Zelditch 2002; Ridgeway 2019; Weber 1958.
22. Ollivier 2008.
23. García 2017. My approach also builds on the robust literature that identifies social class as a major influence on immigrant assimilation and incorporation. See, for instance, Agius Vallejo 2012; Itzigsohn 2009; Portes and Zhou 1993.
24. Flores and Schachter 2018.
25. Ibid.
26. Bratton 2021, 55.
27. Pellerin and Stearns 2001.
28. Interviewing and coding were conducted by a team of researchers and me. I

use the first person throughout the book as a rhetorical strategy to facilitate flow.

29. See Bourdieu's (1973/2018) theory of class reproduction.
30. Social psychologists describe individuals' efforts to "construct and negotiate personal identities" as "identity work." For immigrants, these identity work strategies range from manipulating cultural cues such as dress and appearance to explicitly stating one's preferred social category (García 2019; Kibria 2000; Killian and Johnson 2006; Lamont and Mizrachi 2013; Valenta 2009; Waters 1999).
31. For similar queries among middle-class Mexican Americans and Dominicans, respectively, in traditional destinations (California and Rhode Island), see Agius Vallejo 2020; Itzigsohn 2009; Vasquez 2011.
32. Ridgeway and Kricheli-Katz 2013; Ruggles et al. 2022a; U.S. Census Bureau 2022b. Numbers are calculated for the ten counties in the Atlanta metro area using aggregate county data from the 2017–2021 American Community Survey (ACS) Social Explorer.
33. Jiménez 2010.
34. Aranda, Menjívar, and Donato 2014; Menjívar 2021.
35. Itzigsohn, Giorguli, and Vazquez 2005.
36. Howard 2001; Roth 2013; Sagás 1997; Telles and Paschel 2014; Torres-Saillant 2010.
37. Ibid.
38. Bailey 2001; Candelario 2007; Duany 1998; Howard 2003; Itzigsohn, Giorguli, and Vazquez 2005; Roth 2013; Sagás 2000; Torres-Saillant 2010.
39. Note that Ginetta Candelario (2007) finds this pattern among middle-class Dominicans in Washington, D.C. However, the relative proportion of Dominicans to Mexicans is much higher in D.C. than in Atlanta.
40. Moore 2008.
41. Evans and Moore 2015; Moore 2008; Telles and Sue 2019.
42. O'Brien 2008.
43. Bonilla-Silva 2001.
44. Browne and Odem 2012; Cobas, Duany, and Feagin 2015; Massey 2014; Murji and Solomos 2005; Omi and Winant 1994; Telles and Ortiz 2008. Other institutions that engage in racialization include churches, families, and NGOs (Hagerman 2018).
45. Cobas, Duany, and Feagin 2015; Davis and Moore 2014; Golash-Boza and Darity 2008; Jiménez 2010; Telles and Bailey 2013.
46. Feagin and Cobas 2015.
47. Massey 2014.
48. Chavez 2013.
49. Aranda and Vacquera 2015; Del Real 2019; Martínez-Rosas and Aranda 2018; Massey and Sánchez 2010.
50. Menjívar 2021, 92.

51. Martinez-Cola 2021; Molina 2014; Ngai 2014.
52. Not all northern European groups experienced state-sponsored welcome. For instance, Jewish immigrants and Irish immigrants were treated as outsiders (Brodkin 1998; Ignatiev 2012).
53. No Mexicans were legally classified as "undocumented immigrants" until 1964, when documentation was required and limits on documented Mexican immigrants were set (Fox and Bloemraad 2015; Fox and Guglielmo 2012; Molina 2014; Ngai 2014; Telles and Ortiz 2008).
54. Wong 2006.
55. Donato and Amuedo-Dorantes 2020; Hopkins 2010; Massey and Pren 2012.
56. Marrow 2020; Massey 2008; McDermott 2011; Winders 2013.
57. Weise 2015; Winders 2013.
58. Commins and Wills 2017; Ebert, Estrada, and Lore 2014; Hopkins 2010; Marrow 2020, 101; Ramakrishnan and Wong 2010; Vallas, Zimmerman, and Davis 2009; Winders 2005.
59. Abrego et al. 2017; Aranda, Menjívar, and Donato 2014; Armenta 2017; Cobas, Duany, and Feagin 2015; De Genova 2002; Waters and Kasinitz 2015.
60. Armenta 2017; Chavez 2012; Dreby 2015; Golash-Boza 2015; Waters and Kasinitz 2015.
61. Abrego et al. 2017; Winders 2014.
62. Bloch 2014; Menjívar 2021; Yarbrough 2010.
63. Brown 2013; Dreby 2015; Provine et al. 2016; Stuesse and Coleman 2014; Waters and Kasinitz 2015.
64. Bohon et al. 2011; Dreby 2015; Flores and Schachter 2018.
65. Abrego et al. 2017; Hopkins 2010; Menjívar 2016; Provine et al. 2016; Stuesse and Coleman 2014.
66. Coleman and Kocher 2019.
67. Coleman and Kocher 2019; Menjívar and Abrego 2012; Santos et al. 2021; Stuesse and Coleman 2014.
68. Donato and Rodríguez 2014.
69. Gómez Cervantes 2021; Johnson 1983.
70. Chacón and Coutin 2018, 162.
71. Badie 2004.
72. Gibbins 2005; Winders 2007.
73. Badie 2004.
74. Marrow 2020.
75. Henriksen 2007.
76. López-Sanders and Brown 2020.
77. Carey, Branton, and Martinez-Ebers 2014; López-Sanders and Brown 2020; Rumbaut 2008; Santa Ana et al. 2007; Voss and Bloemraad 2011.
78. McDermott 2011; Santa Ana et al. 2007.
79. Brown, Jones, and Dow 2016; Diamond 1998; Kaufmann 2003; Meier et al. 2004.

80. Hopkins 2010.
81. Hopkins 2010; López-Sanders and Brown 2020.
82. Bohn and Lofstrom 2012; Donato and Amuedo-Dorantes 2020; Hopkins 2010; Ovink, Ebert, and Okamoto 2016; Provine et al. 2016.
83. Browne and Odem 2012.
84. Ibid., 325.
85. López-Sanders 2017.
86. Menjívar and Enchautegui 2015.
87. Ellis, Wright, and Townley 2014; Menjívar and Enchautegui 2015.
88. Menjívar and Enchautegui 2015.
89. Leerkes, Bachmeier, and Leach 2013.
90. Rosales 2020, 46.
91. Del Real 2019; López-Sanders 2017.
92. Liptak 2012.
93. Arrocha 2012.
94. National Conference of State Legislatures 2022.
95. Provine et al. 2016.
96. TRACImmigration 2021.
97. Gonzales 2010.
98. Canizales and Agius Vallejo 2021.
99. Reilly 2016.
100. Bosworth, Parmar, and Vázquez 2018; Ebert and Ovink 2014; Marquez et al. 2022.
101. Marrow 2020.
102. Jones 2019; Marrow 2020; Silver 2018.
103. Aranda, Menjívar, and Donato 2014; Asad and Claire 2018; Brown et al. 2018; García 2017; López-Sanders 2017; Menjívar 2021.
104. Canizales and Agius Vallejo 2021; Dreby 2015.
105. Dreby 2015.
106. Quillian 2006.
107. Agius Vallejo 2020; Fernández-Kelly 2008; Zhou et al. 2008.
108. Portes and Rumbaut 2014.
109. Badillo 2013; Brown-Nagin 2011; Odem and Browne 2011; Rodriguez 2020.
110. Ruggles et al. 2022a, 2022b, 2022c.
111. Suro and Singer 2002.
112. Throughout the book, "black" refers to both black immigrants and U.S.-born individuals; "African American" refers to U.S.-born blacks only. The term "Latine immigrant" includes those who identify as black.
113. Ambinakudige et al. 2017; Jaret, Hayes, and Adelman 2009.
114. Wickert 2016.
115. U.S. Census Bureau 1991, 2001.
116. Metro Atlanta Chamber of Commerce 2020.
117. Ruiz and Krogstad 2018.

118. Winders 2014, 5.
119. Rose 2018; see also Stuesse and Coleman 2014.
120. Moore 2008.
121. Bridges 2018, 70; see also Lacy 2007.
122. Goffman 1963.
123. Stillerman 2023, 8.
124. Stigmatization through legislation has been termed "structural stigma" (Corrigan et al. 2005). Restrictive immigration policy fits the definition of "structural stigma," given that it not only is undergirded by restrictive immigration legislation that "intentionally restrict[s] the opportunities of people" but also "yield[s] unintended consequences that hinder the options of people"—such as documented Latines (ibid., 481).
125. Corrigan et al. 2005; Pescosolido and Martin 2015; Lamont et al. 2016.
126. Link and Phelan 2001, 367.
127. Ibid., 370.
128. Lebrón et al. 2018.
129. Agius Vallejo 2020; Feagin and Cobas 2015; Massey and Sánchez 2010; Valdez 2020.
130. Vasquez 2011, 241. For a discussion of Indian American hotel owners' simultaneous experience in the United States of economic success and social disadvantage, see Dhingra 2012.
131. Khachikian and Bandelj 2019; Lin and Zhou 2005.
132. Agius Vallejo 2012, 666.
133. Cheng 2013; Dreby 2015; Gonzales 2016; Montejano 1987; Schildkraut et al. 2019; Telles 2021; Xie and Gough 2011.
134. Feagin and Cobas 2015; Fernández-Kelly 2008; Flores-González 2017; Itzigsohn 2009; Jiménez 2010. For exceptions, see McDermott 2011; Schleef and Cavalcanti 2010; Winders 2013.
135. Pierrette Hondagneu-Sotelo and Manuel Pastor (2021) study Latine immigrants in South Central, a predominantly black section of Los Angeles. They show a lot of distancing toward blacks in the first generation, but more cooperation and admiration built out of exposure contact and a sense of place in the second generation.
136. American Community Survey 2017–2021 (U.S. Census Bureau 2022a). Atlanta's demographics are similar to those of other new immigrant destinations in the South, such as Nashville, Tennessee, and Richmond, Virginia.
137. U.S. Census Bureau 2021.
138. Ibid.
139. Vasquez 2011, 135.
140. Itzigsohn, Giorguli, and Vazquez 2005; Jiménez 2008; Massey and Sánchez 2010.
141. Agius Vallejo and Canizales 2016; Feagin and Cobas 2015.

142. Tropp et al. 2018.
143. Pescosolido and Martin 2015.
144. Scholars report similar findings among second-generation middle-class Mexicans in traditional gateway locations (Adem et al. 2022; Dowling 2014; Vasquez 2011). Similar patterns are also found among middle-class South Asians in Atlanta and Philadelphia.
145. Tropp et al. 2018.
146. Landgrave and Weller 2022.
147. Barlow and Lahey 2018; Brezina and Winder 2003; Freeman et al. 2011; Gaddis 2017; Penner and Saperstein 2013; Sanchez and Garcia 2012; Weeks and Lupfer 2004.
148. Brezina and Winder 2003; Durante and Fiske 2017; Fiske and Marcus 2012.
149. Tropp et al. 2018; Wilkenson, Cutaia, and Bingham 2016.
150. For a recent discussion, see Monk 2022.
151. Burke and Stets 2021; Hogg 2018; Tajfel and Turner 1979.
152. Burke and Stets 2021; Telles 2021.
153. Snow and Anderson 1987.
154. Burke and Stets 2021; Hogg 2018.
155. Burke and Stets 2021, 254.
156. Burke and Stets 2021; Snow and Anderson 1987.
157. Lamont and Mizrachi 2013.
158. Social identity theory assumes that, because identity work is oriented toward the goal of maintaining a positive identity, it is strategic in a broad sense.
159. Telles 2021.
160. Dowling and Newby 2010.
161. Mallet and Pinto-Coelho 2018.
162. Dixon 2019. The small number of Afro-Mexicans tends to be rendered invisible in the Mexican heritage belief systems (Sue 2013).
163. Monk 2022.
164. Bailey 2001; Torres-Saillant 2010.
165. Candelario 2007; Itzigsohn 2009.
166. Itzigsohn 2009; Massey and Sánchez 2010.
167. Using middle-class attire and comportment to signal authorized status has been termed "legal passing" by Angela García (2019).
168. Ibid.
169. "First generation" refers to individuals who migrated to the United States. "Second generation," "third generation," and "later generation" refer to individuals who were born in the United States and whose parents, grandparents, or great-grandparents were immigrants.
170. We interviewed an additional twenty respondents who did not have a college degree or were born in the United States. These cases are not included in the analyses presented in this book.

171. Du Bois 2015; Frey 2018.
172. Bobo and Hutchings 1996.
173. Some of the responses to stigma that I describe are consistent with findings from studies of middle-class African Americans and studies of middle-class immigrants in traditional destinations (Lamont et al. 2016; Jiménez 2010). I add to this literature by tying my conceptualization of stigma to the racialization of illegality and by including considerations of heritage racial belief systems as a class-based strategy.
174. Zamora 2022.
175. Dazey 2021; Higginbotham 1994.
176. Theiss-Morse, Gonzalez, and O'Toole 2020.
177. Tatum and Browne 2019.
178. Fleming, Lamont, and Welburn 2012; Lamont et al. 2016.
179. Skinner-Dorkenoo et al. 2021.
180. Brettell 2011; Canizales and Agius Vallejo 2021; Cobas, Duany, and Feagin 2015; Cobas, Duany, and Feagin 2015; Essed 2008; Evans and Moore 2015; Feagin and Cobas 2015; Marrow 2011; Stuesse and Coleman 2014.
181. Fleming, Lamont, and Welburn 2012; Lamont et al. 2016.

CHAPTER 2: RACE, CLASS, AND LATINE IMMIGRATION IN ATLANTA: A PORTRAIT

1. Bullard's comment regarding black children in poverty pertains to the city of Atlanta, not the Atlanta metro area.
2. Boissoneault 2017.
3. Bayor 2000.
4. To maintain consistency in geographic coverage from 1980 through 2021, these figures represent the sum of the population counts in the ten counties comprising the Atlanta metro area. The reports include all Latines, regardless of immigration status.
5. Jiménez 2010.
6. Suro and Singer 2002.
7. Browne and Odem 2012; Massey and Sánchez 2010.
8. Hanson 2020.
9. Fox and Guglielmo 2012; Weise 2015.
10. Burns 2009.
11. Franzosi, DeFazio, and Vicari 2012.
12. Woodward 1955/2002.
13. Jones-Correa 2000.
14. Bayor 2000. These laws were part of a larger trend throughout the United States toward adopting restrictive racial covenants (ibid.).
15. Quoted in Atlanta History Center, "Atlanta in 50 Objects," https://www

.atlantahistorycenter.com/exhibitions/atlanta-in-50-objects/jim-crow/ (accessed February 2, 2021).

16. Hobson 2017, 17.
17. Atlanta History Center 2021.
18. Aiello 2014.
19. Du Bois 1903; Itzigsohn and Brown 2020.
20. Atlanta History Center 2021.
21. Guridy 2010.
22. Hobson 2017.
23. Weise 2015.
24. Fox and Guglielmo 2012; Weise 2015.
25. Weise 2015, 8.
26. Olsson 2009/2020; Rodriguez 2020.
27. Weise 2015.
28. Brown-Nagin 2011; Klarman 1997/2004; Kluger 1975/2004; Pratt 2002.
29. Student Nonviolent Coordinating Committee, "Atlanta, Georgia," SNCC Digital Gateway, https://snccdigital.org/location/atlanta-ga/.
30. Brown-Nagin 2011; Harmon 2019.
31. Brown-Nagin 2011.
32. Lewis and D'Orso 2015.
33. Bayor 2000, 46.
34. Bayor 1996; Ruch 2020.
35. Skrentny 2009.
36. Hobson 2017.
37. Garland 1971.
38. Bayor 2000; Stirgus 2020.
39. Williams 2003, 81.
40. Orfield and Ashkinaze 1991.
41. These Mexican migrants were not refugees.
42. Fligstein 2013; Weise 2015.
43. Weise 2015.
44. Ibid., 127.
45. Odem and Lacy 2009.
46. Badillo 2013.
47. Ibid.
48. Weise 2015.
49. Abrego et al. 2017; Donato and Amuedo-Dorantes 2020; Marrow 2020; Zuñiga and Hernández-León 2005.
50. Donato and Amuedo-Dorantes 2020; Winders 2005.
51. Zuñiga and Hernández-León 2005, 249.
52. Furuseth and Smith 2006.
53. Jones 2019.

54. Stuesse 2016.
55. Durand, Massey, and Capoferro 2005.
56. Hernández-León and Zuñiga 2005; Odem and Lacy 2009; Winders 2008.
57. Weise 2015, 216.
58. Golash-Boza 2017.
59. As I discussed in chapter 1, this program provided resources and authorization to train local law enforcement to enforce federal immigration law by requesting documentation of legal status of anyone stopped for a crime and detaining undocumented individuals for apprehension by the Immigration and Naturalization Service (INS, now the U.S. Immigration and Customs Enforcement, or ICE). However, the program was not widely adopted in Georgia until 2005 (Pedroza 2019).
60. Golash-Boza 2017; Provine et al. 2016.
61. Hernández-León and Zuñiga 2005; McDaniel 2018; Weise 2015.
62. Badillo 2013, 130–31.
63. Hernández-León and Zuñiga 2005.
64. Ibid.
65. Hernández-León and Zuñiga 2005.
66. Zuñiga and Hernández-León 2005, 264.
67. Odem and Lacy 2009; Suro and Singer 2002.
68. Bailey 2000; Candelario 2007; Duany 1998; Grasmuck and Pessar 2020; Itzigsohn 2009; Levitt 2001; Roth 2008.
69. Candelario 2007.
70. Levitt 2001, 47.
71. Candelario 2007; Grasmuck and Pessar 2020.
72. Frey 2018; Agius Vallejo and Canizales 2021.
73. Whitfield 2020; Toone 2018.
74. Peters 2021. In fact, the city has been ranked the number-one tech hub in the Southeast "for the quality and quantity of its tech talent . . . drawn in part by Atlanta's Black tech talent."
75. Richards and Ellis 2020.
76. Braxton 2019.
77. Ruggles et al. 2022a.
78. Kim and Bozarth 2021; Tudhope 2020.
79. Yang 2020.
80. I discuss the complex status of Dominican immigrants as "black immigrants" with regard to middle-class Dominican immigrants in chapters 3 and 4.
81. Focusing on college-educated migrants in Silicon Valley, Rafael Alarcón (2007) claims that skilled migrants are incorporated into the U.S. economy in two ways: they arrive in the United States on a postdoc and are hired by large corporations, or they work for multinational companies outside the United States and are then transferred to a U.S. branch.

82. Bayor 2000, 46.
83. Riley 2013.
84. Badger 2016; Raymond, Wang, and Immergluck 2016.
85. Author's calculations based on Ruggles 2022a.
86. Brown University Diversity and Disparities Project, "Racial/Ethnic Composition and Segregation," https://s4.ad.brown.edu/projects/diversity/Data/Download5.htm.
87. Respondents were asked an open-ended question about why they chose to live in their current neighborhood. They could offer multiple responses.
88. Krysan and Crowder 2017.
89. Lacy 2015.
90. Alexander 2016.
91. Frey 2018.
92. Alexander 2016; Barshay 2019; Groeger, Waldman, and Eads 2018; Turner et al. 2016.
93. Tarasawa 2009.
94. U.S. Office of Civil Rights, "Civil Rights Data Collection," ED.gov, https://ocrdata.ed.gov/flex/Reports.aspx?type=school (accessed June 1, 2020).
95. These estimates were calculated by concatenating data for the ten counties in the Atlanta metro area, using data provided by the Annie E. Casey Foundation (2021).
96. I thank an anonymous reviewer for posing these questions.
97. Traditional destination metropolitan areas are taken from Singer (2008), which provides an update of traditional gateways in 2014 that includes Dallas and Washington, D.C. Although the boundaries of the metropolitan areas changed for each decade with population growth, IPUMS USA provides a code for comparable metropolitan areas from 2000 to 2019. I therefore focus on 2000 onwards for the temporal comparison. For an explanation of the noncomparability of metropolitan area data over time, see IPUMS USA, "Incompletely Identified Metropolitan Areas," https://usa.ipums.org/usa/volii/incompmetareas.shtml.
98. Tran and his colleagues (2018) use the term "hyperselectivity" to define situations in which the average (mean) educational attainment of immigrants from a specific country of origin exceeds the mean education level of their heritage country.
99. Lee and Zhou 2015.
100. Tran et al. 2018.
101. Lozano et al. 2001.
102. Wiarda and Kryzanek 2019, 58.
103. Argue and Velema 2022; Lancee and Bol 2017; Walton et al. 2009; Zeng and Xie 2004.
104. Evans and Moore 2015; Moore 2008.
105. Oropesa and Jensen 2010; Portes and Rumbaut 2014.

106. Economic Innovation Group, "Distressed Communities Index," https://eig.org/dci (accessed February 26, 2021); Nunn, Parsons, and Shambaugh 2019; Pooley 2015; American Community Survey 2017–2021 (U.S. Census Bureau 2022c). For a discussion of these trends in new immigrant gateways throughout the U.S. Southeast, see Winders 2005.
107. Blumer 1958; Bobo and Hutchings 1996.
108. Abascal 2020, 298.
109. Quoted in Lippard 2016, 2.
110. Lippard 2016.
111. Budiman 2020; Lippard 2016.
112. Budiman 2020.
113. Allen 2006.
114. Redmon 2013.
115. Browne and Odem 2012; Odem and Lacy 2009.
116. These statements are based on my analysis of data from the National Conference of State Legislatures. For a more in-depth comparison of how black and white Democrats voted on restrictive immigration policy, see Browne and Odem 2012.
117. See appendix B for a description of how these bills are categorized.
118. Gibbins 2005; Winders 2007.
119. Bohon et al. 2011; Flores and Schachter 2018, 2019.
120. Cummings 2018.
121. See the work of Flores and Schachter (2018), who show that the most common stereotype of undocumented Latines is "criminal."
122. King 2023.
123. McDaniel 2018; City of Atlanta, GA 2023.
124. Provine et al. 2016.

CHAPTER 3: NEGOTIATING RACIAL IDENTITIES

1. Itzigsohn, Giorguli, and Vazquez 2005; Jiménez 2008; Massey and Sánchez 2010; Saperstein 2006.
2. Browne and Odem 2012; Flores-González 2017; Rodriguez 2000.
3. Browne and Odem 2012; Vasquez and Wetzel 2009. This is consistent with the claim in Fleming, Lamont, and Welburn (2012, 411) that responses to stigma are "fed by collective myths and memories about national identity."
4. Fleming, Lamont, and Welburn 2012. See also Lamont et al. 2016.
5. Telles and Garcia 2013.
6. Surveys in Latin America show that the majority of both the Mexican and Dominican populations embrace *mestizaje* beliefs about race and class (Telles and Bailey 2013). Wendy Roth (2012) and Peggy Levitt (2001) claim that social

media, TV, films, and returning migrants expose Latin American residents to U.S. racial categories before they migrate. However, my respondents did not appear to have adopted U.S. race-based categories when they arrived in the United States. They still relied on their heritage belief systems to make sense of race.

7. Telles and Bailey 2013; Wade 2005.
8. Telles 2014; Telles and Paschel 2014; Torres-Saillant 2010.
9. Hernández 2016.
10. Beck, Mijeski, and Stark 2011; Cadena 2001; Hooker 2005; Paschel and Sawyer 2008; Telles and Bailey 2013.
11. Beck, Mijeski, and Stark 2011; Cadena 2001; Hooker 2005; Lewis 2000; Telles 2013.
12. Moreno Figueroa 2010; Telles 2014.
13. Dixon 2019; Telles 2014. There is a debate in the literature over the extent to which skin tone, race, and class influence social mobility in Mexico. Flores and Telles (2012) find evidence that class is the strongest predictor of Mexican stratification.
14. Telles 2014, 29.
15. Villarreal 2010.
16. Telles (2014) and others contend that color does not just refer to skin tone and argue for the interchangeability of "race" and "color" in the English language (Dixon 2019; Hoetink 2000; Wade 1997).
17. Amado 2012; Austerlitz 1997; Beltran 2004; Cadena 2001; Ribero 2013; Telles 2014; Wade 2005.
18. Wade 2005.
19. Vasconcelos 1925/1993.
20. Sue 2013.
21. Cadeau 2022; Sue 2013, 2021.
22. Gómez 2022, 81.
23. Lewis 2000.
24. Nutini 1997; Villarreal 2010, 652.
25. Sue 2013, 6.
26. Villarreal 2010.
27. Dixon 2019.
28. Hoetink 2000. Enslaved persons were also brought to Mexico from Africa, but their numbers were small compared to those taken to the Dominican Republic (Sue 2009).
29. Candelario 2007; Roth 2012.
30. Sagás 1997.
31. Ibid.
32. Bailey 2001; Candelario 2007; Duany 1998; Howard 2001; Torres-Saillant 2010; Sagás 1997.

33. Duany 1996; García-Peña 2015.
34. Candelario 2007; Howard 2001.
35. Candelario 2007.
36. Casas et al. 2014; Telles and Bailey 2013.
37. The "one-drop rule" was based on the nineteenth-century belief that black blood was different from white blood and that "one drop" of black blood rendered an individual black (Bonilla-Silva 2004).
38. Hernández 2021; López 2013; Mora 2014; Roth 2013.
39. Oboler 2021; Rodriguez 2000.
40. Massey and Sánchez 2010. The ability to identify as both "black" and "Latine" or as "white" and "Latine" in the U.S. racial system has prompted scholars to consider "Latine" a "racialized ethnic category" (Cobas, Duany, and Feagin 2015; Golash-Boza and Darity 2008; Grosfoguel 2004; Hitlin, Brown, and Elder 2007; Rodriguez 2000).
41. Bonilla-Silva 2006.
42. Ibid.
43. Masuoka and Junn 2013; O'Brien 2008; Vargas 2015; Yancey 2003.
44. Basler 2014; Vega 2014.
45. Dowling 2014.
46. This finding corresponds to studies showing that first-generation Latin American and Caribbean immigrants are more likely to identify with their country of origin when they can draw prestige from this association (Rumbaut 1994; Waters 1994).
47. We drew these dimensions from the published literature (see especially Roth 2016; Itzigsohn, Giorguli, and Vazquez 2005). The dimensions of race we explore often do not align with each other. Racial identity may change with specific circumstances and with the prompts that interviewers use in the open-ended questions.
48. Focusing on Mexicans, Julie Dowling (2014) claims that belief systems are more central to "racial labeling" than skin color, discrimination, or assimilation. My study extends this work by showing that belief systems also predominate among Dominicans in Atlanta. As I discuss later, Lio's white Dominican identity was an exception to this pattern.
49. This perspective is similar to that of Roth's (2012) Dominican respondents.
50. Alba 2005.
51. Duany 2000; Itzigsohn 2005; Massey and Sánchez 2007; Masuoka 2008; Telles 2014.
52. Respondents could select multiple labels, so totals do not add to 100 percent. The respondents in my sample could identify as Dominican or Mexican/Latino/Hispanic, even when they also indicated a "white" or "black" identity. Census respondents could designate multiple categories as well, including "white," "black," and "other." A national designation (Dominican or Mexican) was not available as a response in the race question on the census.

53. This finding is consistent with the literature, which shows that national origin is a preferred identity category for first-generation Latine immigrants (Jones-Correa and Leal 1996; Masuoka 2008).
54. This pattern is consistent with published studies, which show that, across the class spectrum, Mexicans strongly identify with a national label and a secondary labeling as "Latino" (Masuoka 2008).
55. Itzigsohn 2009.
56. Duany 1998.
57. This perspective reflects patterns found in the literature; see Taylor et al. 2012.
58. None of the Mexican respondents claimed an "indigenous" identity.
59. For example, see Hernández 2021. My results are similar to findings from José Itzigsohn, Silvia Giorguli, and Obed Vazquez's (2005) study of first-generation Dominicans. In response to the survey question "Are you white, black, or other (specify)?," a much lower proportion (3 percent) of their Dominican sample selected a "white" identity when the race question was posed this way and offered no other options.
60. Oboler 1995; Roth 2020.
61. For similar findings about rejecting whiteness, see Frank, Akresh and Lu 2010.
62. Bailey 2001; Candelario 2007; Roth 2008.
63. Bailey 2000, 2001; Candelario 2007; Dowling and Newby 2010; Itzigsohn and Dore-Cabral 2000; Itzigsohn, Giorguli, and Vazquez 2005; Levitt 2001; Roth 2012.
64. Hamilton 2019; Waters 1999.
65. Bailey 2000; Toribio 2000.
66. Steinberg 2005.
67. Itzigsohn, Giorguli, and Vazquez 2005.
68. Candelario 2007; Dixon 2019; Telles and Paschel 2014.
69. We measured skin tone only for a subset of the Dominican respondents (see the methodological appendix). We used a skin tone scale developed by Massey and Martin for the New Immigrant Survey (NIS) in which interviewers matched respondents' skin tone to photos of hands in varying shades. The scale can be found at "NIS Skin Color Scale," https://nis.princeton.edu/downloads/nis-skin-color-scale.pdf.
70. Dowling 2014; Roth 2012; Telles and Paschel 2014.
71. Roth 2012; Wade 2005.
72. Candelario 2007, 263.
73. Wade (2005, 239, emphasis added) also discusses mestizaje identity as "a lived process that operates within person and within *networks of family*."
74. Candelario 2007. Our respondents' evoking of their genetic heritage is consistent with Roth's (2012) finding that this racial categorization (or "schema") predominates among well-educated Dominicans.
75. Dowling 2014.
76. Torres-Saillant 2010.

77. Candelario 2007; Waters 1994.
78. Melamed et al. 2019; Roth 2012.
79. Hamilton 2019; Waters 1999.
80. Roth 2013, 94.
81. Candelario 2007.
82. Mora 2014.
83. Ibid.
84. For a discussion of moral distinctions in the construction of race- and nation-based boundaries among working-class men, see Lamont 2001.
85. Martínez and Gonzalez 2021; Massey and Sánchez 2010.
86. Itzigsohn, Giorguli, and Vazquez 2005.
87. Dulitzky 2005.

CHAPTER 4: STIGMA AND THE IMAGE OF THE "TYPICAL LATINE"

1. This chapter builds on Browne, Tatum, and González (2021).
2. Aas and Boswort 2014; Armenta 2017; Deckard et al. 2020; Valenta 2009.
3. Goffman 1963.
4. Lamont and Mizrachi 2013.
5. Hegtvedt and Johnson 2018.
6. Monk 2015, 2022.
7. Jiménez 2008; Menjívar 2021; Simmons et al. 2018; Zepeda-Millán 2017.
8. Parts of the discussion of the figure are reprinted from Browne, Tatum, and González 2021.
9. "Juan Valdez" was dropped from promotional materials in the 1990s but recently was readopted by the Colombian growers' association (McAteer 2018; Molleda and Roberts 2008).
10. BackYardSounds 2011.
11. This is one of the few instances in my interviews where the respondent specifically noted the gender of the typical Latine. While Jade described the "typical Mexican" as a man, most of my respondents did not mention gender. I therefore do not have sufficient data to assess the role of gender in the typical image.
12. Flores and Schachter 2019.
13. Jiménez 2010. Jiménez emphasizes that non-Mexicans continue to assume that all Mexicans are immigrants because the Mexican immigrant population is constantly "replenished" in localities where later generations of immigrants live.
14. Ibid. For a discussion of similar strategies used by African Americans in responding to stigma, see Lamont et al. 2016.
15. For a study of how middle-class blacks signal their education and profession

as a strategy to combat negative stereotypes and "everyday racism," see Lamont and Fleming 2005; Lamont et al. 2016.

16. Flores and Schachter 2018.
17. Deckard and Browne 2015.
18. Selma was undocumented with a high school diploma. Though not included in the analyses of middle-class Latine immigrants in this book, she appears here to illustrate class distinctions in approaches to authorized legal status.
19. García 2019.
20. Flores and Schachter 2018.
21. Kaiser and Miller 2001; Roth 2008; Ruggiero et al. 2000.
22. Kaiser and Miller 2001.
23. Brettell 2011, chap. 12; Dovidio et al. 2010; Feagin and Cobas 2015; Findling et al. 2019; Hegtvedt and Johnson 2018; Marrow et al. 2022; Veenman 2010.
24. Brettell 2011.
25. These overall rates of discrimination among my middle-class Mexican respondents are higher than the rates of discrimination among Mexican immigrants reported in other studies, which range from 24 percent to 40 percent (Brettell 2011; Marrow et al. 2022). My findings on discrimination experienced by Dominicans show rates lower than those reported in the literature, which range from 46 percent to 75 percent (Roth 2008). This wide variation in reports of discrimination across studies is likely to be due to differences in sample characteristics (class, geography, skin tone) and differences in question wording.
26. Jones 2019.
27. These statements are based on chi-square values for cross-tabulations of year of interview with experiences of mistreatment and perceptions of group discrimination.
28. I thank an anonymous Russell Sage Foundation reviewer for highlighting these points.
29. Bonilla-Silva 2006.
30. For a discussion of this attitude among Dominicans, see Roth 2008.
31. Chambers 2017; Roth 2008.
32. O'Brien 2008; Warikoo and Bloemraad 2018. The colorblind perspective used by my Mexican and Dominican respondents accords with Nicholas Vargas's (2015) research on Latine who identify as white. He found that Latines who identify as white but are not categorized as white by others ("contested white identities") are more likely to rely on a colorblind racial ideology than white-identified Latine whose identities are not contested. This move by those whose status as white is not secure, in Vargas's interpretation, is an effort to move closer to whiteness. My interviews compare the colorblind perspectives of first-generation immigrants from Mexico and the Dominican Republic whose identities are attached to these countries rather than to whiteness.
33. O'Brien 2008.

34. Ibid.
35. Senft et al. 2021.
36. Evans and Moore 2015. Jackson and Wingfield (2013) and Fleming, Lamont, and Welburn (2012) refer to these strategies as aspects of "managing the self" in the face of stigmatization.
37. American Psychological Association 2023.
38. For a study of how some Dominicans in New York perceive "color discrimination" in the United States and the Dominican Republic while others claim that there is no color discrimination, see Roth 2008.
39. Jones 2019.
40. This is the strategy that Crystal Fleming, Michèle Lamont, and Jessica Welburn (2012) find is most common among African Americans.
41. Jiménez 2010.
42. Browne, Tatum, and González 2021.
43. Higginbotham 1994.
44. Martinez-Cola 2021.
45. Dazey 2021; Martinez-Cola 2021.

CHAPTER 5: LEVERAGING COSMOPOLITAN ORIENTATIONS AND RESOURCES

1. Cobas and Feagin 2008; Davis and Moore 2014; Levitt 2001; Peterson and Kern 1996; Rössel and Schroedter 2015; Telles and Ortiz 2008. This chapter builds on Tatum and Browne 2019.
2. Johnston and Baumann 2007.
3. Bourdieu 1984; Lamont and Lareau 1988.
4. For a discussion of the state being at the center of developing "migrant cultural capital," see Kim 2018.
5. Igarashi and Saito 2014; Lechner and Boli 2019; Prieur and Savage 2013.
6. Callero 2008; Watson 2018.
7. Those following this definition include Igarashi and Saito 2014; Merton 1968; Prieur and Savage 2013; Rössel and Schroedter 2015; Vertovec and Cohen 2002; Watson 2018; Weenink 2008.
8. Calhoun 2020, 5.
9. Prieur and Savage 2013; Rössel and Schroedter 2015.
10. Weenink 2008.
11. Prieur and Savage 2013.
12. For discussions of cosmopolitan orientations among working-class individuals, see Alarcón 2007; Hannerz 1990; Holt 1997; Lamont and Aksartova 2002; Warikoo 2004. I focus on the elite forms of cosmopolitan cultural capital, which include high educational credentials and the economic means to

sustain the elements of a cosmopolitan lifestyle, such as world travel and fine dining.

13. Maxwell and Yemini 2019, 617.
14. Jones-Correa et al. 2011; Kaufman 2003; McClain et al. 2007; McDermott 2011; Warikoo 2004.
15. In many of our interviews, respondents equated "American" with "white."
16. Tatum and Browne 2019; see also Jiménez and Horowitz 2013.
17. Theiss-Morse, Gonzalez, and O'Toole 2020.
18. Mootz 2009; Walle 1990.
19. Lamont and Aksartova 2002; Zeng 2014.
20. Lamont and Mizrachi 2013; Sherman 2005; Sykes and Matza 1957.
21. Bourdieu and Passeron 1990.
22. Watson 2018, 8.
23. Ball and Nikita 2014; Heiman et al. 2012; Rössel and Schroedter 2015.
24. I am using the term "middle-class orientation" as a synonym for Bourdieu's concept of "habitus," that is, an approach to the world that encompasses worldviews, styles of comportment, dispositions, tastes, and expectations.
25. Ball and Nikita 2014.
26. Hughes 2003.
27. Portes and Rumbaut 2001.
28. Hughes 2003, 16.
29. Hughes 2003.
30. Warikoo 2004.
31. Itzigsohn 2009; Levitt 2001; Portes and Zhou 1993; Smith 2006; Waters et al. 2010.
32. Portes and Rumbaut 2001; Rumbaut, Massey, and Bean 2006; Tran 2010.
33. For a discussion of the friendship network in relation to assimilation, see Greenman and Xie 2008.
34. Lamont and Aksartova 2002; Warikoo 2004.
35. Zamora 2018, 1901.
36. Capetillo-Ponce 2010; Hero and Preuhs 2013; Jones 2019; Jones-Correa et al. 2011; Kaufman 2003; McClain et al. 2007; McDermott 2011.
37. McDermott 2011; Ribas 2015; Tropp et al. 2018.
38. Bobo and Hutchings 1996.
39. Jones-Correa et al. 2011; Kaufman 2003; McDermott 2011; Meier et al. 2004; Ribas 2015. Note that Rodney Hero and Robert Preuhs (2013) find little evidence for threat at the level of national politics.
40. Jones 2019.
41. Okamoto et al. 2020; Tropp et al. 2018.
42. Lareau 2003.
43. Berrey 2021.

44. Lamont and Aksartova 2002.
45. Berrey 2021.
46. Evans 2021.
47. Berrey 2021.
48. Ibid.
49. Kun and Pulido 2014.
50. Maxwell and Yemini 2019; Weenink 2008.
51. Maxwell and Yemini 2019, 617.
52. Nussbaum 1994.
53. Calhoun 2020; Nussbaum 1994; Watson 2018.
54. Lamont and Aksartova 2002, 3.
55. Link and Phelan 2001, 375.
56. For a similar discussion of the impact of responding to stigma on the health and well-being of African Americans, see Lamont et al. 2016.

CHAPTER 6: UNDERSTANDING THE RACIALIZATION OF ILLEGALITY THROUGH A MIDDLE-CLASS LENS

1. Kontonis 2021.
2. I thank an anonymous reviewer for pointing out this pattern and its relevance to my study.
3. Respondents' positive views of Atlanta did not appear to be connected to their lighter skin tones.
4. Tropp et al. 2018. It also is likely that this is a self-selected group: Dominicans and Mexicans who have had negative experiences in Atlanta are likely to have the resources to move out of Georgia.
5. Greenman and Xie 2008, 5.
6. Ibid., 7.
7. Jiménez 2010; Portes and Zhou 1993.
8. Adem et al. 2022.
9. Marrow 2020.
10. Goffman 1963; Link and Phelan 2001; Miller and Kaiser 2001.
11. Brettell 2011; Cobas, Duany, and Feagin 2015; Essed 2008; Pérez, Fortuna, and Alegría 2008.
12. Evans and Moore 2015, 441.
13. Festinger 1957.
14. Link and Phelan 2001; Lamont et al. 2016.
15. See Lamont (2001) for a discussion of morality-based rationales for constructing group boundaries.
16. Chiswick and Miller 2009; Shirmohammadi, Beigi, and Stewart 2019; Subedi and Rosenberg 2016.

17. Alamillo 2019; Basler 2014; McCann and Jones-Correa 2020; Soto-Vásquez and Sánchez-Santos 2022.
18. Cadava 2020.
19. Murphy 2022.
20. Brown 2013; Brown, Jones, and Dow 2016.
21. Howarth 2006.
22. Del Real 2019; Lamont 2019.
23. Fernández-Kelly 2008, 11.
24. Jiménez 2010.
25. I thank an anonymous reviewer for raising this point.
26. Pescosolido and Martin 2015, 101.
27. Waters and Kasinitz 2015.
28. Lamont 2019, 663.

APPENDIX B: CODING FOR GEORGIA IMMIGRATION BILLS, 2005–2016

1. Browne et al. 2018, 1701.
2. Browne et al. 2018.
3. NAACP 2023.
4. Hero and Preuhs 2013, 105, fig. 4.I.

APPENDIX C: METHODS

1. Jonsson 2006.
2. We interviewed additional respondents who were born and raised in the United States or who did not have a college degree. I do not include them in the analyses in the book.
3. Selina Gallo-Cruz was instrumental during the interview phase of the study. She recruited respondents and conducted, translated, and transcribed many of the interviews.
4. Lacy 2004.
5. Yan, Curtin, and Jans 2010.
6. Much of this coding was conducted by my coauthor, Katharine Tatum.
7. Browne and Odem 2012; Odem and Browne 2011.
8. Browne, Tatum, and González 2021.
9. Tatum and Browne 2019.
10. Clark Brinson assisted in coding respondent relations with African Americans.
11. Mellor et al. 2014; Reay 1996.
12. Mellor et al. 2014, 4.
13. Ibid., 5.
14. Reay 1996.

15. Ibid.
16. De Onís 2017.
17. Oboler 2021.
18. Ibid., 68.
19. Mora, Perez, and Vargas 2022; Oboler 1992.
20. Salinas and Lozano 2021.
21. De Onís 2017.
22. Mora, Perez, and Vargas 2022.
23. Marrow 2011, 270.

References

Aas, Katja Franko, and Mary Bosworth. 2014. *The Borders of Punishment: Migration, Citizenship, and Social Exclusion*. Oxford: Oxford University Press.

Abascal, Maria. 2020. "Contraction as a Response to Group Threat: Demographic Decline and Whites' Classification of People Who Are Ambiguously White." *American Sociological Review* 85(2): 298–322.

Abrego, Leisy, Mat Coleman, Daniel E. Martínez, Cecilia Menjívar, and Jeremy Slack. 2017. "Making Immigrants into Criminals: Legal Processes of Criminalization in the Post-IIRIRA Era." *Journal on Migration and Human Security* 5(3): 694–715.

Adem, Muna, Sehlley Rao, Helen Marrow, Melissa García, and Dina Okamoto. 2022. "A Relational Approach to Perceived Discrimination: The Case of South Asian Indians." *Social Psychology Quarterly* (August 19). DOI: https://doi.org/10.1177/01902725221121825.

Agius Vallejo, Jody. 2012. "Socially Mobile Mexican Americans and the Minority Culture of Mobility." *American Behavioral Scientist* 56(5): 666–81.

———. 2020. *Barrios to Burbs: The Making of the Mexican Middle Class*. Stanford, Calif.: Stanford University Press.

Agius Vallejo, Jody, and Stephanie L. Canizales. 2016. "Latino/a Professionals as Entrepreneurs: How Race, Class, and Gender Shape Entrepreneurial Incorporation." *Ethnic and Racial Studies* 39(9): 1637–56.

———. 2021. "Ethnoracial Capitalism and the Limits of Ethnic Solidarity." *Social Problems* (December 3). DOI: https://doi.org/10.1093/socpro/spab067.

Aiello, Thomas, 2014. "The First Fissure: The Du Bois–Washington Relationship from 1898–1899." *Phylon* 51(10): 76–87.

Alamillo, Rudy. 2019. "Hispanics Para Trump? Denial of Racism and Hispanic Support for Trump." *DuBois Review: Social Science Research on Race* 16(2): 457–87.

Alarcón, Rafael. 2007. "The Free Circulation of Skilled Migrants in North America." In *Migration without Borders: Essays on the Free Movement of People*, edited by Antoine Pécoud and Paul de Guchteneire. New York: Berghahn Books/UNESCO.

Alba, Richard. 2005. "Bright vs. Blurred Boundaries: Second-Generation Assimilation and Exclusion in France, Germany, and the United States." *Ethnic and Racial Studies* 28(1): 20–49.

Alba, Richard D., and Victor Nee. 1997. "Rethinking Assimilation Theory for a New Era of Immigration." *International Migration Review* 31(4): 826–74.

———. 2003. *Remaking the American Mainstream: Assimilation and Contemporary Immigration*. Cambridge, Mass.: Harvard University Press.

Alexander, Michael. 2016. "The Diversity Explosion in Metro Atlanta's Schools 2016." Atlanta Regional Commission report. https://app.box.com/s/3xmubhlgfpej3lnnetvodup5hfvhifge (accessed June 1, 2020).

Allen, Ann. 2006. "Peach State Poll Respondents: Immigration Is Good for Country." University of Georgia, *UGA Today*, September 25. https://news.uga.edu/peach-state-poll-respondents-immigration-is-good-for-country/.

Amado, María L. 2012. "The 'New Mestiza,' the Old Mestizos: Contrasting Discourses on Mestizaje." *Sociological Inquiry* 82(3): 446–59.

Ambinakudige, Shrinidhi, Domenico Parisi, Giorgio Carlo Cappello, and Aynaz Lotfata. 2017. "Diversity or Segregation? A Multi-Decadal Spatial Analysis of Demographics of Atlanta Neighborhoods." *Spatial Demography* 5: 123–44.

American Psychological Association. 2023. *American Psychological Association Dictionary of Psychology*. https://dictionary.apa.org/complex.

Annie E. Casey Foundation. 2021."Kids Count Data Book." June 21. https://www.aecf.org/resources/2021-kids-count-data-book.

Aranda, Elizabeth, Cecilia Menjívar, and Katharine M. Donato. 2014. "The Spillover Consequences of an Enforcement-First U.S. Immigration Regime." *American Behavioral Scientist* 58(13): 1687–95.

Aranda, Elizabeth, and Elizabeth Vaquera. 2015. "Racism, the Immigration Enforcement Regime, and the Implications for Racial Inequality in the Lives of Undocumented Young Adults." *Sociology of Race and Ethnicity* 1(1): 88–104.

Argue, Andrew J., and Thijs A. Velema. 2022. "University Prestige, Cultural Distance of the Place of Education, and Wage Differences between High-Skilled U.S. Immigrants with Foreign and Domestic Credentials." *Research in Social Stratification and Mobility* 77(February): 100650. DOI: https://doi.org/10.1016/j.rssm.2021.100650.

Armenta, Amada. 2017. "Racializing Crimmigration: Structural Racism, Colorblindness, and the Institutional Production of Immigrant Criminality." *Sociology of Race and Ethnicity* 3(1): 82–95.

Arrocha, William. 2012. "From Arizona's SB 1070 to Georgia's HB 87 and Alabama's HB 56: Exacerbating the Other and Generating New Discourses and Practices of Segregation." *California Western Law Review* 48: 245–78.

Asad, Asad L., and Matthew Clair. 2018. "Racialized Legal Status as a Social Determinant of Health." *Social Science and Medicine* 199(February): 19–28.

Atlanta History Center. 2021. *Black Citizenship in the Age of Jim Crow.* Exhibition held

February 17, 2021. https://www.atlantahistorycenter.com/blog/each-one-teach-one/.

Austerlitz, Paul. 1997. Merengue: *Dominican Music and Dominican Identity*. Philadelphia: Temple University Press.

BackYardSounds. 2011. "Classic Juan Valdez Colombian Coffee (1982)." YouTube. https://www.youtube.com/watch?v=m_INwKKJKK4.

Badger, Emily. 2016. "This Can't Happen by Accident." *Washington Post*, May 2. https://www.washingtonpost.com/graphics/business/wonk/housing/atlanta/.

Badie, Rick. 2004. "Panelists Denounce Illegal Immigrants." *Atlanta Journal-Constitution*, February 3.

Badillo, David A. 2013. "Shaping Twenty-First-Century Civil Rights Advocacy: Latinos in Metro Atlanta." *Norteamérica* 8(suppl.): 119–39.

Bailey, Benjamin. 2000. "Language and Negotiation of Ethnic/Racial Identity among Dominican Americans." *Language in Society* 29(4): 555–82.

———. 2001. "Dominican-American Ethnic/Racial Identities and United States Social Categories." *International Migration Review* 35(3): 677–708. DOI: https://doi.org/10.1111/j.1747-7379.2001.tb00036.x.

Ball, Stephen J., and Dimitra Pavlina Nikita. 2014. "The Global Middle Class and School Choice: A Cosmopolitan Sociology." *Zeitschrift für Erziehungswissenschaft* 17(3): 81–93.

Barlow, M. Rose, and Joanna N. Lahey. 2018. "What Race Is Lacey? Intersecting Perceptions of Racial Minority Status and Social Class." *Social Science Quarterly* 99(5): 1680–98.

Barshay, Jill. 2019. "An Analysis of Achievement Gaps in Every School in America Shows That Poverty Is the Biggest Hurdle." *The Hechinger Report*. New York: Columbia University. https://hechingerreport.org/an-analysis-of-achievement-gaps-in-every-school-in-america-shows-that-being-poor-is-the-biggest-hurdle/.

Basler, Carleen. 2014. "White Dreams and Red Votes: Mexican Americans and the Lure of Inclusion in the Republican Party." In *Retheorizing Race and Whiteness in the 21st Century: Changes and Challenges*, edited by Charles A. Gallagher and France Winddance Twine. New York: Routledge.

Bayor, Ronald H. 1996. *Race and the Shaping of Twentieth-Century Atlanta*. Chapel Hill: University of North Carolina Press.

———. 2000. "Atlanta: The Historical Paradox." In *The Atlanta Paradox*, edited by David L. Sjoquist. New York: Russell Sage Foundation.

Beck, Scott H., Kenneth J. Mijeski, and Meagan M. Stark. 2011. "¿Qué Es Racismo?: Awareness of Racism and Discrimination in Ecuador." *Latin American Research Review* 46(1): 102–25.

Beltran, Cristina. 2004. "Patrolling Borders: Hybrids, Hierarchies, and the Challenge of Mestizaje." *Political Research Quarterly* 57(4): 597–607.

Berger, Joseph, Cecilia L. Ridgeway, and Morris Zelditch. 2002. "Construction of Status and Referential Structures." *Sociological Theory* 20(2): 157–79.

Berrey, Ellen. 2021. "The Enigma of Diversity." In Berrey, *The Enigma of Diversity: The Language of Race and the Limits of Racial Justice.* Chicago: University of Chicago Press.

Bloch, Katrina Rebecca. 2014. "'Anyone Can Be an Illegal': Color-Blind Ideology and Maintaining Latino/Citizen Borders." *Critical Sociology* 40(1): 47–65.

Blumer, Herbert. 1958. "Race Prejudice as a Sense of Group Position." *Pacific Sociological* 1(1, Spring).

Bobo, Lawrence, and Vincent L. Hutchings. 1996. "Perceptions of Racial Group Competition: Extending Blumer's Theory of Group Position to a Multiracial Social Context." *American Sociological Review* 61(6): 951–72.

Bohn, Sarah, and Magnus Lofstrom. 2012. "Employment Effects of State Legislation against the Hiring of Unauthorized Immigrant Workers." IZA Discussion Paper 6598. Institute for the Study of Labor, May. https://docs.iza.org/dp6598.pdf.

Bohon, Stephanie, Heather Macpherson Parrott, Cameron D. Lippard, and Charles A. Gallagher. 2011. "The Myth of Millions: Socially Constructing 'Illegal Immigration.'" In *Being Brown in Dixie: Race, Ethnicity, and Latino Immigration in the New South*, edited by Cameron D. Lippard and Charles A. Gallagher. Boulder, Colo.: First Forum Press.

Boissoneault, Lorraine. 2017. "What Will Happen to Stone Mountain, America's Largest Confederate Memorial?" *Smithsonian*, August 22. https://www.smithsonianmag.com/history/what-will-happen-stone-mountain-americas-largest-confederate-memorial-180964588/.

Bonilla-Silva, Eduardo. 2001. *White Supremacy and Racism in the Post–Civil Rights Era.* Boulder, Colo.: Lynne Rienner Publishers.

———. 2004. "From Bi-Racial to Tri-Racial: Towards a New System of Racial Stratification in the USA." *Ethnic and Racial Studies* 27(6): 931–50.

———. 2006. *Racism without Racists: Color-Blind Racism and the Persistence of Racial Inequality in the United States.* Lanham, Md.: Rowman & Littlefield Publishers.

Bosworth, Mary, Alpa Parmar, and Yolanda Vázquez, eds. 2018. *Race, Criminal Justice, and Migration Control: Enforcing the Boundaries of Belonging.* Oxford: Oxford University Press.

Bourdieu, Pierre. 1984. *Distinction: A Social Critique of the Judgement of Taste*, translated by Richard Nice. Cambridge, Mass.: Harvard University Press.

———. 1998. "La précarité est aujourd'hui partout" (Precarity is everywhere today). In Bourdieu, *Contre-feux.* Paris: Les Éditions Raisons d'Agir.

———. 2018. "Cultural Reproduction and Social Reproduction." In *Knowledge, Education, and Cultural Change*, edited by Richard Brown. London: Routledge. (Originally published in 1973.)

Bourdieu, Pierre, and Jean-Claude Passeron. 1990. *Reproduction in Education, Society, and Culture.* Thousand Oaks, Calif.: SAGE Publications.

Bratton, Michael. 2021. "Defining, Unpacking, and Contextualizing Class Privilege to Extend the Intersectional Scope of Privilege Studies." *Understanding and Dismantling Privilege* 11(2): 46–83.

Braxton, Greg. 2019. "Tyler Perry Studios, the House 'Medea' Built, Becomes a Landmark for Black Hollywood." *Los Angeles Times*, October 2. https://www.latimes.com/entertainment-arts/tv/story/2019-10-02/tyler-perry-studios-atlanta-dedication (accessed February 24, 2021).

Brettell, Caroline B. 2011. "Experiencing Everyday Discrimination: A Comparison across Five Immigrant Populations." *Race and Social Problems* 3(4): 266–79.

Brezina, Timothy, and Kenisha Winder. 2003. "Economic Disadvantage, Status Generalization, and Negative Racial Stereotyping by White Americans." *Social Psychology Quarterly* 66(4): 402–18.

Bridges, Khiara M. 2018. "Excavating Race-Based Disadvantage among Class-Privileged People of Color." *Harvard Civil Rights–Civil Liberties Law Review* 53: 65.

Brodkin, Karen. 1998. *How Jews Became White Folks and What That Says about Race in America.* New Brunswick, N.J.: Rutgers University Press.

Brown, Hana E. 2013. "Race, Legality, and the Social Policy Consequences of Anti-Immigration Mobilization." *American Sociological Review* 78(2): 290–314.

Brown, Hana E., Jennifer A. Jones, and Andrea Becker. 2018. "The Racialization of Latino Immigrants in New Destinations: Criminality, Ascription, and Counter-mobilization." *RSF: The Russell Sage Foundation Journal of the Social Sciences* 4(5, August): 118–40. DOI: https://doi.org/10.7758/RSF.2018.4.5.06.

Brown, Hana E., Jennifer A. Jones, and Taylor Dow. 2016. "Unity in the Struggle: Immigration and the South's Emerging Civil Rights Consensus." *Law and Contemporary Problems* 79(3): 5.

Browne, Irene, and Mary Odem. 2012. "'Juan Crow' in the *Nuevo South*? Racialization of Guatemalan and Dominican Immigrants in the Atlanta Metro Area." *Du Bois Review* 9(2): 321–37.

Browne, Irene, Beth Reingold, and Anne Kronberg. 2018. "Race Relations, Black Elites, and Immigration Politics: Conflict, Commonalities, and Context." *Social Forces* 96(4): 1691–1720.

Browne, Irene, Katharine Tatum, and Belisa González. 2021. "Presumed Mexican until Proven Otherwise: Identity Work and Intersectional Typicality among Middle-Class Dominican and Mexican Immigrants." *Social Problems* 68(1): 80–99.

Brown-Nagin, Tomiko. 2011. *Courage to Dissent: Atlanta and the Long History of the Civil Rights Movement.* Oxford: Oxford University Press.

Budiman, Abby. 2020. "Key Findings about U.S. Immigrants." Pew Research Center, August 20. https://www.pewresearch.org/short-reads/2020/08/20/key-findings-about-u-s-immigrants/.

Bullard, Robert D. 2007. *The Black Metropolis in the Twenty-First Century: Race, Power, and Politics.* Lanham, Md.: Rowman and Littlefield.

Burke, Peter J., and Jan E. Stets. 2021. "The Microsociology of Self and Identity." In *Theoretical Sociology: The Future of a Disciplinary Foundation*, edited by Seth Abrutyn and Kevin McCaffree. New York: Routledge.

Burns, Rebecca. 2009. *Rage in the Gate City: The Story of the 1906 Atlanta Race Riot.* Athens: University of Georgia Press.

Cadava, Geraldo. 2020. "The Deep Origins of Latino Support for Trump." *The New Yorker*, December 29. https://www.newyorker.com/news/the-political-scene/the-deep-origins-of-latino- support-for-trump.

Cadeau, Sabine F. 2022. *More than a Massacre: Racial Violence and Citizenship in the Haitian-Dominican Borderlands.* Cambridge: Cambridge University Press.

Cadena, Marisol de la. 2001. "Reconstructing Race: Racism, Culture, and Mestizaje in Latin America." *NACLA (North American Congress on Latin America) Report on the Americas* 34(6): 16–23.

Calhoun, Craig. 2020. "The Class Consciousness of Frequent Travellers: Towards a Critique of Actually Existing Cosmopolitanism." In *Enchantments of Modernity: Empire, Nation, Globalization*, edited by Saurabh Dube. New Delhi: Routledge India.

Callero, Peter L. 2008. "The Globalization of Self: Role and Identity Transformation from Above and Below." *Sociology Compass* 2(6): 1972–88.

Callister, Adam Henry, Quinn Galbraith, and Spencer Galbraith. 2019. "Immigration, Deportation, and Discrimination: Hispanic Political Opinion since the Election of Donald Trump." *Hispanic Journal of Behavioral Sciences* 41(2): 166–84.

Candelario, Ginetta E. B. 2007. *Black behind the Ears: Dominican Racial Identity from Museums to Beauty Shops.* Durham, N.C.: Duke University Press.

Canizales, Stephanie L., and Jody Agius Vallejo. 2021. "Latinos and Racism in the Trump Era." *Daedalus* 150(2): 150–64.

Capetillo-Ponce, Jorge. 2010. "Black-Latino/a Relations in Boston: Two Trends of Collective Identification." *Latino Studies* 8(2): 244–70.

Carey, Tony E. Jr., Regina P. Branton, and Valerie Martinez-Ebers. 2014. "The Influence of Social Protests on Issue Salience among Latinos." *Political Research Quarterly* 67(3): 615–27.

Casas, Regina Martínez, Emiko Saldívar, René D. Flores, and Christina A Sue. 2014. "The Different Faces of Mestizaje: Ethnicity and Race in Mexico." In *Pigmentocracies: Ethnicity, Race, and Color in Latin America*, edited by Edward Telles. Chapel Hill: University of North Carolina Press.

Chacón, Jennifer M., and Susan Bibler Coutin. 2018. "Racialization through Enforcement." In *Race, Criminal Justice, and Migration Control: Enforcing the Boundaries of Belonging*, edited by M. Bosworth, A. Parmar, and Y. Vázquez. New York: Oxford University Press.

Chambers, Glenn A. 2017. "Color-Blind Nationalism, U.S. Empire, and the Conundrum of Race in the Late Nineteenth- and Twentieth-Century Spanish Caribbean." *Latin American Research Review* 52(5): 895–900.

Chavez, Leo R. 2012. *Shadowed Lives: Undocumented Immigrants in American Society*, 3rd ed. Boston: Cengage Learning.

———. 2013. *The Latino Threat: Constructing Immigrants, Citizens, and the Nation.* Stanford, Calif.: Stanford University Press.

Cheng, Wendy. 2013. *The Changs Next Door to the Díazes: Remapping Race in Suburban California.* Minneapolis: University of Minnesota Press.

Chiswick, Barry R., and Paul W. Miller. 2009. "Educational Mismatch: Are High-Skilled Immigrants Really Working at High-Skilled Jobs and the Price They Pay if They Aren't?" SULCIS Working Paper 2010:7. Stockholm University Linnaeus Center for Integration Studies.

City of Atlanta, GA. 2023. "Mayor's Office of International & Immigrant Affairs: Welcoming Atlanta." https://www.welcomingatlanta.com/ (accessed September 2, 2023).

Clark, William A. V. 2003. *Immigrants and the American Dream: Remaking the Middle Class.* New York: Guilford Press.

Cobas, José A., Jorge Duany, and Joe R. Feagin. 2015. *How the United States Racializes Latinos: White Hegemony and Its Consequences.* New York: Routledge.

Cobas, José A., and Joe R. Feagin. 2008. "Language Oppression and Resistance: The Case of Middle Class Latinos in the United States." *Ethnic and Racial Studies* 31(2): 390–410.

Coleman, Mat, and Austin Kocher. 2019. "Rethinking the 'Gold Standard' of Racial Profiling: §287(g), Secure Communities, and Racially Discrepant Police Power." *American Behavioral Scientist* 63(9): 1185–1220.

Commins, Margaret M., and Jeremiah B. Wills. 2017. "Reappraising and Extending the Predictors of States' Immigrant Policies: Industry Influences and the Moderating Effect of Political Ideology." *Social Science Quarterly* 98(1): 212–29.

Corrigan, Patrick W., Amy C. Watson, Mark L. Heyrman, Amy Warpinski, Gabriela Gracia, Natalie Slopen, and Laura L. Hall. 2005. "Structural Stigma in State Legislation." *Psychiatric Services* 56(5): 557–63.

Cummings, William. 2018. "Georgia Republican Who Campaigned for Governor in 'Deportation Bus' Reports to Jail." *USA Today*, December 27. https://www.usatoday.com/story/news/politics/onpolitics/2018/12/27/michael-williams-georgia-jail-insurance-fraud/2420141002/.

Davis, Tiffany Y., and Wendy Leo Moore. 2014. "Spanish Not Spoken Here: Accounting for the Racialization of the Spanish Language in the Experiences of Mexican Migrants in the United States." *Ethnicities* 14(5, October): 676–97.

Dazey, Margot. 2021. "Rethinking Respectability Politics." *British Journal of Sociology* 72(3): 580–93.

Deckard, Natalie Delia, and Irene Browne. 2015. "Constructing Citizenship: Framing Unauthorized Immigrants in Market Terms." *Citizenship Studies* 19(6–7): 664–81.

Deckard, Natalie Delia, Irene Browne, Cassaundra Rodriguez, Marisela Martinez-Cola, and Sofia Gonzalez Leal. 2020. "Controlling Images of Immigrants in the Mainstream and Black Press: The Discursive Power of the 'Illegal Latino.'" *Latino Studies* 18(4): 581–602.

De Genova, Nicholas P. 2002. "Migrant 'Illegality' and Deportability in Everyday Life." *Annual Review of Anthropology* 31(1): 419–47. DOI: https://doi.org/ 10.1146 /annurev.anthro.31.040402.085432.

———. 2004. "The Legal Production of Mexican Illegality." *Latino Studies* 2: 160–85.

Del Real, Deisy. 2019. "'They See Us Like Trash': How Mexican Illegality Stigma Affects the Psychological Well-being of Undocumented and U.S.-Born Young Adults of Mexican Descent." In *Immigration and Health*, vol. 19, edited by Reanne Frank. Bingley, U.K.: Emerald Publishing.

De Onís, Catalina Kathleen M. 2017. "What's in an 'X'?: An Exchange about the Politics of 'Latinx.'" *Chiricú Journal: Latina/o Literatures, Arts, and Cultures* 1(2): 78–91.

Dhingra, Pawan. 2012. *Life behind the Lobby: Indian American Motel Owners and the American Dream.* Stanford, Calif.: Stanford University Press.

Diamond, Jeff. 1998. "African-American Attitudes towards United States Immigration Policy." *International Migration Review* 32(2): 451–70.

Dixon, Angela R. 2019. "Colorism and Classism Confounded: Perceptions of Discrimination in Latin America." *Social Science Research* 79: 32–55.

Dixon, Angela R., and Edward E. Telles. 2017. "Skin Color and Colorism: Global Research, Concepts, and Measurement." *Annual Review of Sociology* 43: 405–24.

Donato, Katharine M., and Catalina Amuedo-Dorantes. 2020. "The Legal Landscape of U.S. Immigration: An Introduction." RSF: *The Russell Sage Foundation Journal of the Social Sciences* 6(3, November): 1–16. DOI: https://doi.org/10.7758 /rsf.2020.6.3.01.

Donato, Katharine M., and Leslie Ann Rodríguez. 2014. "Police Arrests in a Time of Uncertainty: The Impact of 287(g) on Arrests in a New Immigrant Gateway." *American Behavioral Scientist* 58(13): 1696–1722.

Dovidio, John F., Agata Gluszek, Melissa-Sue John, Ruth Ditlmann, and Paul Lagunes. 2010. "Understanding Bias toward Latinos: Discrimination, Dimensions of Difference, and Experience of Exclusion." *Journal of Social Issues* 66(1): 59–78.

Dowling, Julie A. 2014. *Mexican Americans and the Question of Race.* Austin: University of Texas Press.

Dowling, Julie A., and C. Alison Newby. 2010. "So Far from Miami: Afro-Cuban Encounters with Mexicans in the U.S. Southwest." *Latino Studies* 8(2): 176–94.

Dreby, Joanna. 2015. *Everyday Illegal: When Policies Undermine Immigrant Families*. Berkeley: University of California Press.

Duany, Jorge. 1996. "Transnational Migration from the Dominican Republic: The Cultural Redefinition of Racial Identity." *Caribbean Studies* 29(2): 253–82.

———. 1998. "Reconstructing Racial Identity: Ethnicity, Color, and Class among Dominicans in the United States and Puerto Rico." *Latin American Perspectives* 25(3): 147–72.

———. 2000. "Neither White nor Black: The Politics of Race and Ethnicity among Puerto Ricans on the Island and in the U.S. Mainland." In *Neither Enemies nor Friends: Latinos, Blacks, Afro-Latinos*, edited by Anani Dzidzienyo and Suzanne Oboler. New York: Palgrave Macmillan.

Du Bois, W.E.B. 1903. *The Talented Tenth*. New York: James Pott and Company.

———. 2015. *The Souls of Black Folk*. New Haven, Conn.: Yale University Press. (Originally published in 1903.)

Dulitzky, Ariel E. 2005. "A Region in Denial: Racial Discrimination and Racism in Latin America." In *Neither Enemies nor Friends: Latinos, Blacks, Afro-Latinos*, edited by Anani Dzidzienyo and Suzanne Oboler. New York: Palgrave Macmillan.

Durand, Jorge, Douglas S. Massey, and Chiara Capoferro. 2005. "The New Geography of Mexican Immigration." In *New Destinations: Mexican Immigration in the United States*, edited by Víctor Zúñiga and Rubén Hernández-Leó. New York: Russell Sage Foundation.

Durante, Federica, and Susan T. Fiske. 2017. "How Social-Class Stereotypes Maintain Inequality." *Current Opinion in Psychology* 18(December): 43–48.

Ebert, Kim, Emily P. Estrada, and Michelle Halla Lore. 2014. "When Organizations Matter: Threatening Demographics, Supportive Politics, and Immigration Lawmaking." *Du Bois Review: Social Science Research on Race* 11(2): 387–417.

Ebert, Kim, and Sarah M. Ovink. 2014. "Anti-Immigrant Ordinances and Discrimination in New and Established Destinations." *American Behavioral Scientist* 58(13): 1784–804.

Ellis, Mark, Richard Wright, and Matthew Townley. 2014. "The Great Recession and the Allure of New Immigrant Destinations in the United States." *International Migration Review* 48(1): 3–33.

Essed, Philomena. 2008. "Everyday Racism." In *A Companion to Racial and Ethnic Studies*, edited by David Theo Goldberg and John Solomos. Oxford: Blackwell Publishers.

Evans, Louwanda, and Wendy Leo Moore. 2015. "Impossible Burdens: White Institutions, Emotional Labor, and Micro-Resistance." *Social Problems* 62(3): 439–54.

Evans, Shani Adia. 2021. "'I Wanted Diversity, but Not So Much': Middle-Class White Parents, School Choice, and the Persistence of Anti-Black Stereotypes." *Urban Education* (July 22). DOI: https://doi.org/10.1177/00420859211031952.

Feagin, Joe R., and José A. Cobas. 2015. *Latinos Facing Racism: Discrimination, Resistance, and Endurance.* New York: Routledge.

Fernández-Kelly, Patricia. 2008. "The Back Pocket Map: Social Class and Cultural Capital as Transferable Assets in the Advancement of Second-Generation Immigrants." *Annals of the American Academy of Political and Social Science* 620(1): 116–37.

Festinger, Leon. 1957. *A Theory of Cognitive Dissonance*, vol. 2. Stanford, Calif.: Stanford University Press.

Findling, Mary G., Sara N. Bleich, Logan S. Casey, Robert J. Blendon, John M. Benson, Justin M. Sayde, and Carolyn Miller. 2019. "Discrimination in the United States: Experiences of Latinos." *Health Services Research* 54: 1409–18.

Fiske, Susan T., and Hazel Rose Markus. 2012. *Facing Social Class: How Societal Rank Influences Interaction.* New York: Russell Sage Foundation.

Fleming, Crystal M., Michèle Lamont, and Jessica S. Welburn. 2012. "African Americans Respond to Stigmatization: The Meanings and Salience of Confronting, Deflecting Conflict, Educating the Ignorant, and 'Managing the Self.'" *Ethnic and Racial Studies* 35(3): 400–417.

Fligstein, Neil, 2013. *Going North: Migration of Blacks and Whites from the South, 1900–1950.* New York: Academic Press.

Flores, René D., and Ariela Schachter. 2018. "Who Are the 'Illegals'? The Social Construction of Illegality in the United States." *American Sociological Review* 83(5): 839–68.

———. 2019. "Examining Americans' Stereotypes About Immigrant Illegality." *Contexts* 18(2): 36–41.

Flores, René, and Edward Telles. 2012. "Social Stratification in Mexico: Disentangling Color, Ethnicity, and Class." *American Sociological Review* 77(3): 486–94.

Flores-González, Nilda. 2017. *Citizens but Not Americans: Race and Belonging among Latino Millennials.* New York: New York University Press.

Fox, Cybelle, and Irene Bloemraad. 2015. "Beyond 'White by Law': Explaining the Gulf in Citizenship Acquisition between Mexican and European Immigrants, 1930." *Social Forces* 94(1): 181–207.

Fox, Cybelle, and Thomas Guglielmo. 2012. "Defining America's Racial Boundaries: Blacks, Mexicans, and European Immigrants, 1890–1945." *American Journal of Sociology* 118(2): 327–79.

Frank, Reanne, Ilana Redstone Akresh, and Bo Lu. 2010. "Latino Immigrants and the U.S. Racial Order: How and Where Do They Fit In?" *American Sociological Review* 75(3): 378–401. DOI: https://doi.org/10.1177/0003122410372216.

Franzosi, Roberto, Gianluca DeFazio, and Stefania Vicari. 2012. "Ways of Measuring Agency: An Application of Quantitative Narrative Analysis to Lynchings in Georgia (1875–1930)." *Sociological Methodology* 42(1): 1–42.

Freeman, Jonathan B., Andrew M. Penner, Aliya Saperstein, Matthias Scheutz, and

Nalini Ambady. 2011. "Looking the Part: Social Status Cues Shape Race Perception." *PLOS ONE* 6(9): e25107.

Frey, William H. 2018. *Diversity Explosion: How New Racial Demographics Are Remaking America*. Washington, D.C.: Brookings Institution Press.

Furuseth, Owen J., and Heather A. Smith. 2006. "From Winn-Dixie to Tiendas: The Remaking of the New South." In *Latinos in the New South: Transformations of Place*, edited by Heather A. Smith and Owen J. Furuseth. Abingdon, U.K.: Ashgate Publishing.

Gaddis, S. Michael. 2017. "How Black Are Lakisha and Jamal? Racial Perceptions from Names Used in Correspondence Audit Studies." *Sociological Science* 4: 469–89.

García, Angela S. 2019. *Legal Passing: Navigating Undocumented Life and Local Immigration Law*. Berkeley: University of California Press.

García, San Juanita. 2017. "Racializing 'Illegality': An Intersectional Approach to Understanding How Mexican-Origin Women Navigate an Anti-Immigrant Climate." *Sociology of Race and Ethnicity* 3(4): 474–90.

García-Peña, Lorgia. 2015. "Translating Blackness: Dominicans Negotiating Race and Belonging." *The Black Scholar* 45(2):10–20.

Garland, Phyl. 1971. "Atlanta: Black Mecca of the South." *Ebony* Magazine. 26(12): 152–57.

Gibbins, Roger. 2005. "Meaning and Significance of the Canadian-American Border." In *Borders and Border Politics in a Globalizing World*, edited by Paul Ganster and David E. Lorey. Lanham, Md.: SR Books/Rowman & Littlefield Publishers.

Goffman, Erving. 1963. *Stigma: Notes on the Management of Spoiled Identity*. New York: Prentice-Hall.

Golash-Boza, Tanya. 2015. *Immigration Nation: Raids, Detentions, and Deportations in Post-9/11 America*. New York: Routledge.

———. 2017. "Structural Racism, Criminalization, and Pathways to Deportation for Dominican and Jamaican Men in the United States." *Social Justice* 44(2/3): 136–62.

Golash-Boza, Tanya, and William Darity Jr. 2008. "Latino Racial Choices: The Effects of Skin Colour and Discrimination on Latinos' and Latinas' Racial Self-Identifications." *Ethnic and Racial Studies* 31(5): 899–934.

Gómez, Laura E. 2022. *Inventing Latinos: A New Story of American Racism*. New York: New Press.

Gómez Cervantes, Andrea. 2021. "'Looking Mexican': Indigenous and Non-indigenous Latina/o Immigrants and the Racialization of Illegality in the Midwest." *Social Problems* 68(1): 100–117.

Gonzales, Alfonso. 2010. "Beyond the Consensus: Oppositional *Migrante* Politics in the Obama Era." *NACLA Report on the Americas* 43(6): 15–19.

Gonzales, Roberto G. 2016. *Lives in Limbo: Undocumented and Coming of Age in America.* Berkeley: University of California Press.

Grasmuck, Sherri, and Patricia R. Pessar. 2020. *Between Two Islands: Dominican International Migration.* Berkeley: University of California Press.

Greenman, Emily, and Yu Xie. 2008. "Is Assimilation Theory Dead? The Effect of Assimilation on Adolescent Well-being." *Social Science Research* 37(1): 109–37.

Groeger, Lena V., Annie Waldman, and David Eads. 2018. "Miseducation: Georgia: Atlanta City School District." *Pro Publica*, updated October 2018. https://projects.propublica.org/miseducation/district/1300120 (accessed April 18, 2023).

Grosfoguel, Ramán. 2004. "Race and Ethnicity or Racialized Ethnicities? Identities within Global Coloniality." *Ethnicities* 4(3): 315–36.

Guridy, Frank A. 2010. *Forging Diaspora: Afro-Cubans and African Americans in a World of Empire and Jim Crow.* Chapel Hill: University of North Carolina Press.

Hagerman, Margaret A. 2018. *White Kids: Growing Up with Privilege in a Racially Divided America.* New York: New York University Press.

Hamilton, Tod G. 2019. *Immigration and the Remaking of Black America.* New York: Russell Sage Foundation.

Hannerz, Ulf. 1990. "Cosmopolitans and Locals in World Culture." *Theory, Culture, and Society* 7(2/3): 237–51.

Hanson, Victor Davis. 2020. "Do We Want Mexifornia?" *City Journal* (Manhattan Institute for Policy Research), Spring. https://www.city-journal.org/html/do-we-want-mexifornia-12236.html.

Harmon, David Andrew. 2019. *Beneath the Image of the Civil Rights Movement and Race Relations: Atlanta, Georgia, 1946–1981.* New York: Routledge.

Hegtvedt, Karen A., and Cathryn Johnson. 2018. *Social Psychology: Individuals, Interaction, and Inequality.* Thousand Oaks, Calif.: Sage Publications.

Heiman, Rachel, Carla Freeman, Mark Liechty, Krisztina Fehérváry, Carla Jones, and Cindi Katz, eds. 2012. *The Global Middle Classes: Theorizing through Ethnography*: Santa Fe, N.M.: SAR Press.

Henriksen, Ken. 2007. "Textual Representations of the Border and Border Crossers: Constructing Latino Enemies in the New York Times." In *The Politics, Economics, and Culture of Mexican-Us Migration*, edited by Edward Ashbee, Helene Balslev Clausen, and Carl Pedersen. New York: Palgrave Macmillan.

Hernández, Tanya Katerí. 2016. "Envisioning the United States in the Latin American Myth of 'Racial Democracy Mestizaje.'" *Latin American and Caribbean Ethnic Studies* 11(2): 189–205.

———. 2021. "Latino Anti-Black Bias and the Census Categorization of Latinos: Race, Ethnicity, or Other?" In *Critical Dialogues in Latinx Studies: A Reader*, edited by Ana Y. Ramos-Zayas and Mérida M. Rúa. New York: New York University Press.

Hernández-León, Rubén, and Víctor Zúñiga. 2005. "Appalachia Meets Aztlan: Mexican Immigration and Intergroup Relations in Dalton, Georgia." In *New Destinations: Mexican Immigration in the United States*, edited by Víctor Zúñiga and Rubén Hernández-León. New York: Russell Sage Foundation.

Hero, Rodney E., and Robert R. Preuhs. 2013. *Black-Latino Relations in U.S. National Politics: Beyond Conflict or Cooperation*. Cambridge: Cambridge University Press.

Higginbotham, Evelyn Brooks. 1994. *Righteous Discontent: The Women's Movement in the Black Baptist Church, 1880–1920*. Cambridge, Mass.: Harvard University Press.

Hitlin, Steven, J. Scott Brown, and Glen H. Elder Jr. 2007. "Measuring Latinos: Racial vs. Ethnic Classification and Self-Understandings." *Social Forces* 86(2): 587–611.

Hobson, Maurice. 2017. *The Legend of the Black Mecca: Politics and Class in the Making of Modern Atlanta*. Chapel Hill: University of North Carolina Press.

Hoetink, Harry. 2000. "The Dominican Republic in the Twentieth Century: Notes on Mobility and Stratification." *Nieuwe West-Indische Gids* (*New West Indian Guide*) 74(3/4): 209–33.

Hogg, Michael A. 2018. "Social Identity Theory." In *Social Identity Theory: Contemporary Social Psychological Theories*, edited by Peter J. Burke. Stanford, Calif.: Stanford University Press.

Holt, Douglas B. 1997. "Poststructuralist Lifestyle Analysis: Conceptualizing the Social Patterning of Consumption in Postmodernity." *Journal of Consumer Research* 23(4): 326–50.

Hondagneu-Sotelo, Pierrette, and Manuel Pastor. 2021. *South Central Dreams: Finding Home and Building Community in South L.A.* New York: New York University Press.

Hooker, Juliet. 2005. "Indigenous Inclusion/Black Exclusion: Race, Ethnicity, and Multicultural Citizenship in Latin America." *Journal of Latin American Studies* 37(2): 285–310.

Hopkins, Daniel J. 2010. "Politicized Places: Explaining Where and When Immigrants Provoke Local Opposition." *American Political Science Review* 104(1): 40–60.

Howard, David. 2001. *Coloring the Nation: Race and Ethnicity in the Dominican Republic*. Oxford: Signal Books.

———. 2003. "Reappraising Race? Dominicans in New York City." *International Journal of Population Geography* 9(4): 337–50.

Howarth, Caroline. 2006. "Race as Stigma: Positioning the Stigmatized as Agents, Not Objects." *Journal of Community and Applied Social Psychology* 16(6): 442–51.

Hughes, Diane. 2003. "Correlates of African American and Latino Parents' Messages to Children about Ethnicity and Race: A Comparative Study of Racial Socialization." *American Journal of Community Psychology* 31(1/2): 15–33.

Igarashi, Hiroki, and Hiro Saito. 2014. "Cosmopolitanism as Cultural Capital: Exploring the Intersection of Globalization, Education, and Stratification." *Cultural Sociology* 8(3): 222–39.

Ignatiev, Noel. 2012. *How the Irish Became White.* New York: Routledge.

Itzigsohn, José. 2009. *Encountering American Faultlines: Race, Class and the Dominican Experience in Providence.* New York: Russell Sage Foundation.

Itzigsohn, José, and Karida L. Brown. 2020. *The Sociology of W.E.B. Du Bois.* New York: New York University Press.

Itzigsohn, José, and Carlos Dore-Cabral. 2000. "Competing Identities? Race, Ethnicity, and Panethnicity among Dominicans in the United States." *Sociological Forum* 15(2): 225–47).

Itzigsohn, José, Silvia Giorguli, and Obed Vazquez. 2005. "Immigrant Incorporation and Racial Identity: Racial Self-Identification among Dominican Immigrants." *Ethnic and Racial Studies* 28(1): 50–78.

Jackson, Brandon A., and Adia Harvey Wingfield. 2013. "Getting Angry to Get Ahead: Black College Men, Emotional Performance, and Encouraging Respectable Masculinity." *Symbolic Interaction* 36(3): 275–92.

Jaret, Charles, Melissa M. Hayes, and Robert M. Adelman. 2009. "Atlanta's Future: Convergence or Divergence with Other Cities?" In *Past Trends and Future Prospects of the American City: The Dynamics of Atlanta,* edited by David L. Sjoquist. Lanham, Md.: Lexington Books.

Jiménez, Tomás R. 2008. "Mexican Immigrant Replenishment and the Continuing Significance of Ethnicity and Race." *American Journal of Sociology* 113(6): 1527–67.

———. 2010. *Replenished Ethnicity: Mexican Americans, Immigration, and Identity.* Berkeley: University of California Press.

Jiménez, Tomás R., and Adam L. Horowitz. 2013. "When White Is Just Alright: How Immigrants Redefine Achievement and Reconfigure the Ethnoracial Hierarchy." *American Sociological Review* 78(5): 849–71.

Johnson, Sheri Lynn. 1983. "Race and the Decision to Detain a Suspect." *Yale Law Journal* 93(2): 214–58.

Johnston, Josée, and Shyon Baumann. 2007. "Democracy versus Distinction: A Study of Omnivorousness in Gourmet Food Writing." *American Journal of Sociology* 113(1): 165–20.

Jones, Jennifer A. 2019. *The Browning of the New South.* Chicago: University of Chicago Press.

Jones-Correa, Michael. 2000. "The Origins and Diffusion of Racial Restrictive Covenants." *Political Science Quarterly* 115(4): 541–68.

Jones-Correa, Michael, and David L. Leal. 1996. "Becoming 'Hispanic': Secondary Panethnic Identification among Latin American–Origin Populations in the United States." *Hispanic Journal of Behavioral Sciences* 18(2): 214–54.

Jones-Correa, Michael, Edward Telles, Mark Sawyer, and Gaspar Rivera-Salgado.

2011. "Commonalities, Competition, and Linked Fate." *Just Neighbors* 74(4): 63–95.

Jonsson, Patrik. 2006. "Backlash Emerges against Latino Culture." *Christian Science Monitor*, July 19.

Kaiser, Cheryl R., and Carol T. Miller. 2001. "Stop Complaining! The Social Costs of Making Attributions to Discrimination." *Personality and Social Psychology Bulletin* 27(2): 254–63.

Kaufmann, Karen M. 2003. "Cracks in the Rainbow: Group Commonality as a Basis for Latino and African-American Political Coalitions." *Political Research Quarterly* 56(2): 199–210.

Khachikian, Oshin, and Nina Bandelj. 2019. "Immigrant Socioeconomic Mobility in the United States: Mechanisms of Inequality and the Role of Ethnic Capital." *Sociology Compass* 13(8): e12723.

Kibria, Nazli. 2000. "Race, Ethnic Options, and Ethnic Binds: Identity Negotiations of Second-Generation Chinese and Korean Americans." *Sociological Perspectives* 43(1): 77–95.

Killian, Caitlin, and Cathryn Johnson. 2006. "'I'm Not an Immigrant!': Resistance, Redefinition, and the Role of Resources in Identity Work." *Social Psychology Quarterly* 69(1): 60–80.

Kim, Anna Joo, and Ashley Bozarth. 2021. "Refuge City: Creating Places of Welcome in the Suburban U.S. South." *Journal of Urban Affairs* 43(6): 851–71.

Kim, Jaeeun. 2018. "Migration-Facilitating Capital: A Bourdieusian Theory of International Migration." *Sociological Theory* 36(3): 262–88.

King, D. A. 2023. "Georgiafornia: Georgia Budget and Policy Institute Now Openly Advocating for Drivers Licenses for Illegal Aliens." Blog. Dustin Inman Society. https://newdustininmansociety.org/?s=Mexifornia (accessed September 1, 2023).

Klarman, Michael. 2004. *From Jim Crow to Civil Rights: The Supreme Court and the Struggle for Racial Equality.* Oxford: Oxford University Press. (Originally published in 1997.)

Kluger, Richard. 2004. *Simple Justice: The History of* Brown v. Board of Education *and Black America's Struggle for Equality.* New York: First Vintage Books. (Originally published in 1975.)

Kontonis, Paul. 2021. "Important Reasons for Reaching the U.S. Hispanic Market." Commpro, October 25. https://www.commpro.biz/news/important-reasons-for-reaching-the-us-hispanic-market?rq=Hispanic (accessed July 29, 2023).

Krysan, Maria, and Kyle Crowder. 2017. *Cycle of Segregation: Social Processes and Residential Stratification.* New York: Russell Sage Foundation.

Kun, Josh, and Laura Pulido. 2014. *Black and Brown in Los Angeles: Beyond Conflict and Coalition.* Berkeley: University of California Press.

Lacy, Karyn R. 2004. "Black Spaces, Black Places: Strategic Assimilation and Identity Construction in Middle-Class Suburbia." *Ethnic and Racial Studies* 27(6): 908–30.

———. 2007. *Blue-Chip Black: Race, Class, and Status in the New Black Middle Class.* Berkeley: University of California Press.

———. 2015. "Race, Privilege and the Growing Class Divide." *Ethnic and Racial Studies* 38(8): 1246–49.

Lamont, Michèle. 2001. "The Dignity of Working Men: Morality and the Boundaries of Race, Class and Immigration." *Symbolic Interaction* 24(4): 505–8.

———. 2019. "From 'Having' to 'Being': Self-Worth and the Current Crisis of American Society." *British Journal of Sociology* 70(3): 660–707.

Lamont, Michèle, and Sada Aksartova. 2002. "Ordinary Cosmopolitanisms: Strategies for Bridging Racial Boundaries among Working-Class Men." *Theory, Culture, and Society* 19(4): 1–25.

Lamont, Michèle, and Crystal Marie Fleming. 2005. "Everyday Antiracism: Competence and Religion in the Cultural Repertoire of the African American Elite." *Du Bois Review: Social Science Research on Race* 2(1): 29–43.

Lamont, Michèle, and Annette Lareau. 1988. "Cultural Capital: Allusions, Gaps and Glissandos in Recent Theoretical Developments." *Sociological Theory* 6(2): 153–68.

Lamont, Michèle, and Nissim Mizrachi. 2013. "Ordinary People Doing Extraordinary Things: Responses to Stigmatization in Comparative Perspective." *Ethnic and Racial Studies* 35(3): 13–29.

Lamont, Michèle, Graziella Moraes Silva, Jessica Welburn, Joshua Guetzkow, Nissim Mizrachi, Hanna Herzog, and Elisa Reis. 2016. *Getting Respect: Responding to Stigma and Discrimination in the United States, Brazil, and Israel.* Princeton, N.J.: Princeton University Press.

Lancee, Bram, and Thijs Bol. 2017. "The Transferability of Skills and Degrees: Why the Place of Education Affects Immigrant Earnings." *Social Forces* 96(2): 691–716.

Landgrave, Michelangelo, and Nicholas Weller. 2022. "Do Name-Based Treatments Violate Information Equivalence? Evidence from a Correspondence Audit Experiment." *Political Analysis* 30(1): 142–48.

Lareau, Annette. 2003. *Unequal Childhoods: Class, Race, and Family Life.* Berkeley: University of California Press.

LeBrón, Alana M. W., Amy J. Schulz, Cindy Gamboa, Angela Reyes, Edna A. Viruell-Fuentes, and Barbara A. Israel. 2018. "'They Are Clipping Our Wings': Health Implications of Restrictive Immigrant Policies for Mexican-Origin Women in a Northern Border Community." *Race and Social Problems* 10(3): 174–92.

Lechner, Frank J., and John Boli, eds. 2019. *The Globalization Reader*, 6th ed. Chichester, U.K.: John Wiley & Sons Ltd.

Lee, Jennifer, and Frank D. Bean. 2010. *The Diversity Paradox: Immigration and the Color Line in Twenty-First Century America.* New York: Russell Sage Foundation.

Lee, Jennifer, and Min Zhou. 2015. *The Asian American Achievement Paradox.* New York: Russell Sage Foundation.

Leerkes, Arjen, James D. Bachmeier, and Mark A. Leach. 2013. "When the Border Is 'Everywhere': State-Level Variation in Migration Control and Changing Settlement Patterns of the Unauthorized Immigrant Population in the United States." *International Migration Review* 47(4): 910–43.

Levitt, Peggy. 2001. *The Transnational Villagers.* Berkeley: University of California Press.

———. 2004. *The Global Villagers.* Berkeley: University of California Press.

Lewis, John, and Michael D'Orso. 2015. *Walking with the Wind: A Memoir of the Movement.* New York: Simon & Schuster.

Lewis, Laura A. 2000. "Blacks, Black Indians, Afromexicans: The Dynamics of Race, Nation, and Identity in a Mexican Moreno Community (Guerrero)." *American Ethnologist* 27(4): 898–926. DOI: https://doi.org/10.1525/ae.2000.27.4.898.

Lin, Mingang, and Min Zhou. 2005. "Community Transformation and the Formation of Ethnic Capital: Immigrant Chinese Communities in the United States." *Journal of Chinese Overseas* 1(2): 260–84.

Link, Bruce G., and Jo C. Phelan. 2001. "Conceptualizing Stigma." *Annual Review of Sociology* 27(1): 363–85.

Lippard, Cameron D. 2016. "Playing the 'Immigrant Card': Reflections of Color-Blind Rhetoric within Southern Attitudes on Immigration." *Social Currents* 3(1): 24–42.

Lippard, Cameron D., and Charles Andrew Gallagher. 2011. *Being Brown in Dixie: Race, Ethnicity, and Latino Immigration in the New South.* Boulder, Colo.: First Forum Press.

Liptak, Adam. 2012. "Blocking Parts of Arizona Law, Justices Allow Its Centerpiece." *New York Times.* June 25. https://www.nytimes.com/2012/06/26/us/supreme-court-rejects-part-of-arizona-immigration-law.html.

López, Nancy. 2013. "Killing Two Birds with One Stone? Why We Need Two Separate Questions on Race and Ethnicity in the 2020 Census and Beyond." *Latino Studies* 11(3): 428–38.

López-Sanders, Laura. 2011. "Is Brown the New Black? Mediated Latino Incorporation in New Immigrant Destinations." PhD. diss., Department of Sociology, Stanford University Press.

———. 2017. "From 'God Sent' to 'God Damned': Nativist Shocks and Race Relations in New Immigrant Destinations." Annual meeting of the American Sociological Association. Montreal, August 12–15.

López-Sanders, Laura, and Hana E. Brown. 2020. "Political Mobilisation and Public Discourse in New Immigrant Destinations: News Media Characterisations of Immigrants during the 2006 Immigration Marches." *Journal of Ethnic and Migration Studies* 46(4): 820–38.

Lovato, Roberto. 2008. "Juan Crow in Georgia." *The Nation,* May 8.

Lozano, Rafael, Beatriz Zurita, Francisco Franco, Teresita Ramirez, Patricia Hernandez, and José Luis Torres. 2001. "Mexico: Marginality, Need, and Resource Allocation at the County Level." In *Challenging Inequities in Health: From Ethics to Action,* edited by Timothy Evans, Margaret Whitehead, Abbas Bhuiya, Finn Diderichsen, and Meg Wirth. Oxford: Oxford University Press.

Mallet, Marie L., and Joanna M. Pinto-Coelho. 2018. "Investigating Intra-Ethnic Divisions among Latino Immigrants in Miami, Florida." *Latino Studies* 16(1): 91–112.

Marquez, Beatriz Aldana, Apryl A. Williams, Nancy Plankey-Videla, and Selene I. Diaz. 2022. "The Discourse of Deservingness: Racialized Framing during Rumored ICE Raids." *Ethnicities* 22(2): 14687968211018215.

Márquez, Cecilia. 2019. "Juan Crow and the Erasure of Blackness in the Latina/o South." *Labor* 16(3): 79–85.

Marrow, Helen. 2011. *New Destination Dreaming: Immigration, Race, and Legal Status in the Rural American South.* Stanford, Calif.: Stanford University Press.

Marrow, Helen B. 2020. "Hope Turned Sour: Second-Generation Incorporation and Mobility in U.S. New Immigrant Destinations." *Ethnic and Racial Studies* 43(1): 99–118.

Marrow, Helen, Dina G. Okamoto, Melissa J. García, Muna Adem, and Linda R. Tropp. 2022. "Skin Tone and Mexicans' Perceptions of Discrimination in New Immigrant Destinations." *Social Psychology Quarterly* 85(2): 374–85.

Martínez, Daniel E., and Kelsey E. Gonzalez. 2021. "Panethnicity as a Reactive Identity: Primary Panethnic Identification among Latino-Hispanics in the United States." *Ethnic and Racial Studies* 44(4): 595–617.

Martinez-Cola, Marisela. 2021. *The Bricks before* Brown v. the Board of Education: *The Chinese American, Native American, and Mexican Americans' Struggle for Educational Equality.* Athens: University of Georgia Press.

Martínez-Rosas, Girsea, and Elizabeth Aranda. 2018. "Racialization and Strategies of Resistance among Undocumented Latino Young Adults in the United States." In *Latino Peoples in the New America*, edited by José A. Cobas et al. New York: Routledge.

Massey, Douglas S., ed. 2008. *New Faces in New Places: The Changing Geography of American Immigration.* New York: Russell Sage Foundation.

———. 2014. "The Racialization of Latinos in the United States." In *The Oxford Handbook of Ethnicity, Crime, and Immigration*, edited by Sandra Bucerius and Michael Tonry. Oxford: Oxford University Press.

Massey, Douglas S., and Karen A. Pren. 2012. "Unintended Consequences of US Immigration Policy: Explaining the Post-1965 Surge from Latin America." *Population and Development Review* 38(1): 1–29.

Massey, Douglas S., and Magaly Sánchez R. 2007. "Latino and American Identities as Perceived by Immigrants." *Qualitative Sociology* 30(1): 81–107.

———. 2010. *Brokered Boundaries: Immigrant Identity in Anti-Immigrant Times.* New York: Russell Sage Foundation.

Masuoka, Natalie. 2008. "Defining the Group: Latino Identity and Political Participation." *American Politics Research* 36(1): 33–61.

Masuoka, Natalie, and Jane Junn. 2013. *The Politics of Belonging: Race, Public Opinion, and Immigration.* Chicago: University of Chicago Press.

Maxwell, Claire, and Miri Yemini. 2019. "Modalities of Cosmopolitanism and Mobility: Parental Education Strategies of Global, Immigrant, and Local Middle-Class Israelis." *Discourse: Studies in the Cultural Politics of Education* 40(5): 616–32.

McAteer, Oliver. 2018. "DDB Welcomes Back Iconic Juan Valez after 30-Year Absence." *Campaign UK*. https://www.campaignlive.co.uk/article/ddb-welcomes-back-iconic-juan-valdez-30-year-absence/1491632.

McCann, James A., and Michael Jones-Correa. 2020. *Holding Fast: Resilience and Civic Engagement among Latino Immigrants*. New York: Russell Sage Foundation.

McClain, Paula D., Monique L. Lyle, Niambi M. Carter, Victoria M. DeFrancesco Soto, Gerald F. Lackey, Kendra Davenport Cotton, Shayla C. Nunnally, Thomas J. Scotto, Jeffrey D. Grynaviski, and J. Alan Kendrick. 2007. "Black Americans and Latino Immigrants in a Southern City: Friendly Neighbors or Economic Competitors? 1." *Du Bois Review: Social Science Research on Race* 4(1): 97–117.

McDaniel, Paul. 2018. "Shared Humanity, City Branding, and Municipal Immigrant Integration Initiatives in the Southeastern United States." *Southeastern Geographer* 58(3): 250–81.

McDermott, Monica. 2011. "Black Attitudes and Hispanic Immigrants in South Carolina." In *Just Neighbors: Research on African American and Latino Relations in the United States*, edited by Edward Telles, Mark Sawyer, and Gaspar Rivera-Salgado. New York: Russell Sage Foundation.

Meier, Kenneth J., Paula D. McClain, J. L. Polinard, and Robert D. Wrinkle. 2004. "Divided or Together? Conflict and Cooperation between African Americans and Latinos." *Political Research Quarterly* 57(3): 399–409.

Melamed, David, Christopher W. Munn, Leanne Barry, Bradley Montgomery, and Oneya F. Okuwobi. 2019. "Status Characteristics, Implicit Bias, and the Production of Racial Inequality." *American Sociological Review* 84(6): 1013–36.

Mellor, Jody, Nicola Ingram, Jessie Abrahams, and Phoebe Beedell. 2014. "Class Matters in the Interview Setting? Positionality, Situatedness and Class." *British Educational Research Journal* 40(1): 135–49.

Menjívar, Cecilia. 2016. "Immigrant Criminalization in Law and the Media: Effects on Latino Immigrant Workers' Identities in Arizona." *American Behavioral Scientist* 60(5–6): 597–616.

———. 2021. "The Racialization of 'Illegality.'" *Daedalus* 150(2): 91–105.

Menjívar, Cecilia, and Leisy Abrego. 2012. "Legal Violence: Immigration Law and the Lives of Central American Immigrants." *American Journal of Sociology* 117(5): 1380–1421.

Menjívar, Cecilia, and M. E. Enchautegui. 2015. "Confluence of the Economic Recession and Immigration Laws in the Lives of Latino Immigrant Workers in the United States." In *Immigrant Vulnerability and Resilience: Comparative Perspectives on Latin American Immigrants during the Great Recession*, edited by María Aysa-Lastra and Lorenzo Cachón. Cham, Switzerland: Springer.

Merton, Robert King. 1968. *Social Theory and Social Structure: Toward the Codification of Theory and Research*. New York: Simon & Schuster.

Metro Atlanta Chamber of Commerce. 2020. "Metro Atlanta Fortune 500 and 1000 Headquarters." https://www.metroatlantachamber.com/wp-content/uploads/2023/07/FORTUNE-500-Companies-11.pdf.

Millar, Kathleen M. 2017. "Toward a Critical Politics of Precarity." *Sociology Compass* 11(6): e12483. DOI: https://doi.org/10.1111/soc4.12483.

Miller, Carol T., and Cheryl R. Kaiser. 2001. "A Theoretical Perspective on Coping with Stigma." *Journal of Social Issues* 57(1): 73–92.

Molina, Natalia. 2014. *How Race Is Made in America: Immigration, Citizenship, and the Historical Power of Racial Scripts.* Berkeley: University of California Press.

Molleda, Juan-Carlos, and Marilyn Roberts. 2008. "The Value of 'Authenticity' in 'Glocal' Strategic Communication: The New Juan Valdez Campaign." *International Journal of Strategic Communication* 2(3): 154–74.

Monk, Ellis P., Jr. 2015. "The Cost of Color: Skin Color, Discrimination, and Health among African-Americans." *American Journal of Sociology* 121(2): 396–444.

———. 2022. "Inequality without Groups: Contemporary Theories of Categories, Intersectional Typicality, and the Disaggregation of Difference." *Sociological Theory* 40(1): 3–27.

Monogan, Jamie. 2018. "Studying Immigrant Policy One Law at a Time." Harvard Dataverse, V1, UNF:6:fRQplTkR2dGSKAijuUJ2Yg== [fileUNF]. DOI: https://doi.org/10.7910/DVN/F8YTX2.

Montejano, David. 1987. *Anglos and Mexicans in the Making of Texas, 1836–1986.* Austin: University of Texas Press.

Moore, Wendy Leo. 2008. *Reproducing Racism: White Space, Elite Law Schools, and Racial Inequality.* Lanham, Md.: Rowman & Littlefield.

Mootz, Francis J., III. 2009. "Ugly American Hermeneutics." *Nevada Law Journal* 10: 587.

Mora, G. Cristina. 2014. *Making Hispanics: How Activists, Bureaucrats, and Media Constructed a New American.* Chicago: University of Chicago Press.

Mora, G. Cristina, Reuben Perez, and Nicholas Vargas. 2022. "Who Identifies as 'Latinx'? The Generational Politics of Ethnoracial Labels." *Social Forces* 100(3): 1170–94.

Moreno Figueroa, Mónica G. 2010. "Distributed Intensities: Whiteness, Mestizaje and the Logics of Mexican Racism." *Ethnicities* 10(3): 387–401.

Murji, Karim, and John Solomos, eds. 2005. *Racialization: Studies in Theory and Practice.* Oxford: Oxford University Press.

Murphy, Patricia. 2022. "Latino Media CEO's Message: You're Doing It Wrong." *Atlanta Journal-Constitution*, July 19.

NAACP. 2023. "Know the Issues." https://naacp.org/know-issues.

National Conference of State Legislatures. 2022. "NCSL Database: Immigration Laws and Current State Immigration Legislation." https://www.ncsl.org/immigration/immigration-laws-and-current-state-immigration-legislation.

Ngai, Mae M. 2014. *Impossible Subjects: Illegal Aliens and the Making of Modern America*, updated edition. Princeton, N.J.: Princeton University Press.

Nunn, Ryan, Jana Parsons, and Jay Shambaugh. 2019. "An Interactive Exploration of the Geography of Prosperity." Brookings Institution, February 28. https://www.brookings.edu/articles/an-interactive-exploration-of-the-geography-of-prosperity/.

Nussbaum, Martha. 1994. "Patriotism and Cosmopolitanism." *Boston Review*, October 1.

Nutini, Hugo G. 1997. "Class and Ethnicity in Mexico: Somatic and Racial Considerations." *Ethnology* 36(3): 227–38.

O'Brien, Eileen. 2008. *The Racial Middle: Latinos and Asian Americans Living beyond the Racial Divide*. New York: New York University Press.

Oboler, Suzanne. 1992. "The Politics of Labeling: Latino/a Cultural Identities of Self and Others." *Latin American Perspectives* 19(4): 18–36.

———. 1995. *Ethnic Labels, Latino Lives: Identity and the Politics of (Re) Presentation in the United States*. Minneapolis: University of Minnesota Press.

———. 2021. "Disposable Strangers: Mexican Americans, Latinxs, and the Ethnic Label 'Hispanic.'" *Critical Dialogues in Latinx Studies: A Reader*, edited by Ana Y. Ramos-Zayas and Mérida M. Rúa. New York: New York University Press.

Odem, Mary, and Irene Browne. 2011. "Understanding the Diversity of Atlanta's Latino Population: Intersections of Race, Ethnicity, and Class." *Norteamérica* 6(SPE): 71–89.

Odem, Mary E., and Elaine Cantrell Lacy, eds. 2009. *Latino Immigrants and the Transformation of the U.S. South*. Athens: University of Georgia Press.

Okamoto, Dina G., Linda R. Tropp, Helen B. Marrow, and Michael Jones-Correa. 2020. "Welcoming, Trust, and Civic Engagement: Immigrant Integration in Metropolitan America." *Annals of the American Academy of Political and Social Science* 690(1): 61–81.

Ollivier, Michèle. 2008. "Revisiting Distinction." *Journal of Cultural Economy* 1(3): 263–79. DOI: https://doi.org/10.1080/17530350802476970.

Olsson, Tore C. 2009. "Latino Immigration." In *New Georgia Encyclopedia*. September 25, 2009; updated August 11, 2020. https://www.georgiaencyclopedia.org/articles/history-archaeology/latino-immigration/.

Omi, Michael, and Howard Winant. 1994. *Racial Formation in the United States: From the 1960s to the 1990s*. New York: Routledge.

Orfield, Gary, and Carole Ashkinaze. 1991. *The Closing Door: Conservative Policy and Black Opportunity*. Chicago: University of Chicago Press.

Oropesa, R. S., and Leif Jensen. 2010. "Dominican Immigrants and Discrimination in a New Destination: The Case of Reading, Pennsylvania." *City and Community* 9(3): 274–98.

Ovink, Sarah M., Kim Ebert, and Dina Okamoto. 2016. "Symbolic Politics of the

State: The Case of In-State Tuition Bills for Undocumented Students." *Socius* 2(May 18). DOI: https://doi.org/10.1177/2378023116647969.

Paschel, Tianna S., and Mark Q. Sawyer. 2008. "Contesting Politics as Usual: Black Social Movements, Globalization, and Race Policy in Latin America." *Souls* 10(3): 197–214.

Pedroza, Juan. 2019. "Where Immigration Enforcement Agreements Stalled: The Location of Local 287(g) Program Applications and Inquiries (2005–2012)." *SocArXiv* (January): 4. DOI: https://doi.org/10.31235/osf.io/2a8kz.

Pellerin, Lisa A., and Elizabeth Stearns. 2001. "Status Honor and the Valuing of Cultural and Material Capital." *Poetics* 29(1): 1–24.

Penner, Andrew M., and Aliya Saperstein. 2013. "Engendering Racial Perceptions: An Intersectional Analysis of How Social Status Shapes Race." *Gender and Society* 27(3): 319–44.

Pérez, Debra Joy, Lisa Fortuna, and Margarita Alegría. 2008. "Prevalence and Correlates of Everyday Discrimination among U.S. Latinos." *Journal of Community Psychology* 36(4): 421–33. DOI: https://doi.org/10.1002/jcop.20221.

Perlmann, Joel, and Roger Waldinger. 1997. "Second Generation Decline? Children of Immigrants, Past and Present—a Reconsideration." *International Migration Review* 31(4): 893–922.

Pescosolido, Bernice A., and Jack K. Martin. 2015. "The Stigma Complex." *Annual Review of Sociology* 41: 87–116.

Peters, Andy. 2021. "Black Talent Luring Tech Titans to Atlanta." *Atlanta Journal-Constitution*, March 7.

Peterson, Richard A., and Roger M. Kern. 1996. "Changing Highbrow Taste: From Snob to Omnivore." *American Sociological Review* 61(5): 900–907.

Pooley, Karen. 2015. "Segregation's New Geography: The Atlanta Metro Region, Race, and the Declining Prospects for Upward Mobility." *Southern Spaces*, April 15. https://southernspaces.org/2015/segregations-new-geography-atlanta-metro-region-race-and-declining-prospects-upward-mobility/.

Portes, Alejandro, and Rubén G. Rumbaut. 2001. *Legacies: The Story of the Immigrant Second Generation*. Berkeley: University of California Press.

———. 2014. *Immigrant America: A Portrait, Updated, and Expanded*. Berkeley: University of California Press.

Portes, Alejandro, and Min Zhou. 1993. "The New Second Generation: Segmented Assimilation and Its Variants." *Annals of the American Academy of Political and Social Science* 530(1): 74–96.

Pratt, Robert A. 2002. *We Shall Not Be Moved: The Desegregation of the University of Georgia*. Athens: University of Georgia Press.

Prieur, Annick, and Mike Savage. 2013. "Emerging Forms of Cultural Capital." *European Societies* 15(2): 246–67.

Provine, Doris Marie, Monica W. Varsanyi, Paul G. Lewis, and Scott H. Decker. 2016.

Policing Immigrants: Local Law Enforcement on the Front Lines. Chicago: University of Chicago Press.

Quillian, Lincoln. 2006. "New Approaches to Understanding Racial Prejudice and Discrimination." *Annual Review of Sociology* 32: 299–328.

Ramakrishnan, S. Karthick, and Tom Wong. 2010. "Partisanship, Not Spanish: Explaining Municipal Ordinances Affecting Undocumented Immigrants." In *Taking Local Control: Immigration Policy Activism in U.S. Cities and States*, edited by Monica Varsanyi. Stanford, Calif.: Stanford University Press.

Raymond, Elora, Kyungsoon Wang, and Dan Immergluck. 2016. "Race and Uneven Recovery: Neighborhood Home Value Trajectories in Atlanta before and after the Housing Crisis." *Housing Studies* 31(3): 324–39. DOI: https://doi.org/10.1080/02673037.2015.1080821.

Reay, Diane. 1996. "Insider Perspectives or Stealing the Words out of Women's Mouths: Interpretation in the Research Process." *Feminist Review* 53(1): 57–73.

Redmon, Jeremy. 2013. "Poll in Georgia Finds Conditional Support for Immigration Plan." *Atlanta Journal-Constitution*, September 20.

Reilly, Katie. 2016. "Here Are All the Times Donald Trump Insulted Mexico." *Time Magazine*, August 31. https://time.com/4473972/donald-trump-mexico-meeting-insult/.

Ribas, Vanesa. 2015. *On the Line: Slaughterhouse Lives and the Making of the New South.* Berkeley: University of California Press.

Ribero, Ana Milena. 2013. "'In Lak'ech (You Are My Other Me)': Mestizaje as a Rhetorical Tool That Achieves Identification and Consubstantiality." *Arizona Journal of Interdisciplinary Studies* 2(Spring): 22–41.

Richards, Janelle, and Rehema Ellis. 2020. "Black Tech Entrepreneurs Move to the South, a Great Migration in Reverse." *NBC News*, March 1. https://www.nbcnews.com/news/nbcblk/black-tech-entrepreneurs-move-south-great-migration- reverse-n1145156 (accessed May 8, 2023).

Ridgeway, Cecilia. 2019. *Status: Why Is It Everywhere? Why Does It Matter?* New York: Russell Sage Foundation.

Ridgeway, Cecilia L., and Tamar Kricheli-Katz. 2013. "Intersecting Cultural Beliefs in Social Relations: Gender, Race, and Class Binds and Freedoms." *Gender and Society* 27(3): 294–318.

Riley, Betsy. 2013. "Neighborhood: Cascade." *Atlanta*, February 3. https://www.atlantamagazine.com/neighborhoods/cascade/ (accessed February 25, 2021).

Rodriguez, Clara E. 2000. *Changing Race: Latinos, the Census, and the History of Ethnicity in the United States.* New York: New York University Press.

Rodriguez, Iliana Yamileth. 2020. "Constructing Mexican Atlanta: 1980–2016." PhD diss., Yale University.

Romero, Mary. 2008. "Crossing the Immigration and Race Border: A Critical Race Theory Approach to Immigration Studies." *Contemporary Justice Review* 11(1): 23–37.

Rosales Rocío. 2020. *Fruteros: Street Vending, Illegality, and Ethnic Community in Los Angeles*: University of California Press.

Rose, Joel. 2018. "How Metro Atlanta Became a 'Pioneer' of Immigration Enforcement." *Morning Edition*, National Public Radio, February 13.

Rössel, Jörg, and Julia H. Schroedter. 2015. "Cosmopolitan Cultural Consumption: Preferences and Practices in a Heterogenous, Urban Population in Switzerland." *Poetics* 50: 80–95.

Roth, Wendy D. 2008. "'There Is No Racism Here': Understanding Latinos' Perceptions of Color Discrimination through Sending-Receiving Society Comparison." In *Racism in the 21st Century: An Empirical Analysis of Skin Color*, edited by Ronald E. Hall. New York: Springer.

———. 2012. *Race Migrations: Latinos and the Cultural Transformation of Race.* Stanford, Calif.: Stanford University Press.

———. 2013. "A Single Shade of 'Negro': Henry Louis Gates' Depictions of Blackness in the Dominican Republic." *Latin American and Caribbean Ethnic Studies* 8(1): 92–96.

———. 2016. "The Multiple Dimensions of Race." *Ethnic and Racial Studies* 39(8): 1310–38.

———. 2020. "Unsettled Identities amid Settled Classifications? Toward a Sociology of Racial Appraisals." In *Why Do We Still Talk about Race?*, edited by Martin Bulmer and John Solomos. New York: Routledge.

Ruch, John. 2020. "How Race and Racism Shaped Growth and Cityhood in North Metro Atlanta." *Reporter Newspapers*, July 3. https://reporternewspapers.net/2020/07/03/how-race-and-racism-shaped-growth-and-cityhood-in-north-metro-atlanta/.

Ruggiero, Karen M., Jennifer Steele, Anne Hwang, and David M. Marx. 2000. "'Why Did I Get a "D"?' The Effects of Social Comparisons on Women's Attributions to Discrimination." *Personality and Social Psychology Bulletin* 26(10): 1271–83.

Ruggles, Steven, Sarah Flood, Ronald Goeken, Megan Schouweiler, and Matthew Sobek. 2022a. "IPUMS USA: Version 12.0 (American Community Survey 2017–2021)." Minneapolis, Minn.: IPUMS.

———. 2022b. "IPUMS USA: Version 12 (American Community Survey 2010–2015)." Minneapolis, Minn.: IPUMS.

———. 2022c. "IPUMS USA: Version 12 (American Community Survey 2005–2010)." Minneapolis, Minn.: IPUMS.

Ruiz, Neil, and Jens Manuel Krogstad. 2018. "East Coast and Texas Metros Had the Most H-1B Visas for Skilled Workers from 2010–2016." Pew Research Center, March 29. https://www.pewresearch.org/short-reads/2018/03/29/h-1b-visa-approvals-by-us-metro-area/.

Rumbaut, Rubén G. 1994. "The Crucible Within: Ethnic Identity, Self-Esteem, and Segmented Assimilation among Children of Immigrants." *International Migration Review* 28(4): 748–94.

———. 2008. "Reaping What You Sow: Immigration, Youth, and Reactive Ethnicity." *Applied Development Science* 12(2): 108–11.

Rumbaut, Rubén G., Douglas S. Massey, and Frank D. Bean. 2006. "Linguistic Life Expectancies: Immigrant Language Retention in Southern California." *Population and Development Review* (January): 447–60.

Sagás, Ernesto. 1997. "The Development of Antihaitianismo into a Dominant Ideology during the Trujillo Era." In *Ethnicity, Race, and Nationality in the Caribbean*, edited by J. M. Carrin. San Juan, Puerto Rico: Institute of Caribbean Studies, University of Puerto Rico.

———. 2000. *Race and Politics in the Dominican Republic.* Gainesville: University Press of Florida.

Salinas, Cristobal, and Adele Lozano. 2021. "The History and Evolution of the Term Latinx." In *Handbook of Latinos and Education: Theory, Research, and Practice*, 2nd ed., edited by Enrique Murillo. New York: Routledge.

Sanchez, Diana T., and Julie A. Garcia. 2012. "Putting Race in Context: Socioeconomic Status Predicts Racial Fluidity." In *Facing Social Class: How Societal Rank Influences Interaction*, edited by Susan T. Fiske and Hazel Rose Markus. New York: Russell Sage Foundation.

Santa Ana, Otto, Sandra L. Treviño, Michael J. Bailey, Kristen Bodossian, and Antonio de Necochea. 2007. "A May to Remember: Adversarial Images of Immigrants in U.S. Newspapers during the 2006 Policy Debate." *Du Bois Review: Social Science Research on Race* 4(1): 207–32.

Santos, Carlos E., Germán A. Cadenas, Cecilia Menjívar, and Jesús Cisneros. 2021. "The Development and Evaluation of the Stigma of Illegality and Marginalization of Latinx (SIML) Scale: Links to Psychological Distress." *Du Bois Review: Social Science Research on Race* 18(2): 1–25.

Saperstein, Aliya. 2006. "Double-Checking the Race Box: Examining Inconsistency between Survey Measures of Observed and Self-Reported Race." *Social Forces* 85(1): 57–74.

Schildkraut, Deborah J., Tomás R. Jiménez, John F. Dovidio, and Yuen J. Huo. 2019. "A Tale of Two States: How State Immigration Climate Affects Belonging to State and Country among Latinos." *Social Problems* 66(3): 332–55.

Schleef, Debra J., and Hilquias B. Cavalcanti. 2010. *Latinos in Dixie: Class and Assimilation in Richmond, Virginia.* Albany: State University of New York Press.

Senft, Nicole, Belinda Campos, Michelle N. Shiota, and Yulia E. Chentsova-Dutton. 2021. "Who Emphasizes Positivity? An Exploration of Emotion Values in People of Latino, Asian, and European Heritage Living in the United States." *Emotion* 21(4): 707–19.

Sherman, Rachel. 2005. "Producing the Superior Self: Strategic Comparison and Symbolic Boundaries among Luxury Hotel Workers." *Ethnography* 6(2): 131–58.

Shirmohammadi, Melika, Mina Beigi, and Jim Stewart. 2019. "Understanding Skilled Migrants' Employment in the Host Country: A Multidisciplinary Review and a Conceptual Model." *International Journal of Human Resource Management* 30(1): 96–121.

Silver, Alexis M. 2018. *Shifting Boundaries: Immigrant Youth Negotiating National, State, and Small-Town Politics*. Stanford, Calif.: Stanford University Press.

Simmons, William Paul, Daniel Alvord, and Valdez Elizabeth Salerno. 2018. "Immigration Enforcement, the Racialization of Legal Status, and Perceptions of the Police: Latinos in Chicago, Los Angeles, Houston, and Phoenix in Comparative Perspective." *Du Bois Review* 15(1): 107–28.

Singer, Audrey. "2008. Twenty-First-Century Gateways: An Introduction." In *Twenty-First Century Gateways: Immigrant Incorporation in Suburban America*, edited by Audrey Singer, Susan W. Hardwick, and Caroline B. Brettell. Washington, D.C.: Brookings Institution Press.

Skinner-Dorkenoo, Allison L., Apoorva Sarmal, Chloe J. Andre, and Kasheena G. Rogbeer. 2021. "How Microaggressions Reinforce and Perpetuate Systemic Racism in the United States." *Perspectives on Psychological Science* 16(5): 903–25.

Skrentny, John David. 2009. *The Minority Rights Revolution*. Cambridge, Mass.: Harvard University Press.

Smith, Heather A., and Owen J. Furuseth, eds. 2006. *Latinos in the New South: Transformations of Place*. Abingdon, U.K.: Ashgate Publishing.

Smith, Rob. 2006. *Mexican New York: Transnational Lives of New Immigrants*. Berkeley: University of California Press.

Snow, David A., and Leon Anderson. 1987. "Identity Work among the Homeless: The Verbal Construction and Avowal of Personal Identities." *American Journal of Sociology* 92(6): 1336–71.

Soto-Vásquez, Arthur D., and Mariana Sánchez-Santos. 2022. "El Cabal, Vacunas, y Donald Trump: An Analysis of Spanish-Language Disinformation Leading Up to the U.S. Capitol Insurrection." *Cultural Studies ↔ Critical Methodologies* 22(5). DOI: https://doi.org/10.1177/15327086221093949.

Steinberg, Stephen. 2005. "Immigration, African Americans, and Race Discourse." *New Politics* 10(3): 42–54.

Stillerman, Joel. 2023. *Identity Investments: Middle-Class Responses to Precarious Privilege in Neoliberal Chile*. Stanford, Calif.: Stanford University Press.

Stirgus, Eric. 2020. "Atlanta and Black Wealth: Success for Many, but Not for All." *Atlanta Journal-Constitution*, February 22. https://www.ajc.com/news/special-reports/atlanta-and-black-wealth-success-for-many-but-not-for-all/OaxgNw8hUuOuusrwFhShbP/ (accessed February 25, 2021).

Stuesse, Angela. 2016. *Scratching Out a Living: Latinos, Race, and Work in the Deep South*. Berkeley: University of California Press.

Stuesse, Angela, and Mathew Coleman. 2014. "Automobility, Immobility, Altermobility: Surviving and Resisting the Intensification of Immigrant Policing." *City and Society* 26(1): 51–72.

Subedi, Rajendra Prasad, and Mark Warren Rosenberg. 2016. "High-Skilled Immigrants–Low-Skilled Jobs: Challenging Everyday Health." *The Canadian Geographer (Le Géographe Canadien)* 60(1): 56–68.

Sue, Christina. 2009. "An Assessment of the Latin Americanization Thesis." *Ethnic and Racial Studies* 32(6): 1058–70.

———. 2013. *Land of the Cosmic Race: Race Mixture, Racism, and Blackness in Mexico.* Oxford: Oxford University Press.

———. 2021. "Is Mexico beyond Mestizaje? Blackness, Race Mixture, and Discrimination." *Latin American and Caribbean Ethnic Studies* 18(1): 1–28.

Suro, Roberto, and Audrey Singer. 2002. "Latino Growth in Metropolitan America: Changing Patterns, New Locations." Brookings Institution, July. https://www.brookings.edu/wp-content/uploads/2016/06/surosinger.pdf (accessed February 25, 2021).

Sykes, Gresham M., and David Matza. 1957. "Techniques of Neutralization: A Theory of Delinquency." *American Sociological Review* 22(6): 664–70.

Tajfel, Henri, and John Turner. 1979. "An Integrative Theory of Inter-Group Conflict." In *The Social Psychology of Inter-Group Relations*, edited by W. G. Austin and S. Worchel. Monterey, Calif.: Brooks/Cole.

Tarasawa, Beth. 2009. "New Patterns of Segregation: Latino and African American Students in Metro Atlanta High Schools." *Southern Spaces* (January). https://web.archive.org/web/20181015141852id_/https://southernspaces.org/node/42513.

Tatum, Katharine, and Irene Browne. 2019. "The Best of Both Worlds: One-Up Assimilation Strategies among Middle-Class Immigrants." *Poetics* 75: 101317.

Taylor, Paul, Mark Hugo Lopez, Jessica Hamar Martínez, and Gabriel Velasco. 2012. "When Labels Don't Fit: Hispanics and Their Views of Identity." Pew Hispanic Center, April 4. https://www.pewresearch.org/hispanic/2012/04/04/when-labels-dont-fit-hispanics-and-their-views-of-identity/.

Telles, Edward. 2014. *Pigmentocracies: Ethnicity, Race, and Color in Latin America.* Chapel Hill: University of North Carolina Press.

———. 2021. "Identity and Immigration: Core Concepts." In *Contested Concepts in Migration Studies*, edited by Ricard Zapata-Barrero, Dirk Jacobs, and Riva Astorians. New York: Routledge.

Telles, Edward, and Stanley Bailey. 2013. "Understanding Latin American Beliefs about Racial Inequality." *American Journal of Sociology* 118(6): 1559–95.

Telles, Edward, and Denia Garcia. 2013. "Mestizaje and Public Opinion in Latin America." *Latin American Research Review* 48(3): 130–52.

Telles, Edward, and Vilma Ortiz. 2008. *Generations of Exclusion: Mexican Americans, Assimilation, and Race.* New York: Russell Sage Foundation.

Telles, Edward, and Tianna Paschel. 2014. "Who Is Black, White, or Mixed Race? How Skin Color, Status, and Nation Shape Racial Classification in Latin America." *American Journal of Sociology* 120(3): 864–907.

Telles, Edward, and Christina A. Sue. 2019. *Durable Ethnicity: Mexican Americans and the Ethnic Core.* Oxford: Oxford University Press.

Theiss-Morse, Elizabeth, Frank J. Gonzalez, and Alison O'Toole. 2020. "Hierarchy, American Identity, and Support for Anti-Poverty Efforts." In *Liberal Nationalism and Its Critics: Normative and Empirical Questions*, edited by Gina Gustavsson and David Miller. Oxford: Oxford University Press.

Toone, Stephanie. 2018. "Forbes: These Are the Top Cities Where African-Americans Are Doing the Best Economically." *Atlanta Journal-Constitution*, January 17. https://www.ajc.com/news/the-cities-where-african-americans-are-doing-the-best-economically/aV6HMTUklKq4Hem3dYXQNK/ (accessed August 31, 2023).

Toribio, Almeida Jacqueline. 2000. "Language Variation and the Linguistic Enactment of Identity among Dominicans." *Linguistics* 38(6): 1133–59.

Torres-Saillant, Silvio. 2010. "Introduction to Dominican Blackness." Research monograph. CUNY Dominican Studies Institute.

Tran, Van C. 2010. "English Gain vs. Spanish Loss? Language Assimilation among Second-Generation Latinos in Young Adulthood." *Social Forces* 89(1): 257–84.

Tran, Van C., Jennifer Lee, Oshin Khachikian, and Jess Lee. 2018. "Hyper-Selectivity, Racial Mobility, and the Remaking of Race." *RSF: The Russell Sage Foundation Journal of the Social Sciences* 4(5, August): 188–209. DOI: https://doi.org/10.7758/RSF.2018.4.5.09.

Transactional Records Access Clearinghouse (TRACImmigration). 2021. "Latest Data: Immigration and Customs Enforcement Removals: ICE Data through June 2020." https://trac.syr.edu/phptools/immigration/remove/ (accessed June 17, 2022).

Tropp, Linda R., Dina G. Okamoto, Helen B. Marrow, and Michael Jones-Correa. 2018. "How Contact Experiences Shape Welcoming: Perspectives from U.S.-Born and Immigrant Groups." *Social Psychology Quarterly* 81(1): 23–47.

Truby, J. Scott. 2020. "Economy, Growth among Top Metro Atlanta Stories of the Past Decade." *Atlanta Journal-Constitution*, January 2. https://www.ajc.com/news/local-govt--politics/economy-growth-among-top-metro-atlanta-stories-the-past-decade/NW2fgJDNPvmHMvTIX2qasL/ (accessed March 9, 2021).

Tudhope, Andrea. 2020. "Clarkston Has Welcomed Thousands of Refugees. Hear What Residents Have to Say." *Weekend Edition*, WABE, February 26. https://www.wabe.org/clarkston-has-welcomed-thousands-of-refugees-hear-what-residents-have-to-say/.

Turner, Cory, Reema Khrais, Tim Lloyd, Alexandra Olgin, Laura Isensee, Becky Vevea, and Dan Carsen. 2016. "Why America's Schools Have a Money Problem." *Morning Edition*, National Public Radio, April 18. https://www.npr.org/2016/04/18/474256366/why-americas-schools-have-a-money-problem (accessed March 6, 2021).

USAID: IDEA International Data and Economic Analysis. 2023. "Educational Attainment Rate, Completed Bachelor's or Equivalent Education or Higher,

Population 25+, Both Sexes (Percentage), 2016–2020." https://idea.usaid.gov/query (accessed December 2, 2023).

U.S. Census Bureau. 1991. "Table T14. Detailed Hispanic Origin." Decennial Census of Population and Housing Data: 1990. Social Explorer. https://www.socialexplorer.com/tables/C1990 (accessed December 6, 2021).

———. 2001. "Table T18. Hispanic or Latino by Specific Origin." Decennial Census of Population and Housing Data: 2000. Social Explorer. https://www.socialexplorer.com/tables/C2000 (accessed December 6, 2021).

———. 2021. "Table AB2000CSA01. Annual Business Survey: Statistics for Employer Firms by Industry, Sex, Ethnicity, Race, and Veteran Status for the U.S., States, and Metro Areas: 2020." Annual Business Survey (ABS) 2020. https://data.census.gov/table?q=ab2000*&t=Race+and+Ethnicity&g=310XX00US12060,31080&n=00&tid=ABSCS2020.AB2000CSA01 (accessed September 1, 2023).

———. 2022a. "Table A04001. Hispanic or Latino by Race." American Community Survey 2021 (5-year sample). Social Explorer. https://www.socialexplorer.com/tables/ACS2021_5yr/R13437091 (accessed September 1, 2023).

———. 2022b. "Table A07001. Place of Birth for the Foreign-Born Population." American Community Survey 2021 (5-year sample). Social Explorer. https://www.socialexplorer.com/tables/ACS2021_5yr/R13437091 (accessed September 1, 2023).

———. 2022c. "Table A13002: Poverty Status of Families by Family Type and Presence of Children Under 18 Years." American Community Survey Population Estimates 2021 (5-year sample). Social Explorer. https://www.socialexplorer.com/tables/ACS2021_5yr/R13437091 (accessed September 1, 2023).

Valdez, Zulema. 2020. "The Great Recession and Precarious Wealth among Middle-Class Mexican-Origin Entrepreneurs." *Journal of Ethnic and Migration Studies* 46(18): 3874–91.

Valenta, Marko. 2009. "Immigrants' Identity Negotiations and Coping with Stigma in Different Relational Frames." *Symbolic Interaction* 32(4): 351–71.

Vallas, Steven P., Emily Zimmerman, and Shannon N. Davis. 2009. "Enemies of the State? Testing Three Models of Anti-Immigrant Sentiment." *Research in Social Stratification and Mobility* 27(4): 201–17.

Vargas, Nicholas. 2015. "Latina/os Whitening? Which Latina/os Self-Classify as White and Report Being Perceived as White by Other Americans?" *Du Bois Review: Social Science Research on Race* 12(1): 119–36.

Vasconcelos, José. 1993. *La raza* cósmica. Universidad Nacional Autónoma de México, Centro de Estudios Latinoamericanos. (Originally published in 1925.)

Vasquez, Jessica M. 2011. *Mexican Americans across Generations.* New York: New York University Press.

Vasquez, Jessica M., and Christopher Wetzel. 2009. "Tradition and the Invention of Racial Selves: Symbolic Boundaries, Collective Authenticity, and Contemporary

Struggles for Racial Equality." *Ethnic and Racial Studies* 32(9): 1557–75. DOI: https://doi.org/10.1080/01419870802684232.

Veenman, Justus. 2010. "Measuring Labor Market Discrimination: An Overview of Methods and Their Characteristics." *American Behavioral Scientist* 53(12): 1806–23.

Vega, Irene I. 2014. "Conservative Rationales, Racial Boundaries: A Case Study of Restrictionist Mexican Americans." *American Behavioral Scientist* 58(13): 1764–83.

Vertovec, Steven, and Robin Cohen. 2002. *Conceiving Cosmopolitanism: Theory, Context, and Practice.* Oxford: Oxford University Press.

Villarreal, Andrés. 2010. "Stratification by Skin Color in Contemporary Mexico." *American Sociological Review* 75(5): 652–78.

Voss, Kim, and Irene Bloemraad. 2011. *Rallying for Immigrant Rights: The Fight for Inclusion in 21st Century America*. Berkeley: University of California Press.

Wade, Peter. 1997. *Race and Ethnicity in Latin America*. Chicago: Pluto Press.

———. 2005. "Rethinking Mestizaje: Ideology and Lived Experience." *Journal of Latin American Studies* 37(2): 239–57. DOI: https://doi.org/10.1017/S0022216X05008990.

Walle, Alf H. 1990. "Beyond the Ugly American." *Management Decision* 28(7). DOI: https://doi.org/10.1108/EUM0000000000060.

Walton, Emily, David T. Takeuchi, Jerald R., Herting, and Margarita Alegria. 2009. "Does Place of Education Matter? Contextualizing the Education and Health Status Association among Asian Americans." *Biodemography and Social Biology* 55(1): 30–51.

Warikoo, Natasha. 2004. "Cosmopolitan Ethnicity: Second-Generation Indo-Caribbean." In *Becoming New Yorkers: Ethnographies of the New Second Generation*, edited by Philip Kasinitz, John H. Mollenkopf, and Mary C. Waters. New York: Russell Sage Foundation.

Warikoo, Natasha, and Irene Bloemraad. 2018. "Economic Americanness and Defensive Inclusion: Social Location and Young Citizens' Conceptions of National Identity." *Journal of Ethnic and Migration Studies* 44(5): 736–53.

Waters, Mary C. 1994. "Ethnic and Racial Identities of Second-Generation Black Immigrants in New York City." *International Migration Review* 28(4): 795–820.

———. 1999. *Black Identities: West Indian Immigrant Dreams and American Realities.* New York and Cambridge, Mass.: Russell Sage Foundation and Harvard University Press.

Waters, Mary C., and Philip Kasinitz. 2015. "The War on Crime and the War on Immigrants: Racial and Legal Exclusion in the Twenty-First-Century United States." In *Fear, Anxiety, and National Identity: Immigration and Belonging in North America and Western Europe*, edited by Nancy Foner and Patrick Simon. New York: Russell Sage Foundation.

Waters, Mary C., Van C. Tran, Philip Kasinitz, and John H. Mollenkopf. 2010. "Segmented Assimilation Revisited: Types of Acculturation and Socioeconomic Mobility in Young Adulthood." *Ethnic and Racial Studies* 33(7): 1168–93.

Watson, Lesley. 2018. "Situating the Self in Global Context: Reconceptualizing Transnational and Cosmopolitan Identities." *Sociology Compass* 12(7): e12592.

Weber, Max. 1958. "Class, Status, and Party." In *Max Weber: Essays in Sociology*, edited by Hans Heinrich Gerth and C. Wright Mills. New York: Oxford University Press.

Weeks, Matthew, and Michael B. Lupfer. 2004. "Complicating Race: The Relationship between Prejudice, Race, and Social Class Categorizations." *Personality and Social Psychology Bulletin* 30(8): 972–84.

Weenink, Don. 2008. "Cosmopolitanism as a Form of Capital: Parents Preparing Their Children for a Globalizing World." *Sociology* 42(6): 1089–1106.

Weise, Julie. 2015. *Corazón de Dixie: Mexicanos in the U.S. South since 1910*. Chapel Hill, N.C.: University of North Carolina Press.

Whitfield, Chandra Thomas. 2020. "Called to Dance Ballet." *Atlanta Journal-Constitution*, December 12.

Wiarda, Howard, and Michael Kryzanek. 2019. *The Dominican Republic: A Caribbean Crucible*. New York: Routledge.

Wickert, David. 2016. "Atlanta Olympics: How Olympics Drew Latinos to Atlanta." *Atlanta Journal-Constitution*, July 19. https://www.ajc.com/news/local-govt--politics/how-the-olympics-helped-lure-latinos-atlanta/REVqYgdV8LjAypmA3zdSeO/.

Wilkenson, Betina Cutaia, and Natasha Bingham. 2016. "Getting Pushed Back Further in Line? Racial Alienation and Southern Black Attitudes toward Immigration and Immigrants." *PS: Political Science & Politics* 49(2): 221–27.

Williams, Terry. 2003. "Money Talks." *Atlanta*, March. https://books.google.com/books?id=FuECAAAAMBAJ&lpg=PA24&pg=PA81#v=onepa ge&q&f=false (accessed February 25, 2021).

Winders, Jamie. 2005. "Changing Politics of Race and Region: Latino Migration to the U.S. South." *Progress in Human Geography* 29(6): 683–99.

———. 2007. "Bringing Back the (B) Order: Post-9/11 Politics of Immigration, Borders, and Belonging in the Contemporary Us South." *Antipode* 39(5): 920–42.

———. 2008. "An 'Incomplete' Picture? Race, Latino Migration, and Urban Politics in Nashville, Tennessee." *Urban Geography* 29(3): 246–63.

———. 2011. "Representing the Immigrant: Social Movements, Political Discourse, and Immigration in the U.S. South." *Southeastern Geographer* 51(4): 596–614.

———. 2013. *Nashville in the New Millennium: Immigrant Settlement, Urban Transformation, and Social Belonging*. New York: Russell Sage Foundation.

———. 2014. "Criminalizing Settlement: The Politics of Immigration in the American South." In *Oxford Handbook on Race, Ethnicity, Immigration, and Crime*, edited by Sandra M. Bucerius and Michael Tonry. Oxford: Oxford University Press.

Wong, Carolyn. 2006. *Lobbying for Inclusion: Rights Politics and the Making of Immigration Policy*: Stanford University Press.

Woodward, C. Vann. 2002. *The Strange Career of Jim Crow.* Oxford: Oxford University Press. (Originally published in 1955.)

Xie, Yu, and Margaret Gough. 2011. "Ethnic Enclaves and the Earnings of Immigrants." *Demography* 48(4): 1293–1315.

Yan, Ting, Richard Curtin, and Matthew Jans. 2010. "Trends in Income Nonresponse over Two Decades." *Journal of Official Statistics* 26(1): 145–64.

Yancey, George A. 2003. *Who Is White? Latinos, Asians, and the New Black/Nonblack Divide.* Boulder, Colo.: Lynne Rienner Publishers.

Yang, Yenny. 2020. "Refugee Resettlement in the Most Diverse Square Mile in America: A Study of Clarkston, Georgia." Master's thesis, Harvard Extension School. https://nrs.harvard.edu/URN-3:HUL.INSTREPOS:37365058.

Yarbrough, Robert A. 2010. "Becoming 'Hispanic' in the 'New South': Central American Immigrants' Racialization Experiences in Atlanta, Ga, USA." *GeoJournal* 75(3): 249–60. DOI: https://doi.org/10.1007/s10708-009-9304-7.

Zamora, Sylvia. 2018. "Mexican Illegality, Black Citizenship, and White Power: Immigrant Perceptions of the U.S. Socioracial Hierarchy." *Journal of Ethnic and Migration Studies* 44(11): 1897–1914.

———. 2022. *Racial Baggage: Mexican Immigrants and Race across the Border.* Stanford, Calif.: Stanford University Press.

Zeng, Minhao. 2014. "Subaltern Cosmopolitanism: Concept and Approaches." *Sociological Review* 62(1): 137–48.

Zeng, Zhen, and Yu Xie. 2004. "Asian-Americans' Earnings Disadvantage Reexamined: The Role of Place of Education." *American Journal of Sociology* 109(5): 1075–1108.

Zepeda-Millán, Chris. 2017. *Latino Mass Mobilization: Immigration, Racialization, and Activism.* Cambridge: Cambridge University Press.

Zhou, Min, Jennifer Lee, Jody Agius Vallejo, Rosaura Tafoya-Estrada, and Yang Sao Xiong. 2008. "Success Attained, Deterred, and Denied: Divergent Pathways to Social Mobility in Los Angeles's New Second Generation." *Annals of the American Academy of Political and Social Science* 620(1): 37–61.

Zúñiga, Víctor, and Rubén Hernández-León. 2005. *New Destinations: Mexican Immigration in the United States.* New York: Russell Sage Foundation.

Index

Tables and Figures are listed in **boldface**.